D1477522

ORTHODOX AND HERETICAL PERFECTIONISM IN THE JOHANNINE COMMUNITY AS EVIDENT IN THE FIRST EPISTLE OF JOHN

by

John Bogart

UNIVERSITY LIBRARY NOTTINGHAM

Published by
SCHOLARS PRESS
for
The Society of Biblical Literature

Distributed by
SCHOLARS PRESS
University of Montana
Missoula, Montana 59812

ORTHODOX AND HERETICAL PERFECTIONISM IN THE JOHANNINE COMMUNITY AS EVIDENT IN THE FIRST EPISTLE OF JOHN

by
John Bogart
The Church Divinity School of the Pacific

Th. D., 1973
The Graduate Theological Union

Advisor:
Edward C. Hobbs

Copyright © 1977

by

The Society of Biblical Literature

Library of Congress Cataloging in Publication Data

Bogart, John.
  Orthodox and heretical perfectionism in the
Johannine community as evident in the first epistle
of John.

  (Dissertation series ; 33)
  Originally presented as the author's thesis,
Graduate Theological Union, 1973.
  Bibliography: p.
  1. Perfection—Biblical teaching. 2. Bible.
N.T. 1 John—Criticism, interpretation, etc.
I. Title: Orthodox and heretical perfectionism
in the Johannine community . . . II. Series:
Society of Biblical Literature. Dissertation
series ; 33.
BS2545.P55B63 1976   227'.94'06   77-5447
ISBN 0-89130-138-0

Printed in the United States of America
1 2 3 4 5

Printing Department
University of Montana
Missoula, Montana 59812

SOCIETY OF BIBLICAL LITERATURE
DISSERTATION SERIES

edited by
Howard C. Kee
and
Douglas A. Knight

Number 33

ORTHODOX AND HERETICAL PERFECTIONISM IN THE JOHANNINE COMMUNITY AS EVIDENT IN THE FIRST EPISTLE OF JOHN

by
John Bogart

SCHOLARS PRESS
Missoula, Montana

KU-998-709

ORTHODOX AND HERETICAL PERFECTIONISM IN THE JOHANNINE COMMUNITY AS EVIDENT IN THE FIRST EPISTLE OF JOHN

TABLE OF CONTENTS

TO MY TEACHERS

The dedication is not anonymous. Chief among my teachers has been the head of my dissertation committee and my "Doctor-Father" over many years of stimulating and enlightening instruction, Edward C. Hobbs, Ph.D., Professor of the Theology and Hermeneutics of the New Testament at the Graduate Theological Union in Berkeley. He has guided me all through the execution of this work, from its inception as a vague idea to its completion in its final form. His creative insights into Johannine literature and theology have been invaluable to me, not to mention his kind personal interest in all my work in New Testament over a period of twelve years.

Next I must mention Dieter Georgi, formerly of the Graduate Theological Union, and now Frothingham Professor of New Testament at Harvard Divinity School. As one of his students, I gained the methodological knowledge, especially in regard to the origins of gnosticism and to the peculiarities of Johannine theology, without which I could not have written this study. I am especially grateful to him for his encouragement to me to pursue my doctoral studies while I was still in the parochial ministry.

To Sherman Johnson, Dean Emeritus of the Church Divinity School of the Pacific, Berkeley, I, along with many others, owe affectionate gratitude for his patience, wisdom and kindness throughout my doctoral course work. His insights into Johannine theology and his rich background of sound scholarship in the history of the ancient Near East were especially valuable to me.

The other scholars on my dissertation committee, Frederick H. Borsch, Dean of the Church Divinity School of the Pacific, and Professor of New Testament there, Massey H. Shepherd, Jr., Hodges Professor of Liturgics, also of C.D.S.P., Thomas W. Leahy, S.J., Associate Professor of Sacred Scripture at the

Jesuit School of Theology, Berkeley, and John E. Huesman, S.J., Professor of Sacred Scripture, also of J.S.T.B., have all been of great help to me, especially in giving me the practical suggestions necessary for the correction and completion of this manuscript. Also to my many other teachers and fellow students at the Graduate Theological Union, I give my sincere thanks for providing me with the dialogue and the stimulating intellectual environment in which alone any genuine scholarship may flourish.

My special thanks go to Esther Davis, Bursar at the Church Divinity School of the Pacific, who typed and proofread this manuscript in preparation for publication by the Scholars Press. Her efficiency, patience and cheerfulness during this arduous task are much appreciated.

Finally, as form dictates, I must mention my family. My wife, Mary Lou, my daughter, Anne, and my son, Christopher, had nothing directly to do with this work; instead, they provided the love and domestic security which alone enabled me to pursue this work to its completion.

                                        JOHN BOGART

Berkeley, California
August 1, 1976

ABBREVIATIONS

ANL	Anti-Nicene Library
BJRL	Bulletin of the John Rylands Library
ET	English Translation
FRLANT	Forschung zur Religion und Literatur des Alten und Neuen Testaments
JBL	Journal of Biblical Literature
NTS	New Testament Studies
TDNT	Theological Dictionary of the New Testament
ThR	Theologische Rundschau
TU	Texte und Untersuchungen
WMANT	Wissenschaftliche Monographien zum Alten und Neuen Testament
ZNW	Zeitschrift fur die neutestamentliche Wissenschaft und die Kunde der alteren Kirche
ZTK (ZThK)	Zeitschrift fur Theologie und Kirche
IQS	Manual of Disciple (Cave I, Qumran)

INTRODUCTION

This study began with an attempt to solve an exegetical
problem. Even the most cursory reader of the First Epistle of
John is aware of the apparent contradiction between 1:8 and 10,
and 3:6 and 9. In the former passage the author declares that
those who claim, "We have no sin" (1:8 RSV), and "We have not
sinned" (1:10 RSV), deceive themselves, have no truth in them,
make God a liar and do not have his word in them. On the other
hand, in 3:6 the author categorically states, "No one who
abides in him sins..." (RSV), and in 3:9, "No one born of God
commits sin... he cannot sin because he is born of God." (RSV)

This apparent conflict concerns the ethical-religious phenomenon commonly called "perfectionism", *i.e.*, the notion that
a person, by whatever means, is capable of achieving ethical
and/or spiritual perfection in his present, earthly existence.
(*Cf.* Chapter One, Section A 1, for the definition of this term
as it is employed throughout this study.)

In the first passage cited above, the author clearly seems
to be condemning perfectionism, whereas in the second, he appears, just as clearly, to be commending it. Is he being inconsistent, or is there some proper distinction to be made between the presuppositions underlying each passage, which will
obviate the apparent contradiction?

In the effort to solve this exegetical puzzle, this study
was led to ask a number of historical-critical questions, which
finally resulted in the writing of an attempted historical reconstruction of the Johannine community between the time its
Gospel was written and the composition of the First Epistle.
Here briefly is a sketch of the questions raised by this study,
in the order of their appearance:

In Chapter One, the definitions of the important terms to
be used in this study are laid out, and the various methodolog-

ical presuppositions necessary for pursuing this study are made explicit.

Then in Chapter Two, the initial thesis of this study is set forth, namely, *there are two distinct types of perfection-ism to be found in 1 John: the "heretical"* (from the standpoint of the author of 1 John) *type, condemned in 1:8ff., and the "orthodox" type, affirmed in 3:6ff.* It will be shown that the theological, anthropological and eschatological presuppositions underlying each type are radically different from each other. Further, it will be shown that the author of 1 John introduced the doctrine of expiation of sin by the blood of Christ into the Johannine community in order to combat the heretical type of perfectionism. Also it will be seen that the author of 1 John carefully qualified the perfectionist teaching he inher-ited, carefully distinguishing it from the heretical type, es-poused by his opponents. His qualifications, it will turn out, modified his perfectionism to the extent of reducing it to a "gradualism", *i.e.*, the ethic that one achieves *some* measure of moral and spiritual perfection only gradually over the span of a lifetime. No matter how lofty and idealistic such a gradual-istic ethic may be, it is never to be identified as a type of perfectionism, strictly speaking.

This initial thesis, concerning two disparate types of perfectionism in 1 John, however, raises another question, to be put at the end of Chapter Two: What is the origin of each type of perfectionism found in 1 John? Chapters Three and Four are devoted to answering this question.

Chapter Three attempts to demonstrate that the Gospel of John alone provides the sole origin for the orthodox type of perfectionism in 1 John. The chief proof of this is the con-viction in the Gospel of John that the believer, by his faith in Jesus as the One From Above, already possesses the life of the new aeon (cf. 5:24; 11:25). This assurance of spiritual perfection, coupled with the strict ethical dualism of the Gos-pel, provides the historical circumstances for a perfectionist self-understanding of the Johannine community. The believer in John's Gospel is seen as born from above, assured of salvation, already enjoying eternal life, already pure, orthodox in belief and perfect in gnosis. In short, ethically and spiritually

perfect. The Gospel of John alone adequately explains the existence of the orthodox type of perfectionism which turns up in
1 John.

This, however, only answers half of the question put at
the end of Chapter Two. The question remains as to the origin
of the heretical type, plus two further questions, put forward
at the end of Chapter Three: What are the origins of the perfectionism found in John's Gospel *itself*? and How are the two
types related to each other?

Chapter Four undertakes to answer these three remaining
questions by a search into perfectionist tendencies found in
some pre-Johannine literature. Of all the literature surveyed,
only that of Jewish apocalyptic is seen as showing evidence of
a genuine perfectionism. A historical rule, already implied
in Chapter Three, is then established: Perfectionism, in the
strict sense as defined in this study, may arise in any given
community when two necessary concepts or elements are present
at the same time, *viz.*, ethical dualism and imminent eschatological expectation. Both these elements were present in the
Jewish community which produced 1 Enoch, Jubilees and the Testament of the Twelve Patriarchs; and both were also present in
the Johannine community at the time its Gospel was written.
Both traditions exhibit a similar ethical dualism. The eschatology, of course, in each is quite different. The Jewish apocalypticists expected the eschaton soon in the future, whereas
the Johannine Christians, in a sense, believed they were already living in the new age. In both cases, however, the new
age was a vivid reality to both groups, impinging upon their
present existence. This vivid apprehension of the new age,
plus a dualistic-ethical viewpoint, tends historically to pro-
duce an in-grown community, hostile to its environment, and
with a perfectionist self-understanding. Thus, we say, at the
end of Chapter Four, that the parents of Johannine perfectionism were ethical dualism and realized eschatology.

A *caveat* must be entered here. We do not claim that Johannine perfectionism originated out of Jewish apocalyptic. There
would be no way to demonstrate this. However, we claim that
the *Sitze-im-Leben* in both communities were mutually analogous
--both had a dualistic ethic and a vivid eschatological hope

at the same time.

As for the question of the origin of the heretical type of perfectionism, it is maintained in this study that it arose out of a gnostic view of creation and man *radically foreign* to that found in the Gospel of John, and hence probably imported into the community from the outside. We insist that there was not any natural, straight-line development from orthodox Johannine perfectionism into the heretical type. Rather, outside gnostic influence *perverted* it and produced a rival type, against which the author of 1 John reacted. His reaction took the form of a careful modification of Johannine perfection (*cf.* Chapter Two), to the extent of its virtual obliteration.

Thus the third question, the relationship between the two types, is answered already, by saying they were not related *at all* to each other. Each was based on radically different world views. The only relationship they may have had probably came from the historical fact that the heretical perfectionists *had been* Johannine Christians. However, they became gnostics, and very likely considered themselves to be the true interpreters of the Johannine doctrines of perfection.

This then brings us to the final questions, raised at the end of Chapter Four, to which the final chapter, Chapter Five, is devoted to answering: Who were these heretical perfectionists? Who were the other opponents alluded to in 1 John? How were the former related to the latter? And finally, Was the Johannine community "sectarian"?

Chapter Five sketches the various opponents in 1 John, and identifies the heretical perfectionists as part of the *same* group of charismatic, prophetic, itinerant-teachers of a libertine-gnostic persuasion. In other words, our hypothesis is that the author of 1 John fought on only one front.

Finally, this study presumptuously enters the current debate on the "sectarian" nature of the Johannine community, coming down rather firmly on the side of Käsemann and Meeks. We see the perfectionism of John's Gospel as only one indication of the peculiar theology and ethics of the Johannine community, which remove it from the main stream of early Christianity.

The final observation is that the perfectionist self-understanding of the Johannine community at the time its Gospel

was written contributed greatly to its sectarian viewpoint.
However, the gnostic crisis which produced 1 John brought the
Johannine community back into the main stream of early orthodoxy. Perfectionism died out; it is seen only as an ephemeral
phenomenon, alive only when the Gospel was written. It is also
seen as being *sui generis* in the whole New Testament. After its
disappearance, in the strict sense, from the Johannine community (by the time 1 John was written), it turns up only in an
attenuated form in 1 John, or in an exaggerated gnostic form in
the gnostic literature of the second and third centuries.

All this seems a complex picture -- this odyssey through
the birth, life and death of Johannine perfectionism. And complex it is. But it is hoped that this study will throw some
light upon the historical circumstances of that remote and
strange community which produced a literature both compelling
and puzzling to us.

CHAPTER ONE

DEFINITION OF TERMS,
PRESUPPOSITIONS AND METHODOLOGY

A. Definition of Terms

1. "Perfectionism"

"Perfectionism" is the term generally applied to the view
that man is capable of achieving sinlessness in his present existence. This definition primarily concerns the ethical aspect
of perfection, *i.e.*, the achievement of ethical or moral purity;
it may, however, be expanded to include spiritual perfection
also, *i.e.*, the union with God or the beatific vision. The latter aspect would normally include the former, but the former,
ethical perfection, could conceivably exist without the latter.[1]
Also the aspect of ritual or purely cultic perfection could be
brought into this definition, especially when dealing with
ethical systems which include ritual purity as part of their
ethical demands.[2]

This study will be dealing with perfectionism as found in
the Johannine community, and therefore will use the term to include both the ethical sense of sinlessness and the spiritual
sense of union with God -- the latter especially in dealing
with some Johannine texts.[3] Ritual perfection will be referred
to only when dealing with the Priestly strata of the Old Testament and with the sectarian writings from Qumran.

The most decisive factor in this definition of perfectionism is that of the achievement of ethical and spiritual perfection *in the present existence* of a human being. Achievement of
this complete perfection only in the after-life is excluded
from this definition. Also excluded is any concept which views
man as only *gradually* reaching some measure of ethical and/or
spiritual good over a long period of time, or of having only
intermittent periods of sinlessness. An example of such a
"gradualist" ethic may be found in Paul's Letter to the Philippians, 3:12-14,

> Not that I have already obtained this or am already
> perfect; (ἤδη τετελείωμαι) but I press on to make
> it my own, because Christ Jesus has made me his own.
> Brethren, I do not consider that I have made it my
> own; but one thing I do, forgetting what lies behind
> and straining forward to what lies ahead, I press on
> toward the goal for the prize of the upward call of
> God in Christ Jesus.
>
> (RSV)

"Perfectionism" and "perfection", then, are necessarily absolute terms. One cannot be "slightly perfect" any more than
"slightly dead."[4]

The means by which man achieves perfection vary, of course,
according to the ethical-religious system in question: obedience to God's will as revealed in the Torah in Judaism;[5] ac-
quisition of true gnosis in the various gnostic systems;[6] or
being born of God and abiding in Christ in Johannine theology.[7]
But regardless of the means, all perfectionist systems have
this in common: man can become ethically and/or spiritually
perfect in his present, earthly life.

2. "Orthodox" and "Heretical"

These terms obviously can vary considerably in meaning and
content according to the theological predilections of the author employing them. One man's orthodoxy is another man's heresy, as later Church history has shown. Further, these terms
gain a specialized meaning from the late second century on,
especially after the writings of Irenaeus and Hippolytus.[8] It
would be inappropriate and inaccurate to apply them to first
century or early second century New Testament texts with the
same meanings that they acquired in the late second century.

Nevertheless, it can be demonstrated that the mode of
thought or the "mind set" that dichotomously divides all doctrine into well-defined categories labeled either "orthodox"
or "heretical" (with an occasional middle ground labeled "heterodox"), a mind set explicitly evident in Irenaeus *et al.*, is
also evident in the New Testament. The Pastoral Epistles, Jude
and 2 Peter are commonly cited as evidence.[9] To these we may
add 1 and 2 John as well. One need only read such passages
as 1 John 1:6-10; 2:18-27; 3:7,12; 4:1-6; 5:6-12; and 2 John
7-9 in the most cursory manner to see that the author here is
struggling polemically to combat what he considers dangerously

false doctrine. In doing so he states what he believes is the
true faith. Examples like 1 John 3:23 and 5:1, and 2 John 4
(where περιπατοῦντας ἐν ἀληθείᾳ is apparently equivalent to
holding the correct doctrine) illustrate the presence of concise orthodox *formulae*, almost catechetical in nature. The
formulation of such concise statements of true doctrine finds
its *Sitz-im-Leben* often in the struggle over heresy. In this
sense, then, the Johannine Epistles belong to the world of the
late New Testament writings, where such a struggle was increas-
ingly evident.

Of course we wish to avoid terminological anachronisms
(see below, C 1) and not confuse the use of these terms in regard to 1 John with their use in regard to various late second
century authors. Irenaeus *et al*. were dealing with *organized*
schools of commonly recognized heretical teaching, *e.g.*, with
Valentinus and Basilides. The author of 1 John does not provide us with any definite evidence that his opponents were so
organized. (The nature of his opponents will be dealt with in
the final chapter of this study.) Furthermore, it is not clear
that in the late first century the lines between "orthodoxy"
and "heresy" were as clearly drawn as they obviously were by
the end of the second century. The point we wish to make here
is simply that the *tendency* toward drawing such lines -- in
other words, the tendency toward dichotomous or dualistic
thinking concerning doctrine, in light of the struggle with
opponents who taught dubious doctrines -- is already present
in 1 John. It may also be said that there is very likely a
direct line of development between what we find in 1 John, the
Pastorals, and certainly in Jude and 2 Peter, and what finally
appears in Irenaeus.

The objection can arise that the term "orthodox" does not
appear in the New Testament. But since this term originally
meant "straight teaching", we see no great objection to using
it when speaking of what the author of 1 John considers correct doctrine, provided that no implications of an elaborately
organized system of orthodoxy were ascribed to him, as might
be ascribed to the later Patristic writers.

3. The "Johannine Community"

This term refers to that group of Christians who, regardless of the number of authors or redactors, produced the literature known as the Gospel according to John and the First, Second and Third Epistles of John. (For the purposes of this study, the Book of Revelation is excluded.) The term "community" is a neutral one and is preferred to "church" because that term has connotations of organization, polity and tradition which might be anachronous when referring to a group of late first, early second century Christians. This does not mean, however, that the Johannine Christians did not constitute a "church" in the broadest sense of an organized group who celebrated the sacraments and instructed the faithful. This much is apparent from the Johannine literature itself.[10] Whether or not the Johannine community was "a conventicle with gnosticizing tendencies", as E. Käsemann has characterized it,[11] or "sectarian", according to Wayne Meeks,[12] will be dealt with in the final chapter. Also to be discussed there is the whole problem alluded to in 3 John of the relationship between the Johannine community and the rest of Christianity. For now it suffices to make the term "Johannine community" refer to that distinctive group of Christians who produced a theologically distinctive literature.

The singular "community" does not necessarily imply the existence of only one congregation of Johannine Christians in one geographical center. The very existence of 2 and 3 John points to the existence of more than one congregation of likeminded persons. Perhaps there was a center from which the author of the Johannine Epistles wrote; certainly there was more than one place to which he wrote, and where he expected to find loyal disciples. Thus the Johannine community may have been a collection of "churches" (ἐκκλησίας in 3 John 6 and ἐκκλησίᾳ 3 John 9 refer to individual congregations[13]), spread over a geographical area made up of theologically like-minded people.

4. "Gnostic" and "Gnosticizing"

The term "gnostic" is notoriously slippery. Originally it was simply applied to those post-Christian heresies which can be reconstructed from the writings of Irenaeus et al. However, since the research of Bultmann into the possibilities of a pre-Christian gnosticism,[14] said to be evident in Mandean and Manichean literature, and especially since the finds at

Nag Hamadi,[15] the term has been expanded to include a greatly wider range of literature. For our purposes, we will confine the term "gnostic" only to those examples of literature, as mentioned above, in which *an organized system* of gnostic concepts is demonstrably present.[16] For any other literature which shows the presence of only some of these concepts, or which merely employs gnostic-mythic terminology, and which lacks any evidence of an organized system, the term "gnosticizing" will be used.

In this we are following the international agreement of scholars on the use of the terms "gnosis" and "gnosticism", put forth at the Colloquium of Messina, in 1966. A quotation from the English text of the opening part of the proposal would be appropriate here:[17]

> In order to avoid an undifferentiated use of the terms *gnosis* and Gnosticism, it seems to be advisable to identify, by the combined use of the historical and the typological methods, a concrete fact, "Gnosticism", beginning methodologically with a certain group of systems of the Second Century A.D. which everyone agrees are to be designated with this term. In distinction from this, *gnosis* is regarded as "knowledge of the divine mysteries reserved for an elite."

We are using the adjective "gnostic" to refer to gnosticism, not merely gnosis. A footnote in the Messina Proposal refers to the ambiguity of this adjective:[18]

> The adjective "gnostic" could be ambiguous from a strictly scholarly point of view, and in that case it would be necessary to clarify it in relation to the substantives "Gnosticism" and "*gnosis*" (though it points in learned terminology, habitually and historically more legitimately at Gnosticism).

Such clarification has been made here. The theology of Valentinus, as reported in Irenaeus, for example, is "gnostic", *i.e.*, pertaining to an organized gnosticism. The theological language, however, of John 16:28 ("I came from the Father and have come into the world; again I am leaving the world and going to the Father") is "gnosticizing", *i.e.*, pertaining to a use of gnostic-mythic terminology without any evidence of an organized gnostic system of thought.

5. "Opponents"

We use this term rather than any English equivalent of Bultmann's *die Irrlehrer*[19] simply because of its neutrality. (The identification and the characteristics of these opponents, and whether they comprised one group or many, will be dealt with in the final chapter.) Further, our use of the term "opponents" is consistent with the use of the equivalent German term *die Gegner*, used almost universally now, *e.g.*, Dieter Georgi's *Die Gegner des Paulus im zweiter Korintherbrief*.

B. Presuppositions about 1 John

1. The Genre of 1 John

1 John cannot properly be called an epistle because of its lack of the customary greetings at the beginning and the ending.[20] Further, the structure of 1 John, as we shall see, defies classification or even outlining. These facts have been noted by practically every commentator on this writing, and since they all agree on these observable phenomena, it is not necessary to rehearse all their comments here. However, it will be instructive to examine what various commentators say 1 John is, if not an epistle.

B. F. Wescott (1883)[21] notes that 1 John "has no address, no subscription; no name is contained in it of person or place; there is no direct trace of the author, no indication of any special destination." Yet because of its "intense personal feeling" and the author's obviously personal relationship to his readers, he calls it a *pastoral*: "Thus perhaps we can best look at the writing not as a Letter called out by any particular circumstances, but as a Pastoral addressed to those who had been carefully trained and had lived long in the Faith."[22] We take issue with Wescott's assertion about 1 John not being called out by any particular circumstances; our study will show how the problem of heresy called forth this writing. But his estimate of it as a pastoral had held up during the test of time, and as we shall see, has been corroborated by several later commentators.

Hans Windisch (1930),[23] after noting the absence of the customary epistolary characteristics and the presence of a

personal relationship between the author and his readers, calls
1 John "*ein religioser Traktat*", a designation not accepted by
any of the subsequent commentators. Religious tractates, such
as those found in the *Corpus Hermeticum*, have quite a different literary style (dialogue, diatribe) from that of 1 John,
and also lack the concern for specific pastoral problems evident in 1 John, *e.g.*, the struggle with false teachers within
the community, who became recently separated from it, *cf.* 2:19.
Hence this designation is inappropriate.

C. H. Dodd (1946)[24] calls it an "informal tract or homily"
and speaks of its author as a "pastor addressing his flock."
His first comment, like that of Windisch, is imprecise and mis-
leading. Homiletic traits, *i.e.*, paraenesis, may certainly be
found in 1 John, but the term "homily" is hardly adequate for
the whole writing, considering its didactic sections. (See
under Structure, B 2, on the alternation of *didache*, chiefly
christological, with paraenesis in 1 John.) However, Dodd's
perception of the pastoral tone of 1 John is correct.

Rudolf Schnackenburg (1953)[25] dutifully notes the lack of
Protokoll and *Eschatokoll* in 1 John, and rightly rejects the
notion of its being a tractate. He goes on to suggest that the
epistolary form can hardly be proved to be fixed in the Hellenistic period, and that another epistolary form was occasioned
by the oral tradition behind 1 John. Finally, he confesses,
"Letzhin bleibt diese Art für uns ein Rätsell."[26] This unfor-
tunately provides us with no solution to the problem of genre.

Hans Conzelmann, in his splendid article "Was von Anfang
war" (1954),[27] has provided us with an insightful view of our
writing. He sees 1 John as a pastoral, *i.e.*, "ein johanneischer Pastoralbrief", using the analogy of the "Pauline" Pastoral Epistles.[28] 1 John is related to the Gospel of John as
the Pastorals are related to the Pauline Epistles. This assertion is significant not only in helping us designate the genre
of 1 John, but also in tracing the theological development in
the Johannine community between the time of the composition of
the Gospel and the Epistles. This problem, to which Conzelmann
has supplied some excellent tradition-criticism, will be taken
up in this study in Chapters Two and Five.

Willi Marxsen (1964)[29] has given us a useful summary of

our investigations into the literary form of 1 John:

> As the document lacks not only a preface--like Heb.--
> but also a letter ending, its literary form is not easy
> to determine. We certainly cannot describe 1 Jn. as a
> "letter", as it lacks all the concrete details which
> would justify such a description. On the other hand,
> it is quite plain that the author frequently has in
> mind a circle of readers to whom he addresses himself
> directly (ii.1, 7f., 12ff., 18,21, 26, etc.). The doc-
> ument has been spoken of as a "homily", an "admonitory
> letter", a "tract" or a "manifesto", but none of these
> is really an adequate description. It is a document
> the form of which has no parallel elsewhere. All we
> can say is that the author is seeking to address readers
> with whose particular situation he is acquainted. This
> means that his writing repeatedly approaches the form
> of a letter, but he does not actually write a letter.

Marxsen is right in rejecting the terms he names for their
inadequacy, but is disappointingly non-committal in attempting
some positive designation for 1 John. His last sentence quoted
here is useless. Had he employed the methods of Conzelmann he
might have developed a fruitful insight into the pastoral nature of the writing.

W. G. Kümmel (1965)[30] laboriously reviews all the views of
previous commentators on the question of the literary form of
1 John, but fails to advance any theory of his own. He spends
much time dealing with the question of *Vorlage*, *e.g.*, the the-
ories of Dobschütz and Bultmann, and rejects them as improb-
able. However, his unitive view of the writing does not help
us, any more than the various views about *Vorlage*, to answer
the question of genre.

Bultmann (1967)[31] notes that the Ταῦτα ἔγραψα of 5:13 is
a mark of an epistle, much as, we might say, the phrase τοῦ
λόγου τῆς παρακλήσεως in Hebrews 13:22 marks the close of that
generically enigmatic writing with a possible generic title.
In both these cases we find a flesh and blood pastor addressing a historical congregation(s) with a vital pastoral, didactic, apologetic and paraenetic concern. This is most likely
as much as we can say about the literary form or genre of
1 John.

Finally, Massey Shepherd (1971)[32] comments pragmatically:

> Letter, sermon, or treatise--the writing is addressed
> to a specific group of Christian believers, whether
> of one or of several congregations.

The common thread which runs through all these comments

on genre is the difficulty of classification, yet the clarity
of one point: pastoral concern for a specific group. Conzelmann's insight here, foreseen by Westcott and reiterated by
Dodd and Shepherd, is decisive for any consideration of genre.
The designation "pastoral" is probably the best and most adequate for a writing which in fact defies classification.

2. The Structure of 1 John

Pierson Parker, when once dealing with the problem of the
structure of 1 John, commented, "Indeed 1 John makes almost as
good sense when read backward, sentence by sentence."[33] His
hyperbole need not be taken seriously, but it does fairly com-
municate the frustration any commentator experiences when attempting to outline the First Epistle of John. Amos Wilder
alludes to this problem also: "The first epistle does not lend
itself easily to a tabular outline, as appears in the disagree-
ment of those who have sought to analyze the movement of
thought."[34]

Nevertheless every commentator has tried it. Haering,[35]
Westcott,[36] Brooke,[37] Dodd,[38] Schnackenburg,[39] Wilder,[40] Bultmann,[41] and Shepherd,[42] and even the editors of the Jerusalem
Bible[43] have provided us with outlines, all differing from each
other! Probably the most useful one for our purposes is that
of Haering's, reproduced in Brooke's commentary on 1 John in
the ICC. Briefly, Haering recognized that 1 John has three major divisions, each consisting of alternating sections of ethical and christological teaching, and each section somewhat parallel to its counterparts in the other major divisions:

(Prooemium -- 1:1-4)
I. First Division
    A. Ethical Section 1 -- 1:5-2:17
    B. Christological Section 1 -- 2:18-27
II. Second Division
    A. Ethical Section 2 -- 2:28-3:24
    B. Christological Section 2 -- 4:1-6
III.Third Division
    A. Ethical Section 3 -- 4:7-21
    B. Christological Section 3 -- 5:1-12
(Postscript -- 5:13-21)

Hence in this scheme we have a triple presentation of two
major concerns, ethical and christological. The advantage of
Haering's analysis is: (1) It avoids the subjective editorial
titles found in all the other commentators, which though homi-
letically useful, can tend toward eisegesis. (2) It rightly
recognizes the two major concerns of the First Epistle, namely,
ethical and christological instruction, both presented polemically. A summary of the whole writing could be said to be
found in 3:23, Καὶ αὕτη ἐστὶν ἡ ἐντολὴ αὐτοῦ, ἵνα πιστεύσωμεν
τῷ ὀνόματι τοῦ υἱοῦ αὐτοῦ ᾿Ιησοῦ Χριστοῦ καὶ ἀγαπῶμεν ἀλλήλους,
καθὼς ἔδωκεν ἐντολὴν ἡμῖν. (3) It points out the parallelism
of sections, e.g., as Raymond Brown has it:[44]

    Walking in Light (1:5-7) = Children of God (2:28-3:3)
    Opposition to sin (1:8-2:2) = (3:4-10)
    Keeping the commandments (2:3-11) = (3:11-24)
    Resisting the world/Antichrist (2:12-27) = (4:1-6).

Of course, the parallelism is not exact. Each section is
taken up again in a "spiral" fashion, i.e., sometimes a particular theme is developed more than previously, or expressed in
different terms. The absence of exact parallelism here makes
the writing difficult to outline; nevertheless, Haering's analysis is empirically based on the observation of definite breaks
in the writing.

The main presupposition of this study concerning the
structure of 1 John is that 1:5-2:11 forms an original unit,
which consists of six Grundsätze (1:6,8,10; 2:4,6,9 -- see below, B 3 on Sources), surrounded by the author's (or redactor's) interpretive commentary. (This will be analyzed at the
beginning of Chapter Two.) Haering would add 2:12-14 and 15-17
to this unit, but each of these obviously stands by itself in
its literary construction, although also dealing with ethical
themes, as 1:5-2:11 does. Bultmann makes a division between
2:2 and 3, indicating a thematic transition between the ethical instruction on walking in light and not presuming sinlessness (1:5-2:2), and keeping the commandments; but these two
subsections are not essentially different in ethical content.
Further, the themes of φῶς and σκοτία, ethically understood,
appear in 1:5 and 2:10-11, forming an inclusio.

To sum up, the structure of 1 John is that of a three-fold

spiral of ethical and christological instruction polemically
presented. The exact division between major divisions, sections and subsections is not directly relevant to the concerns
of this study, except for showing that 1:5-2:11 forms an original unit. One final observation: the sections sometimes "flow"
into each other, making the discernment of divisions difficult.
For example, the author picks up a term in the last sentence of
one section and uses it in the first sentence of the next: ἡ
ἀγγελία ἣν ἀκηκόαμεν in 1:5 echoes ἀκηκόαμεν ἀπαγγέλλομεν in 1:
3; μένετε ἐν αὐτῷ in 2:27, which concludes the First Division,
is quoted verbatim in 2:28, which begins the Second Division.
The word πνεύματος in 3:24, which concludes the second ethical
section, is taken up at the beginning of the second christological section in 4:1, which exhorts the beloved not to believe
every πνεύματι.

3. Sources (*Vorlage*)

Dobschütz isolated eight *Grundsätze* in 1 John, which form
four sayings in the form of an antithetical parallelism:[45]

-2:29b   πᾶς ὁ ποιῶν τὴν δικαιοσύνην ἐξ αὐτοῦ γεγέννηται
         πᾶς ὁ ποιῶν τὴν ἁμαρτίαν καὶ τὴν ἀνομίαν ποιεῖ

-3;6a   πᾶς ὁ ἐν αὐτῷ μένων οὐχ ἁμαρτάνει
-3:6b   πᾶς ὁ ἁμαρτάνων οὐχ ἑώρακεν αὐτὸν οὐδὲ ἔγνωκεν αὐτόν

-3:7b   ὁ ποιῶν τὴν δικαιοσύνην δίκαιός ἐστιν
-3:8   ὁ ποιῶν τὴν ἁμαρτίαν ἐκ τοῦ διαβόλου ἐστίν

-3:9a   Πᾶς ὁ γεγεννημένος ἐκ τοῦ θεοῦ ἁμαρτίαν οὐ ποιεῖ
-3:10b   πᾶς ὁ μὴ ποιῶν δικαιοσύνην οὐκ ἔστιν ἐκ τοῦ θεοῦ

The antithetical parallelism and the striking similarity
in form of each of these four pairs is plainly observable.
Hence Dobschütz' basic thesis can be granted, without, however,
speculating on the origin or authorship of the *Grundsätze*. The
author's *use* of them and his comments on them, interspersed
among them--in other words, how they *function* for the author
(or redactor)--is of more importance for understanding the nature and purpose of 1 John than is knowing about their origin.
These *Grundsätze*, however, do not immediately concern us in
this study.

Of more concern are these *Grundsätze* isolated by Bultmann:

1:6,7,8,10; 2:4,5,9,10 and 11.[46] Bultmann claims that these
are obviously a source for the author:

> In diesem Abschnitt benutzt der Verfasser offenbar
> eine Quelle, die stilistisch mit der in Joh benut-
> zten Quelle der "Offenbarungsreden" verwandt ist.

We are willing to grant Bultmann's basic thesis that the
author employs a source, as we gladly did for Dobschütz; however, we are not so willing to connect it with Bultmann's highly hypothetical *Offenbarungsreden* of the Gospel of John. That
both the authors of the Gospel and the Epistles employed sources
is readily admitted; but the nature and origin of these sources
remains problematical. Their *use*, as we have stated, by the
author is of far greater import. In Chapter Two we will carefully observe how the author used six *Grundsätze* (1:6,8,10;
2:4,6 and 9), five of which Bultmann counts in his source noted
above. (Bultmann's exclusion of 2:6 from his hypothetical
source is probably due to its lack of complete parallelism to
2:4 and 9; see Chapter Two, *ad loc.*) The main point here is
that we presuppose sources, but are not interested, for the
purposes of this study, in their origin--only their use. This
implies, then, that the chief concern of this study is with
the First Epistle of John *as it now stands*. It was *how* the
final redactor used his sources which will contribute to answering the questions put forth in this study. (See the conclusions of Chapters Two, Three and Four for these major questions.) The concept of considering a document as it stands in
its final redaction was well expressed by C. H. Dodd, when he
spoke thus of the Fourth Gospel:[47] "I conceive it to be the
duty of an interpreter at least to see what can be done with
the document as it has come down to us before attempting to
improve upon it."

4. Author, Date and Occasion

1 John is anonymous. Most commentators assume that it
was written by the "Elder", the author of 2 and 3 John. In
turn this author is taken as a disciple of the original "Master Evangelist" who wrote the bulk of the Fourth Gospel.[48] As
for date, the late first century seems to enjoy a general consensus. These questions, like the question of the origin of
sources, are not paramount ones for this study. It matters

little whether the same hand wrote both the Gospel and the
Epistles, or whether two (or more) different hands did, *provided that the theological differences between them are properly discerned*. It would be to engage in unwarranted psychologizing to base one's argument for the number of authors on the
notion that one author "developed" his thought, or that one
author could not possibly hold varying ideas together in his
mind. Literary similarity or dissimilarity *alone* is an inadequate criterion for determining the authorship of the Johannine
writings. Theological motifs and *sitze-im-Leben* must be taken
into account, as we shall be doing in this study.

As for the occasion of the writing of 1 John, J.A.T. Robinson's fine article "The Destination and Purpose of the Johannine Epistles"[49] provides a useful guide. Speaking in summary
of the emphases peculiar to 1 John, he says, "...they are seen
as necessary correctives to deductions drawn from the teaching
of the fourth Gospel by a gnosticizing movement within Greek-
speaking diaspora Judaism." This is a basic presupposition of
this study, and Robinson's insights furnish the basis for much
of the conclusion of this study in Chapter Five, especially as
to the nature of the opponents in 1 John and the nature of the
Johannine community at the time of its writing. It is a truism
of course to say that 1 John was written to combat opponents
(or "heretics"). The questions which this study will grapple
with are, Who are these opponents? Whence are they and their
ideas? What motivated the author of 1 John to oppose them? And
what does this writing tell us about the Johannine community
and its theology *vis à vis* the rest of Christianity? *These* are
the issues for this study.

5. The Relationship of 1 John to the Gospel of John

Much has been written on this subject in many various com-
mentaries, which need not be repeated here. The seminal article on this problem was written by C.H. Dodd a generation ago,
namely, *The First Epistle of John and the Fourth Gospel* (BJRL,
Vol. 21, No. 1, April, 1937), and it serves as a major presupposition of this study. Its chief virtue lies in its discernment of the differences in theology between the Gospel and the
First Epistle. Dodd lists three major areas of difference,
viz., eschatology, atonement and the doctrine of the Spirit.[50]

We presuppose the thesis that there are real theological differences here and that they are due to a *change in the internal situation of the Johannine community*. (Again, this will be brought out in Chapters Two and Five.) We also presuppose that 1 John was written after the Gospel[51] and that the differences in theology were due to the new challenges of heretical teaching which arose *within* the community and threatened the community's traditional teaching, giving rise to a sort of theological apologia found in 1 John, but not in the Gospel. (The particulars of this presupposition will also be made explicit in Chapters Two and Five.)

C. Methodology

1. Theological and Terminological Anachronisms

It is anachronistic to apply theological terms born in a later age to theological problems of an earlier age. To do so leads inevitably to a distortion of the understanding of the earlier age. This has been done, for example, by E. Käsemann, when he used the sixteenth century term *simul justus et peccator* in speaking of the first century problems in 1 John.[52] On this particular example, E. Schweizer has stated that no elucidation of the problem of sin in 1 John can be obtained by imposing such a late concept on an early problem.[53]

This principle of avoiding theological and terminological anachronisms has already been employed here in our discussion above on the terms "gnostic" and "gnosticizing", "orthodox" and "heretical." Care must always be taken not to interpret the first century through the eyes of any later century. This ought to be axiomatic, but it is surprising and dismaying how often it is ignored.

2. Source and Motif Analysis

We have already dealt with the problem of source criticism (in B 3 above). There is no doubt about the value of source analysis in determining *Vorlage*; but, as has been said already, this study is primarily concerned with the First Epistle of John as it stands in its final redaction. Hence source criticism as such is not of primary importance here.

However, motif analysis is important for this study. The literary source, in the sense of a *Vorlage*, an actual document,

which may lie behind 1 John is not our concern, but rather *the
search for the origins of the theological motifs which form the
heritage of the author of 1 John.* This study is such a search
--specifically, for the origin of the concept of perfectionism
in 1 John, and in turn, of the Gospel of John also. The question, then, is not, "What document or documents did the author
use?", but rather, "What are the theological origins of the
concepts of perfection found in the Johannine literature?" To
answer these questions we must look not merely for *Vorlage*, but
explore perfectionist ideas and tendencies in the Jewish, Christian and gnostic literature which preceded our Epistle. This
task will be taken up in Chapters Three and Four.

How the final redactor of 1 John understood his sources
and how he used and remolded them for his own theological and
polemical purposes is the question of this study, and an attempt to answer this question will lead, we believe, to a
clearer understanding of the life situation in the Johannine
community at the time 1 John was written than would all the
source criticism in the world.

3. Parallels

In Chapter Four of this study parallels to perfectionist
thought in 1 John, from various types of pre-Johannine literature of various religio-cultural backgrounds, will be considered for their possible influence on that thought. But simply
drawing parallels between documents, no matter how close the
theological motifs in them are to each other, does not demonstrate either dependence of one on the other, or interdepen-
dence, or even mutual dependence on a common source. Hence all
the cases of imputed parallels must be examined for any possible corroborating evidence, *e.g.*, direct and demonstrable literary dependence--the *probability* (not the mere possibility)
that the author of document A *knew* document B, and some accom-
panying historical evidence to help verify this probability.
In the case of 1 John, we can be sure only that the author
knew the Gospel of John and the Old Testament.[54] Beyond that
we must approach the phenomena of parallels with caution.

4. Contextual Exegesis

In Chapter Two, the six *Grundsätze* are considered in their
whole context, 1:15-2:11. It is axiomatic that the total struc-

ture and function of a passage must be considered before analyzing any particular parts of it.

5. Theological (*sachlich*) and Linguistic Analysis

Linguistic insights, *e.g.*, the grammar and function of the
words, phrases and clauses of a sentence, problems of syntax,
parallelism, etc. are primary in all exegesis. So also are
form and redactional critical observations. Yet the analysis
of the theological motifs of a given passage must not be ignored. Some commentators (*e.g.*, Nigel Turner, cf. Chapter Two
ad loc.) stop short of this. A good example of theological
analysis can be found in Bultmann's commentary on 1 John, where
speaking of 1:7b as an ecclesiastical redaction of the author's
source, he comments,[55] "Er hebt sich nicht nur durch seine
Prosa vom poetischen Stil der Umgebung ab, sondern er stört
auch sachlich."

Robert Fortna also refers to the "ideological", *i.e.*,
sachlich (=essential, *i.e.*, theological) considerations.[56]
Dodd's chief reasons for ascribing a different author to 1 John
from that of the Gospel are theological, as noted above under
B 5.

6. How Documents May Be Used to Reconstruct History

Reconstructing the life situation (=Sitz-im-Leben) of a
community's literature by analyzing the *form* of the literature
produced by the community is, of course, the major axiom of
form-criticism. In the case of the Johannine community, its
life situation will be reconstructed by analyzing one of the
literary forms found in the First Epistle. (In Chapter Two,
the six sentences, 1:6,8,10; 2:4,6,9.) We have already dealt
with the overall genre of that writing. These methods, we believe, are capable of yielding positive results for a reliable
historical reconstruction.

In the case of reconstructing the history of the Johannine
community, we are fortunate in having more than just one document from it. By carefully observing the theological differences, as well as the vocabulary and stylistic differences, between the Gospel and the Epistles, we will obtain data which
will help us understand what changes in the life situation occurred within the community *between* the writing of the Gospel
and the Epistles.

Further, we may obtain an excellent insight into the life situation of the Johannine community at the time the First Epistle was written by noting the apparent quotations of the author's opponents, and also by analyzing the theological content of the author's arguments against his opponents. To employ an analogy, just as we may learn something of the shape of an object by studying the shadow it casts, so by analyzing the arguments of our author we may, in part, and often only imperfectly, discern his opponents' teachings. In the case of 1 John we are fortunate in having some apparent quotations from the opponents, which we may regard as good secondary sources for their theological views. To these we must now turn in order to discover the nature of the perfectionist controversy which was going on within the Johannine community when 1 John was written.

CHAPTER TWO

ORTHODOX AND HERETICAL PERFECTIONISM IN I JOHN

Introductory Remarks

The purpose of this chapter is to demonstrate that two
distinct types of perfectionism, orthodox and heretical, existed within the Johannine community when 1 John was written.
The essential differences between them will be clearly delineated. Further, it will be shown that the author of 1 John introduced the doctrine of Christ's expiation for sin into his
writing in order to combat the heretical type. The resulting
conflict or theological tension between the doctrine of expiation for sin and the orthodox doctrine of perfection will be
explored. Finally, the important question of the origin of
each type of perfectionism will be raised, to which the rest
of this study will be devoted.

A. The Evidence for Two Types of Perfectionism in 1 John

1. The Analysis of Six *Grundsätze* in 1 John 1:5-2:11

Now let us proceed to find the evidence for the two types
of perfectionism found in 1 John. The approach by which we
choose to demonstrate this will be an analysis of six verses
in 1 John 1:5-2:11, which are strikingly similar in form:[1]

1:6 'Εὰν εἴπωμεν ὅτι   (a)

Κοινωνίαν ἔχομεν μετ' αὐτοῦ,   (b)

καὶ ἐν τῷ σκότει περιπατῶμεν,   (c)

ψευδόμεθα καὶ οὐ ποιοῦμεν τὴν ἀλήθειαν   (d)

1:8 ἐὰν εἴπωμεν ὅτι   (a)

ἁμαρτίαν οὐκ ἔχομεν   (b)

                                                            (c)

ἑαυτοὺς πλανῶμεν καὶ ἡ ἀλήθεια οὐκ ἔστιν ἐν ἡμῖν (d)

25

1:10 ἐὰν εἴπωμεν ὅτι   (a)

     οὐχ ἡμαρτήκαμεν,   (b)

                                                          (c)

     ψεύστην ποιοῦμεν αὐτὸν   (d)

     καὶ ὁ λόγος αὐτοῦ οὐκ ἔστιν ἐν ἡμῖν

2:4 ὁ λέγων ὅτι   (a)

     Ἔγνωκα αὐτόν,   (b)

     καὶ τὰς ἐντολὰς αὐτοῦ μὴ τηρῶν,   (c)

     ψεύστης ἐστιν, καὶ ἐν τούτῳ   (d)

     ἡ ἀλήθεια οὐκ ἔστιν

2:6 ὁ λέγων   (a)

     ἐν αὐτῷ μένειν   (b)

                                   No (c) or (d)

     ὀφείλει καθὼς ἐκεῖνος περιεπάτησεν   (e)

     καὶ αὐτὸς περιπατεῖν.

2:9 ὁ λέγων   (a)

     ἐν τῷ φωτὶ εἶναι   (b)

     καὶ τὸν ἀδελφὸν αὐτοῦ μισῶν   (c)

     ἐν τῇ σκοτίᾳ ἐστὶν ἕως ἄρτι.   (d)

For purposes of analysis, we have enumerated four grammatical elements found, in varying extent, in these six *Grundsätze*
quoted above. They may be conveniently designated thus:

(a) The opening quotation formula.

(b) The apparent quotation of the opponents; (direct in the
first four, indirect in the latter two). Also called
the assertions of the opponents.

(c) The statement of the actual behavior of the opponents.

(d) The statement of the consequences of that behavior,
i.e., the present spiritual state of the opponents.

1:6, 2:4 and 2:9 have all four of these grammatical elements. 1:8 and 1:10 both lack (c). 2:6 lacks (c) and (d),
but instead has a closing clause (e) which may be designated
as a simple statement of the moral obligation of one who makes
the quoted assertion.

Among these six sentences we shall eventually concentrate
on 1:8 and 10, which contain the perfectionist claims refuted

by the author. However, before we undertake that task, we must
first analyze all four of the grammatical elements found in
all the sentences; in doing so, we hope to show how 1:8 and 10
stand out as different from the other four sentences.

To begin, the first and most obvious similarity found in
all six sentences is, of course, the opening quotation formula: ἐὰν εἴπωμεν ὅτι in the first three sentences, and ὁ λέγων
(ὅτι) in the latter three. (The last two lack the ὅτι, which
results in an indirect expression of the apparent quotation.)

The second similarity, found in all six sentences, consists of the apparent quotations of the author's opponents,
which the opening quotation formulae serve to introduce. (The
conjunction ὅτι here indicates a quotation.[2]) If the ὅτι had
been inserted after the ὁ λέγων in 2:6 and 9, the text would
probably have read:

2:6 ὁ λέγων (ὅτι) ἐν αὐτῷ μένω

2:9 ὁ λέγων (ὅτι) ἐν τῷ φωτί εἰμι[3]

However, in spite of this inconsistency in the last two
sentences, and the stylistic variation in the opening quotation formula, all six of these sentences have these two grammatical elements on common, namely, (a) the opening quotation
formula, and (b) the apparent quotation of the opponents.
These two elements adequately indicate by themselves that the
six sentences under discussion are all *Grundsätze*: they share
a common form and hence a common purpose.

Before we go on to discuss the other two grammatical elements in these sentences, we need to ask a question about the
second element, the *apparent* quotation: Is the author actually quoting the opinions of his opponents, or is he merely
characterizing (and hence possibly distorting) what they actually assert? In order to answer this question, we must turn
to the first grammatical element, the introductory quotation
formula, and clear up the meaning of the first person plural
in the first three sentences, *i.e.*, the εἴπωμεν; like all
first person plurals, it is ambiguous. Does the "we" (1) include *both* the speaker (and perhaps his fellow witnesses, referred to by the first person plural in 1:1*ff.*) *and* the audience he is addressing; or (2) does it refer only to the speaker

and his co-witnesses, *excluding* the audience; or (3) does it
refer to the speaker *alone*, who is using an editorial "we"; or
(4) is it merely an impersonal "we", equivalent to the impersonal ὁ λέγων of the last three sentences, *i.e.*, much like the
English expression "they say" or "one says" (*man sagt* in German)? (This last alternative could also include the possibility that the impersonal "we" really means "you", much in the
style of the preacher who says "we must not" when he really
means "*you* must not.")

The first three alternatives must be excluded immediately
because neither the author not his co-witnesses could possibly
admit to walking in darkness, lying, not doing the truth, etc.!
Nor could the author include himself and his co-witnesses in
the condemnations contained in 1:6, 8 and 10. The only alternative left is the last one, namely, that the εἴπωμεν is entirely impersonal, and thus equivalent to the impersonal ὁ
λέγων, which seems to be merely a stylistic variant.[4] R. Bultmann came to this same conclusion on the use of "we" in his
commentary on 1 John, *ad loc*.[5]

Since, then, all six of these sentences use an *impersonal*
formula to introduce the views of the author's opponents, it
is strongly possible that in the second grammatical element,
the *apparent* quotation, the author is only *characterizing*, or
paraphrasing, what *he thinks* his opponents' claims really are,
rather than actually quoting them *verbatim*.[6] This, as noted
above, implies the danger of distortion or misrepresentation
of the opponent's actual statements. We can never know, of
course, what the author's opponents *literally* said, short of
discovering some hitherto unknown manuscripts. Nevertheless,
we need not despair of finding out, with a reasonable measure
of accuracy, what they actually claimed, in spite of any sus-
picions about either the author's accuracy in quoting his opponents or his possible malice in misquoting them.

We may reasonably trust the author of 1 John; he is obviously giving us only what *he thinks* his opponents were asserting, but his impressions, characterizations or paraphrasings
are reliable for this reason: There can be no doubt that his
opponents' claims were actually upsetting the community, and
causing such a disturbance among the faithful that the author

felt obliged, as a good pastor, to write his congregation(s) and set them straight. We hypothesize that it would be incredible that such a disturbance among the faithful could have come about merely by a misunderstanding of what the opponents were really teaching and asserting. The intensity of the disturbance (measured by the intensity of the author's response!) indicates that the disturbance in the community was caused by no phantom threat, but rather by a clear understanding of what the opponents were actually proclaiming. In other words, only the community's understanding that a genuine threat to their orthodox teaching really existed, can adequately account for the intense reaction against it which actually resulted. The author, then, understood all too well (and with fair accuracy) what his opponents were asserting! He may or may not have quoted them *verbatim*; but he already knew the *effect* of their teaching (*i.e.*, the great disturbance within the community), and from that he could fairly ascertain the *cause* of it. This puts the author of 1 John into the same class with Paul, Ignatius and Irenaeus, who knew their opponents' opinions generally with surprising accuracy.

Hence we may say that, even though these six *Grundsätze* contain characterizations or paraphrases of the opponents' assertions, these paraphrases are cast in a striking and vivid form, *i.e.*, in the form of an actual quotation from living, flesh and blood opponents. This vivid form was in keeping with the vivid problem of actual opponents stirring up the congregation(s). In turn, this indicates that the opponents' claims were, as we have surmised, an obvious *present* danger to the community. Certainly the author's sharply dualistic[7] condemnation of his opponents indicates that they had to be countered with appropriately strong measures. The general intensity of 1 John, and its pastoral concern for orthodox teaching, indicates the author's passionate desire to preserve this teaching. His use of the vivid quotation form fits in with the general *Sitz-im-Leben* of 1 John: the refutation of heresy and the pastoral care of the congregation(s). Specifically, the *Sitz-im-Leben* of the quotation form is the peril of false teaching, which required the author to put that teaching in a vivid form which would match the vivid situation of struggle within the

community. Of course, after all this is said and done, the
possibility still exists that perhaps the apparent quotations
were after all *verbatim* quotations from the author's opponents!
We really cannot know for sure. In either case, however, we
simply wish to make this point, which is vital to our whole research, namely, that the apparent quotations (*verbatim* or not)
are *reliable* indicators of the actual, historical teaching of
the opponents in 1 John.

Now after this excursus on the quotation form, let us turn
to the third element, (c) the statement of the opponent's actual behavior, which is found in three of these sentences, 1:6,
2:4 and 2:9. In these three, immediately after the apparent
quotation, there follows a clause beginning with καὶ which describes the opponents' actual behavior, according to the author.
Thus we have, with elements (b) and (c) next to each other, a
juxtaposition of assertion and behavior--of what the opponents
say with what they do:

1:6	κοινωνίαν ἔχομεν μετ᾽αὐτοῦ	assertion
	καὶ ἐν τῷ σκότει περιπατῶμεν	behavior
2:4	Ἔγνωκα αὐτόν	assertion
	καὶ τὰς ἐντολὰς αὐτοῦ μὴ τερῶν	behavior
2:9	ἐν τῷ φωτὶ εἶναι	assertion
	καὶ τὸν ἀδελφὸν αὐτοῦ μισῶν	behavior

In addition to this juxtaposition, the author--in his comments which come before and surround the six *Grundsätze*--care-
fully qualifies the opponents' assertions in this way: he re-
defines them, so that they exclude the actual behavior of the
opponents. Or to put it the other way, the opponents' actual
behavior shows that their assertions, now carefully re-defined
with crucial, qualifying moral provisions, are false. Thus in
1:5 the important theological proposition "God is light" is
qualified by the equally important moral proposition that no
darkness dwells in Him whatever. Bultmann here has correctly
shown that 1:5 does not deal with some sort of metaphysical
truth about the Deity, but rather stresses God's absolute moral
purity.[8] This then implies that to have fellowship with the
Light (=with Him who is morally perfect) absolutely excludes
"walking in darkness", a phrase used several places in the New

Testament, always referring to immoral behavior.[9] The empiri-
cal behavior of which the author accuses his opponents in 1:6
obviously contradicts their claim "to have fellowship with God"
--a claim which has now been crucially qualified and re-defined
in terms of God's absolute moral purity, in the previous verse,
1:5.

The same method of qualification, with its consequent re-
definition, is used with the claims made in 2:4 and 9. In 2:3
"knowing God" is qualified by "keeping his commandments"; in
2:4 the author states that his opponents do not in fact keep
God's commandments and therefore their boast of knowing God is
false. Here we see that 2:3 serves to set the background of
qualification for 2:4, just as 1:5 has for 1:6. In 2:10 "being
in the light" is qualified by "loving one's brother"--*i.e.*, it
is defined in those behavioral terms; but in 2:9 the opponents'
hatred of their brothers shows that their claim to be in the
light is utterly false. These crucial moral qualifications
serve to re-define or explicate the theological propositions
in terms of a demand for right ethical behavior. One's theological assertions must have ethical effect. Thus "fellowship
with God" is defined in terms of "walking in light", *i.e.*, the
claim to be close to God must result in moral purity; "knowing
God" likewise must be thought of and acted out in life in terms
of "keeping his commandments"; and "being in the light" must
also mean "loving one's brother." To sum up, these explications of theology in terms of ethics serve to re-define the
opponent's assertion in order to exclude their actual behavior,
and show them up as liars. The third element (c), the description of the opponents' actual behavior, when juxtaposed with
the second element (b), the opponent's assertions, effects a
startling rhetorical contrast, which serves to highlight the
opponents' hypocrisy. Finally, the juxtaposition of assertion
and behavior, together with the technique of interspersing important theological and moral qualifications in and about the
six *Grundsätze*, serves the overall rhetorical purpose of refutation.

Next there is a fourth grammatical element (d), the statement of the present spiritual condition of the opponents, found
in all our sentences, except 2:6. Each of these five sentences

has a concluding clause which describes the actual spiritual
state of the claimants, in the eyes of the author. (Of these
five, let us postpone, for now, a discussion of 1:8 and 10;
see below, p. 33.) In 1:6 they lie and do not tell the truth;
in 2:4 we find an almost exact parallel to this, except for the
number and the person;[10] and in 2:9 the false claimant is seen
as still in darkness up to the present moment. This fourth
element, then, serves to reinforce the condemnation of the opponents, already implicit in the third element. There the opponents' evident hypocrisy is exposed by the juxtaposition of
their assertions with their behavior; here, in the fourth element, the inevitable results of their hypocrisy are spelled
out. The opponents are in final spiritual darkness up to the
present time.

Both the third and fourth elements are lacking in 2:6, but
this sentence, like the other three, deals essentially with the
same problem of hypocrisy. The author simply states that anyone who dares make the claim of abiding in Christ[11] ought to
live in the same way he did, that is, in absolute sinlessness.[12]
Therefore, even though its form is different from the form
found in 1:6, 2:4 and 2:9, 2:6 deals with the same problem of
hypocrisy in theologically the same way.

Further, it ought to be noted that in all four of these
sentences discussed so far (1:6, 2:4,6,9), the author sees *nothing intrinsically wrong* with any of the assertions found in the
second element (b), the apparent quotations, *provided* that they
are all properly qualified and re-defined, as the author has
so done. Hence, (1) Claiming fellowing with God (1:6) is proper, provided one walks in the light (1:7). This claim the author makes for himself in 1:3, thus inferring his own claim
to moral purity. (In fact, 1:3 provides us with our first evidence in the Epistle that the author affirms some kind of perfectionism.) (2) Claiming to know God (2:4) is right when it
involves keeping his commandments (2:3). (3) Claiming that one
dwells in Christ (2:6) implies that one must live as he lived
(2:6). (This too implies some kind of perfectionism.) And (4)
Claiming to be in the light (2:9) is validated by the love of
one's brother (2:10). *These four claims are all characteristic
of any true member of the Johannine community.* They are def-

initely claims of a perfectionist nature and are found as prominent themes in both the Gospel and First Epistle of John.[13]
*Therefore, the author of 1 John cannot complain that his oppo-
nents claim more than he himself or any other Johannine christian claims;* his complaint in the four of these six *Grundsätze*
which we have been examining is, as we have seen, essentially
the complaint against *hypocrisy.* The author's opponents simply
do not live as they say.

However, this cannot be said of the opponents' assertions
in 1:8 and 10. Here the form is different. The first two elements, the quotation form and the apparent quotation, are both
present in each, but neither has the third element which points
out hypocrisy. They both, however, contain the fourth element,
which describes the opponents' final spiritual state. But here
in 1:8 and 10, *the assertions themselves are categorically denied as intrinsically wrong;* unlike those in the other four
sentences, these two have no qualifying explications surrounding them. This marks them off as not only different in form,
but as dealing with a different problem: not the problem of
hypocrisy, as in the other four, but here, *the problem of heresy.*

It is precisely here that we face a puzzle. As we have
seen, the claim of fellowship with God in 1:3, as well as the
properly Johannine claims in 1:6, 2:4, 6 and 9, definitely imply a perfectionist stance--not to mention 3:6 and 9, which
are explicitly perfectionist! Yet the perfectionism claimed
by the author's opponents in 1:8 and 10 is denied. As we asked
in our Introduction, is the author being inconsistent, or are
there real differences between *two* types of perfectionism? Let
us look now more closely, first of all, at the type of perfectionism denied by the author in 1:8 and 10.

The first assertion, in 1:8 ἁμαρτίαν οὐκ ἔχομεν, is cast
in the present indicative, which here seems to have a durative
function, indicating a permanent state of being, existing not
only in the present, but stretching timelessly into both the
past and the future.[14] This would mean that the author's opponents claim *always to have been sinless, i.e., intrinsically*
sinless, a claim, according to Bultmann, typical of the "gnosticizing false teachers" in 1 John who claim to be in the light

i.e., perfect and sinless.[15]

The second assertion, in 1:10 οὐχ ἡμαρτήκαμεν, is cast in the perfect, which often indicates the continuance of completed action.[16] This would serve to strengthen the opponents' claim to sinlessness, made in the present tense in 1:8--they *never* have sinned at all. No Christian perfectionist would ever make such a claim. The perfection already implied in 1:3 (having fellowship with God) and claimed in the assertions of 1:6, 2:4, 6 and 9 does not imply that the Christian members of the Johannine community never in their past sinned; presumably they were sinners before they were baptized into the Church, after which they claimed a life of perfection, or near perfection, because of their new fellowship with the Father. *Only a gnostic view of man, a view which saw man as intrinsically part of the Divine Essence, or a spark[17] from the Divine Fire, a part of the Father who is above all, could claim that man had never sinned.* It would be a claim of *intrinsic* human perfection, possessed by man as a *right*, not, as in the case of Christian perfectionism, *given* to repentant, sinful man as a *gift* from the forgiving Father. Such a claim of intrinsic perfection betrays a doctrine of human nature radically different from the Judeo-Christian one found throughout the whole Bible, and which hardly needs documenting, namely, that man is sinful and in need of redemption. This doctrine of man's intrinsic sinlessness may properly be designated as gnostic, insofar as it is an important teaching in some gnostic systems.[18] Certainly it is part of a radically different anthropology from that which underlies the whole biblical doctrine of man.

Hence we conclude that the author in 1:8 and 10 is dealing with *an heretical type of perfectionism, based on a definitely gnostic anthropology*, and which he denies, in contrast with the type he affirms in 1:3*ff.*, and especially in 3:6 and 9. This means, then, that *there are two distinct types of perfectionism evident in 1 John*. We must explore their differences further; but first, it would be well to deal with one of the ways the author chooses to refute his opponents' heretical type of perfectionism, namely, by introducing a previously unmentioned (in Johannine literature, *i.e.*, previously unmentioned in the Gospel of John) but important theological concept in 1 John

1:7b, 9; 2:1-2--verses which surround 1:8 and 10, and serve to
interpret them. At this concept we must now turn our attention.

2. The Doctrine of the Expiation for Sin

The theological concept here in question is the doctrine
of Christ's expiation for sin, explicitly stated in 1:7b and
2:1b-2.[19] These verses do not qualify the assertions of the
opponents in 1:8 and 10, but rather *refute* them. The refutation is expressed in terms of Jesus' blood cleansing us from
all sin in 1:7b; in 1:9 it is expressed in terms of confessing
sins and being forgiven by him who is faithful and righteous,
and who cleanses us from all iniquity. In 2:1b the concept of
expiation is developed further in terms of Jesus Christ as the
Righteous One, the Paraklete, *i.e.*, the intercessor on behalf
of sinners.[20] Then in 2:2 (repeated in 4:10) the term ἰλασμός
itself finally occurs, which serves to tie together all these
verses into one basic idea of the atonement, namely, that the
death of Jesus on the cross provided the means for forgiveness
of all sins. This concept of Christ's expiatory sacrifice for
sin is certainly a primitive Christian doctrine, with its roots
deep in the earliest Christian community,[21] and one which is
nearly ubiquitous in the New Testament, being found in a variety of theologically different writings, *e.g.*, Rom. 3:25; 5:8-
9; 1 Cor 15:3; Gal 1:4; Eph 1:7; Col 1:20; 1 Thes 5:10; Heb 1:
3; 9:12; 1 Pet 1:2,19; Rev. 1:5; 7:14. One might add that the
passion narratives in all four Gospels have this concept of the
atonement lying behind them, and though not explicitly present
in the Gospel of John (as we shall see), it seems to be implied
in the saying of Caiaphas about the death of Jesus in John 11:
50. The presence of this common Christian doctrine of the
atonement here in 1 John indicates the author's desire to bring
the Johannine community back into line with the great mainline
Christian thinking about Christ's death, and so close the mouths
of the heretics within the community.

The striking thing about this familiar concept of the
atonement is that it is atypical of the Gospel of John. As
C. H. Dodd has pointed out, this concept of atonement, intro-
duced in 1 John, is quite different from that found in the
Fourth Gospel. Following Dodd, we note that in the Gospel of
John the atonement is spoken of in terms of:[22]

(1) The *glorification* of Christ. Dodd cites John 12:23, 32-33, and 13:31 as illustrations of this.

(2) Christ is *"lifted up"* (his *exaltation*) in order to draw all men to himself. Dodd does not cite this, but it is relevant here: *cf.* 3:14; 8:28 and 12:34.

(3) Dodd points out the *sacrificial overtones* of 6:51a, where Jesus gives his flesh and blood for the life of the world (but not for sin).

(4) In the same place Dodd cites 17:19 which contains the motif of *self-dedication* and *sanctification*. In connection with this, *cf.* 10:36, where Jesus, at the Feast of the Dedication (10:22), refers to himself as being dedicated and sent into the world by the Father. Hence he is the new temple, the new presence of God with men. (*Cf.* Rev 21:3).[23]

(5) Dodd also cites 13:1 where Jesus loves his disciples and *freely lays down his life* for them, as well as 10:5 where he lays down his life for the sheep, and 15:13 for his friends.

(6) Not cited by Dodd, but important here in relation to #5 above, is the Johannine motif of *no one taking Jesus' life from him*, but rather his free giving of himself, especially evident in 10:17-18.

(7) Finally, it should be noted that all through the passion narrative in John, *Jesus is in complete control of the situation at all times*. When the soldiers come to arrest him in the garden, his "I am" sends them reeling back on their heels (18:6). When Peter tries vainly to defend him, Jesus asserts that he will drink his Father's cup without compulsion (18:11). (There is no Gethsemane scene in John.) Jesus boldly answers the High Priest (18:19*ff.*), and Pilate (18:33*ff.*). He carries his own cross (19:17), contrary to the Synoptic tradition. He cooly commends his mother to the beloved disciple (19:27-27), and except for the ironic "I thirst" (19:28), his last words, "It is finished" (19:30) are a cry of triumph. In a sense, there hardly is a "passion" in the Gospel of John; Jesus is never really passive, in spite of his being a captive. Rather

in John, Jesus goes actively to meet his death; it is
the hour for which his whole life on earth was the
preparation (*cf*. 12:23,27; 13:1; 16:25,28,32; 17:1);
and for John it is nothing less than Jesus' triumphant
stride into glory!

Therefore we can readily agree with Dodd that in John's
Gospel the atonement "is not a sacrifice for the expiation of
sin." (See note 22 above.) (The only exception to this is the
Lamb of God motif in 1:29, which Dodd discusses,[24] and which we
will discuss in Chapter Three.) This means that the author of
these verses in 1 John was introducing (or perhaps re-introduc-
ing) the doctrine of expiation for sin, previously (in the Gospel) almost unheard of in the Johannine community. He did so
for the purpose of refuting his opponents' audacious claims to
perfection. We suppose that he introduced it because he apparently deemed it a theological argument sufficiently strong to
refute his opponents' perfectionist heresy. Like the good
scribe in Matthew 13:52, the author of 1 John brought out of
the Johannine treasure things both new and old; in this case,
apparently something old for his special polemic purposes.[25]

Further, Bultmann, in his commentary on 1 John, p. 26*ff*.,
notes how 1:7b is an intrusion into the flow of argument.[26]
Indeed, one is surprised to find, in the midst of a discussion
about being in the light and having fellowship with God, a
strong proclamation of the expiation for sin effected by the
cleansing blood of Jesus! (The jarring effect here would be
similar to the introduction of a revivalist preacher into a
Christian Science testimonial meeting.) Not only is 1:7b lit-
erarily jarring, but it is also theologically different from
its immediate context.

3. Orthodox and Heretical Perfectionism Distinguished

At this point we may safely conclude that the opponents'
claims in 1:8 and 10 are treated quite differently from the way
the others are treated because the author considered them quite
different: heretical, not merely hypocritical. Also, it may be
concluded that the author has introduced the doctrine of expiation of sin for the purpose of vigorously combatting this
gnostic heresy. These conclusions might lead us to think that
the author of 1 John held an "expiationist" view of sin, while

his gnostic opponents alone held a perfectionist view. But it is not that simple. Already, as we have seen, in the whole section of 1:3ff., it is clear that the author claims moral purity for himself and for his followers. They walk in the light, which seems to imply that they are close to Him who is purity itself, and hence participate in that purity. This is a type of perfectionism, since moral purity is obviously equivalent to sinlessness. To reiterate, the claims to have fellowship with God (1:6), to know him (2:4), and to abide in him (2:6), and to be in the light (2:9) are made by any good Johannine Christian, and can be abundantly documented in the Fourth Gospel. (Cf. note 13.)

Furthermore, the author's perfectionism can also be detected in 2:1a, Τεκνία μου, ταῦτα γράφω ὑμῖν ἵνα μὴ ἀμάρτητε. This sentence implies that sin is expected to be quite exceptional in the life of a Johannine Christian, and although the author goes on to state his expiatory doctrine, he is demanding ethical perfection of his audience. Therefore, what we have before us in this section of 1 John is not a stark contrast between the expiationist author and his perfectionist opponents, but rather, as we have indicated, *two types* of perfectionism.

The opponents' type may be designated "heretical" and the author's "orthodox", inasmuch as the latter is the type of perfectionism acceptable to an author who obviously manifests a real concern for correct teaching. The opponents' perfectionism is gnostic. It claims, as we have seen, that man is intrinsically perfect and sinless; he is already part of the Divine Essence, and *ipso facto* is incapable of sin. (Cf, above, notes 17 and 18.)

On the other hand, the author of 1 John holds to a carefully qualified perfectionism. The section 1:3ff., which we have been discussing, lays out this perfectionism in terms of moral purity, which is a gift to man, not his by right. It comes only by virtue of fellowship with God, who is Light, etc. It insists upon unhypocritical behavior, in other words, upon the moral perfection which alone validates the claim to know God. (3:7-8 are further qualifications, surrounding the author's highly qualified perfectionism in 3:6 and 9; cf. below,

Chapter Five, *ad loc.*, on the discussion of the "deceivers.")
This orthodox perfectionism in 1 John refutes the gnostic concept of inherent sinlessness in two ways: first, as we have
seen, by a firm affirmation of the primitive doctrine of expiation, hitherto unused in the Johannine community; and, second, by an emphasis upon the qualifying motifs of *abiding in
God* and *being born of God*, found in 3:6 and 9. These verses,
more than 1:3*ff.*, provide us with the *locus classicus* of orthodox perfectionism in 1 John. It is important for us now to
note these verses carefully, because at first sight they seem
to assert as true what the author has stated previously in 1:8
and 10 to be false. But the contradiction is only apparent. Let
us look now at how various commentators have dealt with this
famous problem of 1 John.

B. The Problem of Apparent Contradiction

1. The Apparent Conflict Between 1:6*ff.* and 3:6 and 9

First, let us set before our eyes the texts which present
the orthodox perfectionism in 1 John:

3:6 πᾶς ὁ ἐν αὐτῷ μένων οὐχ ἁμαρτάνει... (3:6b omitted)
3:9 Πᾶς ὁ γεγεννημένος ἐκ τοῦ θεοῦ ἁμαρτίαν οὐ ποιεῖ,
     ὅτι σπέρμα αὐτοῦ ἐν αὐτῷ μένει καὶ οὐ δύναται
     ἁμαρτάνειν, ὅτι ἐκ τοῦ θεοῦ γεγέννηται

Now let us survey how eight different commentators (in
chronological order of their works) have dealt with this problem.

A. E. Brooke[27] writes the following comment on 1 John 3:6:

In so far as union with the Sinless is realized, sin
ceases to be. The doing of sin shows that the Christ
has never been fully seen or known. The statements
are made absolutely, after the writer's wont. They
must, of course, be interpreted in the light of i.8ff.,
where the writer makes it clear that he does not mean
that those who have realized their union with Christ
have actually attained as yet to a state of complete
sinlessness. Where sin is, the vision of the Christ
has not yet been made perfect. There is nothing to
show that the writer is describing the *general* character of the Christian, which remains unchanged by
separate sinful acts, inasmuch as they are foreign to
it and do not affect it as a whole. The statement is
made absolutely without reference to the modifications
necessary when it is applied to the individual case.

There is much good insight into the theology of 1 John in this statement, especially in the first sentence, where Brooke correctly understands the necessary qualification of union with Christ as the *sine qua non* of the sinless life. Further, he seems to be aware of the apparent conflict between 3:6 and 1:8 when he refers to the "absolute" character of the assertion in 3:6, which nonetheless must be "interpreted in light of i.8ff."

Brooke thus solves the problem of the apparent conflict in two ways: first by implying that it is merely the strong "absolute" rhetorical style of 3:6 which makes it appear in conflict with 1:8, and second, by establishing a somewhat arbitrary hermeneutical rule that 3:6 must "be interpreted in light of i.8 ff."

The first way is typical of many commentators who have followed Brooke: explain 3:6 away in terms of *rhetoric only*, in effect maintaining that the text does not mean what it says, and hence ignoring the whole *theological* question of perfectionism raised in 3:6. Those who believe that grammatical analysis alone can solve all such problems of interpretation, without bothering with theological content, are mightily attracted to this approach. It is, however, an inadequate method of exegesis; this study maintains throughout that the theological content of any sentence under examination is of primary importance to its interpretation. (*Cf*. Chapter One, C 5.)

The second way, appealing to an arbitrary hermeneutic rule of interpreting one sentence in light of another, is also questionable, because of its sheer arbitrariness. Why not interpret 1:8 in light of 3:6? Or better, why not interpret each in light of the other? Brooke does not consider these alternatives, apparently in an effort to harmonize two apparently conflicting concepts of 1 John. The perfectionism explicit in 3:6 was probably suspect to Brooke, so it had to be interpreted in the light of the expiationist doctrine in 1:7b*ff*, which, of course, is perfectly orthodox. Brooke underestimates here the strength of the orthodox version of perfectionism in 3:6, and does not appreciate the dialectical tension which exists between 3:6 and 1:8. Although Brooke has done justice to the all-important qualification of "union with the Sinless" in 3:6, as we have noted, he fails, in the main, to grasp the full theological import of 3:6, and takes the easy road of harmonization with 1:8.

C. H. Dodd raises this problem in his commentary.[28] He notes that "The difficulty may be relieved by observing a distinction of tense in Greek."[29] He then goes on to describe and contrast the grammatical force of both the present and aorist tenses, much in the same way Nigel Turner did later. (See below.) He also refers to passages in Jewish apocalyptic literature, namely, Enoch 5:8*ff.* and Jubilees 5:12 (*Cf.* Chapter Four of this study, below, *ad loc.*), which provide evidence for perfectionist thought. Then he admits, unlike Brooke or Turner, that "The apparent contradiction is probably not to be eliminated (though it may be qualified) by grammatical subtlety."[30]

His basic solution is that the author "is writing from different points of view, and concerning himself with different problems."[31] This sentence shows that Dodd, again unlike Brooke (or Turner), considers the theological issues involved in the apparent conflict and not merely grammatical questions. It also shows that Dodd sees the likelihood of there being more than one front against which the author is struggling. In this case Dodd sees the author of 1 John combatting, on one hand, "the complacency" of those who assumed they were "already perfect in virtue", in 1:8-10, and, on the other hand, "the moral indifference" of others who "thought it did not matter whether they were virtuous or not, provided they were enlightened", in 3:1-10. This is certainly possible. However, it seems that Dodd regards both groups as merely wayward Johannine Christians and not gnostic false teachers (the latter group at least), as do Schnackenburg and Bultmann, for example. (See below.) This is a weakness of Dodd's: he underestimates the virulence of the gnostic heresy which infected the Johannine community at the time 1 John was written. However, he does refer, in his commentary (on 1:8), to gnostic heretics:[32]

> The heretics (if we may read between the lines, with the support of what is known about "Gnostic" teaching) take their stand upon the belief that Christians have been given a new nature superior to that of other men. Consequently, they affirm, Christians are already sinless beings; or if not all Christians, at least those who have attained to superior enlightenment. They have no further need for moral striving: they are already perfect.

This is an excellent description of the gnostic opponents of the author of 1 John, and it is regrettable that Dodd did not carry through his insight here into his analysis of the difference between 1:8-10 and 3:6-9. Had he done so, he probably would have discovered the difference between the two distinct types of perfectionism.

Dodd rightly sees that gnostic heretics are the source of the false teaching being combatted in 1 John 1:8*ff.*: "The heretical teaching might have different effects upon its adherents."[33] But he ascribes the viewpoints against which the author writes in both 1:8*ff.* and 3:6*ff.* to "adherents" of gnostic heresy, which seems to imply wayward members of the community, not the gnostic, heretical teachers themselves. It would seem, rather, that the author in both places has primarily the heretics themselves in mind, not any members who may have been influenced by them. Thus the notion that the author is writing to two different groups is an unnecessary hypothesis. We need to know *who* the opponents were and *what* they professed, and not merely whom they may have influenced, or that perhaps they influenced different persons in different ways. Instead of Dodd's hypothesis of two groups, it seems more likely that there is only one group of heretical perfectionists against which the author is contending (*cf.* Chapter Five), and that first in 1:8 and 10 he attacks their heresy directly, and then in 3:6 and 9 he provides his readers with his own *orthodox* version of perfectionism, with its important qualifications of abiding in Christ and being born of God.

At this point, it would be well in our discussion to consult the comments of Herbert Braun, in his article *Literar-Analyse und theologische Schichtung im ersten Johannesbrief.*[34] He states the following, in the context of the discussion of the theological stratification evident between 1:8-10 and 3:6-10:[35] "Der Versuch, diese einander entgegengesetzten Aussage-Gruppen auf zwei Schichten, also etwas Quelle und Verfasser, zu verteilen, versagt restlos."

Braun will not allow a theological difference to be established by means of source analysis; for him it would be a vain attempt to attribute one passage to a hypothetical source and the other to the author. He notes that Bultmann's source anal-

ysis does not attempt such a facile and superficial solution to
the problem. Further, Braun maintains that the paradox should
not be weakened between these two passages:[36] "Das Paradox
scheint beabsichtigt und darf nicht abgeschwägt werden."

But after all this has been rightly said, what is Braun's
solution to this problem? It seems to be based on the observation that the important qualifications of abiding in Christ
in 3:6, and being born of God in 3:9, are essential to the
author's understanding of perfection and constitute the decisive difference between the orthodox and heretical versions of
perfectionism. Braun sees being born of God as an action, not
a condition:[37] "Aus-Gott-gezeugtsein ist nicht Zustand, sondern Aktion im Konkreten..." The gnostic perfectionists, according to Braun, believe their perfection to be a condition,
a state of being (*Zustand*), whereas the author sees perfection
as the concrete action of abiding in Christ. (The heretics do
not so abide, as is apparent in 2:19, "They went out from us.")
Or, to put it another way, the gnostics have a static view of
human nature while the orthodox have a dynamic one.

Braun further contrasts the difference between the gnostic
and orthodox views in this way:[38]

> Die sehr aufschlussreichen Differenzen zwischen beiden
> Texten (C.H. 13 and 1 John) beginnen damit, dass im
> 1 Joh. die Gotteszeugung in der glaubenden Begegnung
> mit der Verkündigung, im C.H. in der Rückerinnerung
> des Menschen an sein wahres Sein sich realisiert:
> τοῦτο τὸ γένος--οὐ διδάσκεται, ἀλλ' ὅταν θέλῃ ὑπὸ
> τοῦ θεοῦ ἀναμιμνήσκεται. (C.H. 13,2). Definiert der
> I. Joh. den Gottgezeugten als den aktual Liebenden,
> so entfällt dagegen eine konkrete Ethik hier in C.H.
> 13 schon deswegen, weil die Identität des Wiederge-
> borenen (Gotteszeugung und Wiedergeburt stehen in
> C.H. 13 promiscue) mit seiner fruheren Existenz un-
> terbrochen ist: Καὶ εἰμί νῦν οὐχ ὅ πρίν. (C.H. 13,3).

The gnostic self-understanding includes seeing the human
soul as already part of the Divine Essence, as we have noted
above, whereas the Christian understands the soul as sinful
but called by God (by proclamation, not by remembering) to
union with Him.[39] Braun has correctly put his finger on the
essential difference between orthodox and heretical perfectionism, and his viewpoint has been productively followed by
both Schnackenburg and Bultmann, as we shall see.

Rudolf Schnackenburg[40] finds the key to this problem in

44

the eschatological nature of salvation, *i.e.*, in the eschatological tension between the already and the not yet. In his
important *Exkurs 12: Christ und Sünde*, he expresses his view
thus:[41]

> Das Heil, das der von Gott Erzeugte erlangt, ist
> grundsätzlich ein eschatologisches... Diese Span-
> nung zwischen Erwartung und Erfüllung erfordert auch
> in der joh. Theologie den sittlichen Imperativ (3,3).
> Er ist -- in anderen Formulierungen als bei Paulus
> -- sogar sehr kräftig ausgeprägt.

This insight of Schnackenburg's is most helpful in understanding the author's concept of perfection, as well as that of
his opponents. For the author of 1 John, the tension between
perfection and sin still exists, as clearly stated in 3:2, "Beloved, we are now children of God, and it does not yet appear
what we shall be." The Christian in 1 John lives the dynamic
life of the ever-approaching eschaton: he already has been born
of God and abides in Christ, and insofar as he fulfills those
two essential provisions, he is sinless (3:6,9). But there remains a "not yet", a future expectation of the completion or
fulfillment of his moral perfection, and this implies that he
may yet lapse back into sin temporarily and have need of the
forgiveness which comes through Christ's expiatory sacrifice
(1:7b*ff.*).

On the other hand, the gnostic view has broken this eschatological tension; the Christian is already complete; no eschatological fulfillment awaits him. He is statically perfect because his soul is essentially part of the Divine Being. Hence
there is no need to abide in Christ or in his teaching, which
for the author of 1 John, as well as for the Fourth Evangelist,
is equivalent to remaining in the community.[42] Nor does the
gnostic need to be born of God in the radical sense found in
John 3 (Nicodemus), *i.e.*, receiving a new origin from above
(ἄνωθεν), from Christ;[43] he *already* is from God, already his
child.[44] Schnackenburg's analysis here has provided us with
another decisive difference between orthodox and heretical perfectionism (besides the anthropological difference pointed out
by Braun): each has a radically different *eschatological* viewpoint.

Wolfgang Nauck[45] has followed Schnackenburg on the idea of
the eschatological tension in 1 John:[46]

Im *1 Joh* wird dieser Hoffnung einer endgultigen
Befreiung von der satanischen Macht zwar nirgends
explizit Ausdruck gegeben, sie wird aber vorausge-
setzt, wenn der Verfasser in 3, lf. im Zusammenhang
mit den Sätzen über Gerechtigkeit und Sünde von dem
νῦν und dem οὔπω des Christenstandes spricht: Das
Tun der Gerechtigkeit ist das Kennzeichen und die
Frucht der *jetz* im Glauben gegenwärtigen, in der
Taufe geschenkten, aber noch verborgenen Gotteskind-
schaft. Aber sofern diese *noch nicht* in ihrer vollen
Herrlichkeit des Ihm-gleichseins und des Ihn-sehens
erschienen, offenbar geworden ist, ist das Tun der
Gerechtigkeit durch die Anfechtung der Sünde stets
neu in Frage gestellt und kann nur durch das Sich-
heiligen wie jener heilig ist im Glauben an die Über-
windung der Sünde und des Satans durch Christus ge-
schehen. Was Gott am Glaubigen 'im Endgericht offenbar machen will, das ist an Jesus Christus schon
jetzt Wirkichkeit geworden: "Es ist keine Sünde in
ihm."

Nauck properly emphasizes here the author's main theological thrust: moral perfection is possible for the Christian insofar as he is caught up in the eschatological event of Christ.
He *already* participates in the new life (in Nauck's view this
comes through his baptism[47]), but does not *yet* share in the
glory of being-like-him (1 John 3:2).

Nigel Turner represents the school of purely grammatical
exegesis. In his study *Grammatical Insights into the New Testament* (1965), he has neatly solved our problem by a feat of
bright but superficial exegesis. Noting the inceptive force
of some aorists,[48] Turner designates the ἁμάρτῃ of 2:1b as such,
thus allowing the verse to be translated, "and if he *began* to
be a sinner..." On the other hand, the ἁμαρτάνειν of 3:9 is a
present tense, which is known to "express a state rather than
an action."[49] This is all quite well, but it blithely ignores
the crucial historical and theological questions lying behind
the real tension between the view of sin in Chapters 1 and 3
respectively, which we have been struggling with here. It probably should not be expected that a book on grammar alone should
deal with history and theology, yet why does such a book as
Turner's pretend to have solved this problem by grammatical
analysis alone? We would contend, for methodological purposes,
that grammatical analysis is necessary but not sufficient for
responsible exegesis.

Rudolf Bultmann, like Braun and Schnackenburg and Nauck,

quite predictably grasps the paradoxical nature of the problem
before us. In dealing in his commentary on 1 John 1:9, he
writes:[50]

> Aber eben diese Paradoxie, dass mit dem Lichtwandel das
> Sündenbekenntnis ebenso wie das Κοινωίαν ἔχειν μετ
> ἀλλήλων zusammengehört, charakterisiert das christliche
> Sein gegenüber der gnostischen Irrlehre. Ist das Sein
> des Gnostikers ein statisches, so ist das christliche
> Sein ein dynamisches. Dem Gnostiker ist durch seine
> Gnosis seine Zugehörigkeit zum Licht der Gottheit --
> sei sie entdeckt, oder sei sie erlangt -- ein für alle-
> mal zum Besitz geworden. Der Christ hat durch seinen
> Glauben das Licht nie als dauernden esitz erworben. Er
> hat seinen Glauben im περιπατεῖν zu bewähren, ist immer
> unterwegs und steht nie als ein Fertiger vor Gott, son-
> dern ist auf Vergebung angewiesen.

Here we find an excellent and clear contrast between gnostic and Christian anthropologies.

Then on 3:6, Bultmann comments:[51]

> Dieser Satz scheint zunächst im Widerspruch zu 1:8 ff.
> zu stehen, wo die Leser im Gegensatz zu den Irrlehr-
> ern, die behaupten, sündlos zu sein, vor der Einbild-
> ung gewarnt werden, sündlos zu sein. Indessen besteht
> kein wirklicher Wilderspruch; den V. 6a sagt nur die
> grundsätzliche Wahrheit, dass jeder, der "in ihm
> bleibt", d.h. wer ihm treu verbunden bleibt, nicht
> sündigt. Das μένειν ἐν αὐτῷ ist also die Bedingung
> des μὴ ἁμαρτάνειν.

According to Bultmann's view, one might say that the author of 1 John held an existentialist, dynamic view of man before God: as long as he remained in Christ and was born of God
he did not sin; his sinlessness is to be "located" in his *existence*, not in his essence. On the other hand, the author's
gnostic opponents held an essentialist and static view of man:
he *is* part of God and *is in essence* perfect. "Sin" could only
be forgetfulness of his true origin.

Bultmann has not shrunk from facing up to the apparent
contradiction between 1:8*ff.* and 3:6*ff.* His existentialism
here has been helpful in making clear what the decisive difference was between orthodox and gnostic anthropology, and
consequently between orthodox and heretical perfectionism.

Finally, Massey Shepherd observes on 3:9:[52]

> The author does not flinch from using language as
> astonishing as that of his opponents: *No one born
> of God commits sins*; for God's nature, lit. "seed",
> *abides in him* (vs. 9). But he controls his state-

> ment by the context. He does not mean to say that
> the new birth demanded by Jesus in the Gospel pro-
> duces a man who is sinless (cf. 1:10). Rather the
> man who is born of God is set in the right direc-
> tion--of doing what is right and of loving his
> brother. Sin is a matter not of nature but of
> conduct.

Like Braun, Schnackenburg and Bultmann, Shepherd rightly
perceives the eschatological tension in the author's perfectionism. Further, he sees how it is related to the doctrine
of expiation. The gnostic opponents viewed sinlessness as a
matter of nature, whereas the author saw it, and also sin, as
a matter of conduct; here Shepherd has neatly summarized the
decisive difference between gnostic and orthodox anthropology
as evident in 1 John.

2. The Real Conflict in 1 John

As we have seen, the apparent conflict between $1:8ff.$ and
3:6 and 9 is due to the author's condemnation of the heretical
type of perfectionism in the former and his affirmation of the
orthodox type in the latter. Yet when all is said and done,
there remains an inconsistency in 1 John. The author, in his
eagerness to combat heretical perfectionism, came up with three
strategems: (1) the introduction of the old doctrine of Christ's
expiation for sin, (2) the two important qualifications or provisions for sinlessness, in 3:6 and 9, namely, abiding in Christ
and being born of God, and (3) the introduction of a system of
casuistry concerning two kinds of sin, mortal and non-mortal.
The first and third strategems conflicted with the second one.
In other words, by introducing the doctrine of expiation and
the practice of casuistry, he effectively nullified even his
orthodox version of perfectionism. There simply can be no way
of harmonizing even the carefully qualified perfectionism of
3:6 and 9 with the antiperfectionist, gradualist ethic presup-
posed by expiationism and casuistry. (Perfection is, by definition, an absolute.) These two doctrines turned out to be an
"overkill"; they must have effectively countered the gnostic
doctrine of perfection, but, at the same time, they produced
an intolerable tension with the orthodox expression of perfection. Expiation for sin and sinless perfection by abiding in
Christ and being born of God are simply irreconcilable doctrines.

Now in order to save the author of 1 John from the accusation of being confused, unaware of the obvious inconsistency between expiationism and perfectionism, the only apparent alternative would be to say that he genuinely espoused one of these doctrines, while giving the other only formal acceptance out of a sense of loyalty to his church's teaching. Of the two, it would seem more likely that the author espoused the doctrine of expiation, in which case he could not technically be termed a perfectionist, as we have strictly employed the term. (Perhaps he could be termed a "semi-perfectionist" or a "quasi-perfectionist", since he certainly longed after perfection for his congregation(s).)

The tension in the author's mind shows up especially in 5:16*ff.*, where he wrestles with the problem of intercessory prayer. It is here that he makes a "casuistic" compromise by attempting (rather feebly) to make some sort of distinction between "mortal" and "non-mortal" ("venial") sins. No thoroughgoing perfectionist would ever have engaged in such casuistry; a believer was either sinless or not sinless. Likewise, those parts of the New Testament which teach the expiatory sacrifice of Christ for sins do not employ such casuistry. It comes into play here because of the author's attempt to reconcile two different, and ultimately irreconcilable, concepts of sin, which, in turn, are based on two utterly different ethical systems, *viz.*, perfectionism and gradualism. In the perfectionist ethic there would be only one kind of sin, mortal; but in an ethic which in its background had the doctrine of Christ's expiatory sacrifice for sins, venial, as well as mortal, sins could be seen as existing. For this reason it seems probable that the author of 1 John really was an expiationist at heart, since only such a person could believe there were any such thing as non-mortal or venial sins, *i.e.*, ἁμαρτίαν μὴ πρὸς θάνατον, in 5:16. This means, in turn, that the author of 1 John, by introducing the doctrine of Christ's expiation for sin (and consequently the practice of casuistry), modified his orthodox perfectionism to the point that it ceased being a thoroughgoing perfectionism in the strict sense. Yet, as we have suggested, he did not discard it altogether, but rather carefully qualified it, probably out of loyalty to his heritage, *i.e.*, the tradition of the Johannine community.

Now to summarize our findings so far, we may say that perfectionism existed in two distinct types in 1 John, orthodox
and heretical, and each was rooted in radically different anthropologies and eschatologies. The doctrine of Christ's expiation for sin was introduced by the author not only out of a
polemical concern for combatting the heretical type of perfectionism which was disturbing the community, but also out of
the author's personal conviction of its truth. However, out of
loyalty to his Johannine heritage, and to be sure, out of real
spiritual longing for his "children", he retained the doctrine
of perfection, carefully modifying it with the two indispensa-
ble qualifications of being born of God and abiding in Christ.
However, the juxtaposition of these two mutually incompatible
doctrines forced him to construct a compromise, a casuistic
system which made, for the first time in Christian history, a
distinction between mortal and non-mortal sins.

3. The Question of Origins

The question now arises, What is the origin of each type
of perfectionism found in 1 John? To answer this we must now
turn to the source most closely related to the First Epistle
and most likely to be the theological source of at least the
orthodox type of perfectionism, and perhaps of the heretical
type also, namely, the Gospel of John. But our search for origins must take us beyond this work to those pre-Johannine writings which exhibit perfectionist tendencies. Special attention
must be given to any gnostic writings which could be probable
sources of heretical perfectionism. To this search for the
origins of perfectionism in 1 John the next two chapters will
be devoted.

CHAPTER THREE

PERFECTIONISM IN THE GOSPEL OF JOHN

Introductory Remarks

This chapter will approach the problem of discovering perfectionism in the Gospel of John in two ways: first by ascer-
taining the meaning of the concept of sin *peculiar* to the Fourth
Evangelist, and second by exploring the numerous passages which
bear on the character of the believer in John. The first approach may be designated as the negative proof for perfectionism in John, in that the first part of this chapter will attempt to demonstrate the validity of Bultmann's dictum that in
the Gospel of John there is no sin but unfaith. The mere absence of "sin" in the traditional sense of wrongdoing, of course,
is only an argument from silence for perfectionist theology in
the Gospel of John. We will go beyond this, however, and in
the second part, attempt to demonstrate that the believer in
John is considered both morally and spiritually perfect.

PART ONE

SIN IN THE GOSPEL OF JOHN

Introductory Remarks

In his commentary on the Gospel of John, dealing with the
section 15:21-25, Bultmann states,[1] "Sin therefore is not primarily immoral behaviour; it does not consist in any particular
action, but is unbelief, and it will be defined as such explicitly in 16:8."

To test this assertion, let us examine the usage of the
term ἁμαρτ-άνω, ία in the Gospel of John. The usage of this
term may be conveniently divided, for our purposes into two
main categories, (1) pre-Johannine usage, atypical of the

central theological thrust of the Gospel, and (2) the usage
peculiar to John's theological outlook.

A. Pre-Johannine Usage of the Term ἁμαρτ-άνω, ία

Only three examples fall into this category, but they must
be dealt with first, since they appear to contradict Bultmann's
dictum that in the Gospel of John there is no sin but unfaith.

1. 1:29b The Lamb of God

This verse is an amazing complex of diverse scriptural
echoes. There seem to be allusions here to three different
concepts: the paschal lamb,[2] the expiatory sacrifice of Christ,[3]
and the Suffering Servant, metaphorically described as a lamb
in Isaiah 53:7. C. K. Barrett, in his excellent article, *The
Lamb of God*,[4] observed that this "strange amalgam" was fused
together in the Christian eucharist. Be that as it may, certainly it must be said that the combination of the title *Lamb
of God* with the function of taking away the world's sin is a
Christian invention.[5] The offering of the paschal lamb is not
an expiatory sacrifice, nor does any Hebrew sacrifice take away
sin. The juxtaposition of these two disparate symbols--the
paschal lamb and the removal of sin--is entirely of Christian
origin. Barrett has shown in the article just cited that C.H.
Dodd's hypothesis of the Lamb of God as the apocalyptic, messi-
anic lamb[6] "does not do justice to the explanatory clause, 'who
takes away the sin of the world'."[7] The term *sin* here is tied
together with the symbol of the Lamb as Jesus, whose death on
the cross in this one verse seems to have been modelled after
the paschal lamb of deliverance,[8] the lamb of the sin-offer-
ing,[9] and the Suffering Servant.[10] This hardly bears out Bultmann's thesis, since the sin of the world which the Lamb takes
away could not be mere unfaith. Nowhere in John does Jesus
take away unfaith; rather, as the light of the world, who cre-
ates the genuine *krisis* for all men (3:19), he actually cre-
ates, dualistically, the occasion for either faith or unfaith.
Sin here must signify the actual sin of men for which expiatory
sacrifice is deemed necessary. In John no sacrifice of any
sort can take away unfaith--only faith can cancel it out.[11]
Sin in 1:29 is not unfaith.

The only way to mitigate this conclusion, which contradicts Bultmann's generalization about sin in John's Gospel, is

to note that this understanding of sin is *atypical* of the rest
of the Gospel, and is generally left *undeveloped*. To be sure,
as Barrett has noted, the theme of Jesus as the paschal lamb is
developed throughout the Gospel;[12] but the *total* phrase in 1:29
--with its juxtaposition of two disparate elements--is not. It
remains a puzzling anomaly in the Fourth Gospel. Very likely
it is a pre-Johannine theological motif, and hence methodologi-
cally, cannot be cited as evidence for the task of discovering
the concept of sin *peculiar* to the Fourth Evangelist. It should
be no surprise that there are isolated and undeveloped passages
in John which echo pre-Johannine theological motifs. The question here is not what John shares, somewhat tentatively, with
the general Christian tradition, particularly in the interpretation of Old Testament models, but *in what ways he departs
from tradition*. It is in his theological departures that we
discover what is *sui generis* Johannine. The Lamb-of-God-who-
takes-away-the-sin-of-the-world echoes a complex tradition
which the Fourth Evangelist used but did not develop for his
peculiar understanding of sin.

2. 5:14b Healing of the Lame Man

Fortna assigns this to his hypothetical "Gospel of Signs."[13]
Certainly the section 5:2-9a, 14b, is pre-Johannine; the basic
source, as Fortna has isolated it, contains no material which
can be designated as peculiarly Johannine. Furthermore, as
Barrett has observed,[14] the words μηκέτι ἁμάρτανε recall Jesus'
forgiveness of the paralytic in Mark 2:9.[15] Sin here seems to
denote the actual committing of misdeeds. Yet taken as a part
of the whole Gospel, sin here could possibly mean unfaith.
The invalid's lack of faith, evidenced in his feeble excuse
for remaining ill, in v. 7, is possibly his real sin, in the
Johannine sense. The injunction μηκέτι αμάρτανε would then
mean "Do not fall back into unfaith." In this case, the use
of sin in 5:14 would fit into the category of sin as unfaith.
If this is not the case, then the concept of sin here is part
of the pre-Johannine concept of sin as committing actual misdeeds, a concept which finds little corroboration in the rest
of the Gospel.[16] Like the concept of sin in 1:29, it has no
bearing on our investigation into the peculiarly Johannine
concept of sin.

3.   20:23 Authority to Forgive Sins

This is a bolt out of the Matthean blue! Matthew 16:19
comes to mind immediately; indeed, R. Brown has drawn a close
parallel between these two verses. Both, he believes, derive
from "a Hebrew/Aramaic formula well attested in later rabbini-
cal writings with the verbs $'\bar{a}sar$ and $n\bar{a}tar$ or s^e $r\bar{a}h$."[17] The
authority to bind and loose, found in both Matthew and John
makes the disciples plenipotentiaries of Jesus. However, in
light of 17:18, καθὼς ἐμὲ ἀπέστειλας εἰς τὸν κόσμον, κἀγὼ
ἀπέστειλα αὐτοὺς εἰς τὸν κόσμον, this concept is not foreign
to the Gospel of John. (Note the force of the καθὼς = *in the
same way*[18] as the Father sent the Son, so the Son now sends his
disciples.) The disciples according to John do not merely represent Jesus in the world, they *are* Jesus--they re-present him!
By their apostolic labor (*Cf.* 4:34-38) of preaching and teaching they make Jesus again present to their audience, and his
presence is still the coming of the *krisis*-making light into
the world (3:19). Hence those who hear the apostolic word from
the Johannine community are confronted with the decision either
to respond in faith, in which case their sins are loosed, or
turn away in unfaith, with their sins still bound to them. We
would say, then, that the Fourth Evangelist inherited the same
Jewish-Christian tradition of binding and loosing as Matthew
did, but put it in his general theological context of *krisis*,
thus transforming it. The sins spoken of in 20:23 probably referred originally to those misdeeds washed away in baptism, or
to post-baptismal sins, absolved by some ecclesiastical peni-
tential system (as in Matthew or in 1 John 5:16*ff*.). But in
the Gospel of John *sins* even here seem to mean, at least as
well, *the sin* of unfaith, which comes from remaining deaf to
the community's apostolic preaching.

To summarize, it may be said that these three verses are
rooted in pre-Johannine traditions, which viewed sin in the
way normative to the whole Bible, and hence have no bearing on
the concept of perfectionism found in Johannine literature.
Yet they have undergone some theological transformation, in
order to fit them into the overarching concept of sin found in
the Fourth Gospel. To that peculiar understanding of sin we
must now turn.

B. Sin as Unfaith

The following examples of the use of ἁμαρτ-άνω, ία bear
out Bultmann's thesis of sin as unfaith.

1. 8:21,24 "You will die in your sin(s)."

As Bultmann has pointed out,[19] the phrase καὶ ἐν τῇ ἁμαρτίᾳ
(or pl. αις in v. 24) ὑμῶν ἀποθανεῖσθε, is typical of the Old
Testament: Deuteronomy 24:16; Ezekiel 3:19; 18:24,26; Proverbs
24:9. Here in the context of John 8:21-30 it is tied in with
the important motif of Jesus' descent/ascent,[20] e.g., in v.21,
Ἐγὼ ὑπάγω καὶ ζητήσετέ με, καὶ ἐν τῇ ἁμαρτίᾳ ὑμῶν ἀποθανεῖσθε
ὅπου ἐγὼ ὑπάγω ὑμεῖς οὐ δύνασθε ἐλθεῖν. Jesus and his opponents
are from different realms: v.23, Ὑμεῖς ἐκ τῶν κάτω ἐστε, ἐγὼ
ἐκ τῶν ἄνω εἰμί. This motif governs the whole section of 8:21-
30, and serves to interpret the meaning of the term ἁμαρτία.
Jesus' opponents (the Pharisees, 8:13) are from the lower realm
(this world) and hence are incapable of knowing who Jesus is
and from where he originates; only if they are born ἄνωθεν can
they know him who is ἐκ τῶν ἄνω; only if they are born "from
above" (3:3) can they enter into the faith which alone leads
to eternal life. Otherwise they remain in darkness (cf. 8:12)
and unfaith. They judge κατὰ τὴν σάρκα (8:15), and cannot know
the real Jesus. Hence their only sin is unfaith; but that is
the one fatal sin of which all other sins (v. 24 in plural) are
mere reflections.[21] R. Brown (cf. note 21 again) and C. K.
Barrett[22] have both noted that for John here, sin means the
rejection of Jesus. The absence in John's Gospel of any list
of specific charges against the Pharisees, such as found in
Matthew 23, also argues (from silence) that unfaith is their
only sin.

2. 8:34 Sin is slavery

τῆς ἁμαρτίας is found in p[66,75] ℵ B C K etc., f[1] f[13]m 33m
vg syr[p,h,pal], etc.; it is missing in D it[b,d] syr[s], etc., and
is given a C probability rating in the Aland, Black, Metzger,
Wikgren The Greek New Testament.[23] Bultmann calls it "an interpretive gloss"[24] which spoils the meaning and the original
impact of the verse, namely, that sin is slavery. Certainly
the subject of freedom and bondage is the overriding concern
in the section 8:31-38, addressed to that significant group
designated τοὺς πεπιστευκότας αὐτῷ Ἰουδαίους, whom we may take

for former Jewish-Christian members of the Johannine community, who defected and who are hence the object of the greatest scorn found in all Johannine literature.[25] (*Cf*. 8:37*ff*, especially v. 44!) They are characterized as harboring a murderous hate for Jesus (8:37), which most likely meant historically, the mutual hate between the Jewish-Christian defectors and the Johannine community, read back into the life of Jesus. In any case, they, through their unfaith, are slaves according to John (vv. 34-35). They ironically believe themselves to be the seed of Abraham (v. 33), and never to have been bondmen; but because of their refusal to know the truth (*i.e.*, who Jesus is, v.31), and their refusal to *remain* in the faith, they are slaves. Hence they cannot abide in the house for ever; only the son (= members of the Johannine community) remains. Sin here is interpreted only as slavery;[26] no other specific charge is evident. In turn, slavery is due to unfaith.

   3.   8:46   "Who convicts me of sin?"

   Irony is again involved here. It is implied that Jesus has been accused of sin (*cf*. 9:24, where he is so accused because of his breaking of the Sabbath, *cf*. also 9:16); yet the accusation is really upon those who refuse to believe Jesus' words of truth. Verses 45-67 deal with one theme: Jesus has come speaking truth (= revealing heavenly reality), and his opponents have refused to hear him. This theme interprets ἁμαρτίας in v. 46; sin is the refusal to believe Jesus' revelation. The Evangelist in v. 47b adds his deterministic reason for the opponents' refusal to hear [ἐκ τοῦ θεοῦ οὐκ ἐστέ], which, in turn, recalls 8:23. They are not from God, nor from above, and therefore they *cannot* come to faith. They stubbornly remain on the lower level of reality, and refuse the rebirth from above, which alone can make them free to see the highest reality, namely, that *Jesus* is the ultimate revelation of God and the only giver of eternal life. That alone is their sin; but that sin is fatal.

   4.   9:2-3   Against the Rabbinic Style of Argument

   All through Chapter 9, which is the most cohesive section of the whole Gospel, the theme of blindness and of either coming to or refusing to come to the light is brilliantly and

ironically delineated. Martyn's historical analysis of this
chapter is particularly useful.[27] The blind man represents
those Jews who became members of the Johannine community and
then were excommunicated from the synagogue (9:33); "they once
were blind but now they see", *i.e.*, they came out of the old
blindness of Judaism into the light of faith in Jesus. The
really blind persons turn out to be the Pharisees, as the bit-
ter irony of 9:41 indicates. They have refused to see who
Jesus is, to confess him as the Son of Man (9:35), *i.e.*, the
man from above who is to be lifted up.[28] This constitutes
their blindness, and in harmony with what has gone before in
Chapter 8, this is their only sin.

The term *sin* is introduced in Chapter 9 in the context of
a sort of school debate in the rabbinic style (vv. 2-3).[29]
Martyn, speaking of the same type of debate in 6:32, points
out that Jesus has entered into a midrashic discussion in order
to terminate all midrashic discussion.[30] The same can be said
of 9:2-3. The words attributed to Jesus here indicate the Johannine community's *total lack of interest in the question of
sickness as the punishment for sin.*[31] Jesus refuses to answer
the question put to him and goes on instead to restore sight
to the blind man. Only if he had *remained* in the dark world
would he have had sin (*cf.* all of Chapter 8 and 9:41); his res-
toration to sight symbolizes his coming to faith in Jesus,
first as a prophet (v. 17), and finally as the Son of Man (v.
38). Any sin he might have had in the past fades in signifi-
cance or disappears altogether because of this act of faith.
Faith obviates sin; unfaith confirms it.

5. 9:16, 24, 25, 31 Sabbath Controversy

All these verses revolve around the sabbath controversy
of which Jesus is the object. Is Jesus a sinner? The blind
man at first does not know (v. 25); he is satisfied alone to
see again, *i.e.*, to have faith is to become disinterested in
the whole question of sin, which, in contrast, becomes an ob-
session with the blind man's interrogators. All this is splendid Johannine irony. The sarcasm directed against the legalism of the Jewish (or perhaps Jewish-Christian) opponents of
the Johannine community here is tellingly effective. Verses
31-32 are samples of the satirical polemic the Johannine com-

munity used against its enemies. The Evangelist uses rabbinic
logic in order to destroy it! In other words, by using one of
their own propositions, *i.e.*, "God does not hear sinners", and
the common assumption that no man could heal without being
heard by God, the Evangelist destroys the absurd accusation
against Jesus, which, historically, was the accusation of non-
observance of the Torah directed against the Jewish-Christian
members of the Johannine community by their Jewish opponents.
In fact, the whole rabbinic idea of sin, as characterized here
(perhaps unfairly) by John has been destroyed. Only refusing
to see is sin for the Johannine community.

6. 9:34, 41   Born in Sin

These two verses go together to depict the ironic juxtaposition between the two contradictory views of sin. The Pharisees in v. 34 dismiss with scorn the man born blind as an in-
veterate sinner. He cannot teach the truth; his blindness is
due to sin *only in the sense of his former unfaith*, which has
now been done away with, symbolized by the giving of his sight.
The real sinners are those who remain in unfaith; it is *they*
who are blind now, not the man born blind. (Having been born
blind seems to imply that having been born into the Judaism the
Johannine community opposes means having *always* been in unfaith.)
The irony is compounded by the Pharisees' false boast of being
able to see; according to our Gospel, they *never* have seen! If
only they would admit, as the man born blind did, that they
are indeed blind and always have been (*i.e.*, they have never
come to faith in Jesus as the Son of Man, the one who came
ἄνωθεν, who alone can give the blind sight and new birth to
those born into unfaith), then they might come to the light
of faith and begin to participate in the life of the new aeon,
now present in Jesus and in all who have come to faith in him.
But they remain in the blindness of the only sin there is: unfaith.

7. 16:8-9   The Paraklete as the Ἔλεγκος

We come finally to John's explicit identication of sin
with unfaith. The theological context for this is the portrayal of the Paraklete as an Ἔλεγκος, *i.e.*, the prosecuting
attorney who, in God's name, indicts the world for its failure
to believe in Jesus. [32] The verb ἐλέγχειν means "to expose",

"to uncover",[33] and it is the world's sin, the sole sin ὅτι οὐ πιστεύουσιν εἰς ἐμέ, which is exposed by the Paraklete, just as the light coming into the world in 3:19 exposed the evil deeds of those who refused to believe in the light. The evidence here on John's understanding of the term ἁμαρτ-άνω, ία, plus the foregoing evidence, show that as far as this term is concerned, Bultmann's dictum stands.

8. 19:11   Judas as the Epitome of Sin

It is implied here that Pilate has sin. He does not know Jesus' true origin; (cf. 19:9, Πόθεν εἶ σύ;--to which Jesus makes no reply). He does not know what truth is (18:38), even when--ironically--he is staring at him who is the truth (cf. 14:6). In short, his sin is unfaith. Yet, according to John, Judas' sin of betrayal is worse. However, it is not the betrayal as such that makes Judas a sinner, or even his thieving acts of covetousness (cf. 12:6); no moral transgression in itself causes Judas to be designated a sinner. Rather, Judas is portrayed in the Gospel of John as already being totally evil from his very origin: Οὐκ ἐγὼ ὑμᾶς τοὺς δώδεκα ἐξελεξάμην, καὶ ἐξ ὑμῶν εἷς διαβολός ἐστιν; 6:70, cf. 8:44. Out of the intrinsic darkness and total evil of his heart, Judas sins against Jesus. Chapter 13, verses 29-30, make this portrayal dramatically clear: he goes out into the night from which he originated.[34] Thus for John's Gospel, Judas is the epitome of sin, the incarnation of radical unfaith. His sin against Jesus had been determined from the beginning.

9. Light and Darkness in John

Some familiar citations from the Gospel where the terms φῶς and σκοτ-ία, -ός appear in dualistic juxtaposition, bear out the thesis that only unfaith is sin. These are found in 1:5; 3:19; 8:12 and 12:35. Only definitely in one, and perhaps in two of these, do we find any indication of an earlier, moralistic view of sin, as the commission of actual misdeeds. 3:19a reads up to the word φῶς as teaching that men's refusal to believe in Jesus, i.e., "they loved the darkness rather than the light", is the reason for their condemnation. This would fit into the main Johannine view of sin as the stubborn refusal to leave the darkness of unfaith and come into the light of faith. But beginning with the words in 3:19b, ἦν γὰρ αὐτῶν πονηρὰ τὰ ἔργα, and going on through the end of verse 21, we have an older stratum of the theology of sin delineated before us. Here evil deeds are the reason for the desire of men to remain in darkness, and the light has come to expose those evil deeds. The doers of truth (*cf*. Tobit 4:6 for one example of this common Jewish, moralistic expression), on the other hand, come to the light in order to have their good deeds made manifest. (*Cf*. Matt. 5:16.) This is pre-Johannine theology, commonplace in Judaism, in the Jewish Christianity of Matthew and James, and in various other examples of early strata in the New Testament.[35] It is not the view of sin typical of, or peculiar to the Fourth Gospel. The only comment which can be made about its appearance here is that the Fourth Evangelist, or his redactor, did not suppress every example of the community's Jewish-Christian heritage. Just as an older eschatology shows up in 5:25-29, after the radically new Johannine eschatology of 5:24, so here an older view of sin has been attached to the view peculiar to John. Whether or not this is the work of a redactor or of the original Evangelist is a moot question. Certainly it is possible to construct the hypothesis that 3:19b -21 comes from the hand of the "ecclesiastical redactor", but such a hypothesis is not necessary. It is of little importance for our thesis at which stage—early or late—these pre-Johannine, moralistic sentiments appeared alongside statements of peculiar Johannine concepts of sin. The fact remains that they remain unimportant and *undeveloped* throughout the rest of the Gospel. In the main, for John, unfaith is the only sin worth talking about at length—which the Evangelist certainly does!

The only other verse employing the light/darkness dichotomy, which hints at the pre-Johannine view of sin, is 12:35-36. The phrases ὁ περιπατῶν ἐν τῇ σκοτίᾳ and υἱοὶ φωτός γένησθε are reminiscent of paraenetic material found in Eph 5:8 and elsewhere.[36] No doubt the common store of pre-Johannine, Jewish-Christian paraenesis is evident here, as in 3:19b-21. Nevertheless, the same observation applies here as above: this type of paraenesis is conspicuously absent elsewhere in the Gospel of John, and is never developed. Unfaith remains the only sin in John's peculiar theological viewpoint, and Bultmann's thesis is shown as valid by the foregoing analysis.

One further comment is worth making at this point. Bultmann's terms "ethical dualism" or the "dualism of decision"[37]
have certainly stood the test of time in Johannine criticism.
However, as a result of this study, we might suggest the term
"ethical dichotomy" as being a more precise characterizing
phrase for the Fourth Evangelist's ethical outlook. The split
between those who have come to faith in Jesus and those who
have not is *absolute*; most likely this represents the attitude
of the Johannine community to the totally alien world of unfaith about it. (*Cf*. John 15:18-16:4a and 1 John 2:15-17; also
cf. our discussion of this in Chapter Five of this study.) They
consider themselves to be totally in the light, and everyone
else to be totally in the darkness. This dichotomy is based on
ethics only in a very peculiar way: the enemies of the Johannine community (portrayed in the Gospel as the enemies of Jesus
who represents the community) are evil not because of their
evil deeds but because they *originate* in evil, just as the members of the Johannine community have received a new origin
ἄνωθεν by their act of faith in Jesus.[38] This means that the
dichotomy between these two groups is not based primarily on
ethical behavior or misbehavior, but on whether or not a confession of faith is made in Jesus as the One From Above. Thus
we might coin the phrase "*pisteuological* dichotomy" to describe this phenomenon in John's Gospel. And if the split occurs over a confession of faith, then do we not have in John a
doctrinal dichotomy also? The Johannine community is alienated
from the rest of the world over the matter of *christology*, of
identifying *Jesus* and not the Torah or anything else as the One
Who Came Down From Heaven. (*Cf*. 6:32-35.) To be sure, faith
in John's Gospel is more than the orthodox confession of belief,
but as we shall see further on in this Chapter, orthodoxy is
involved in the Johannine view of faith.

Now let us proceed to the positive evidence from the Gospel of John itself, that the *believer* is ethically and spiritually perfect.

PART TWO

THE BELIEVER IN THE GOSPEL OF JOHN

Introductory Remarks

A thorough examination of the Gospel of John reveals the pervasive prominence of the believer. To be sure, the chief subject of this Gospel is Jesus, who is depicted as He-Who-Is-One-With-The-Father, and sent by him to bring eternal life to all believers.[39] The Gospel of John is a christological *tour de force* throughout. But next to Jesus, the believer is the most important character[40] in the Fourth Gospel. Like his Master, he is depicted by an amazing variety of motifs. Just as the various christological motifs finally come together to point to Jesus as He-Who-Is-One-With-The-Father, and consequently able to bring the life of the Father to man,[41] so the following motifs, now to be delineated below, point to the believer as he who is virtually sinless, morally and spiritually perfect, and in possession of the gnosis which brings him the life of the new aeon as a present reality.[42] This gnosis is nothing less than the perfect vision of the Father himself, made visible through the Revealer.[43]

In order to demonstrate this thesis, we have arranged an exhaustive selection of verses from the Gospel of John into five general categories, according to the characteristics of the believer(s).[44] Among these verses are fourteen which contain the explicit phrase ὁ πιστεύων. However, these verses alone do not exhaust the portrayal of the believer in John. There are many other verses, varying in the range of explicitness and implicitness, which also characterize the believer, and thus must be taken into consideration in the task of gathering data pertinent to proving our thesis. Indeed, as already indicated, the believer "pops up all over the place;" he is as ubiquitous as Jesus the Revealer himself, and the whole Gospel seems to have been written for his sake:[45]

> 20:31 But these are written that you may believe
> that Jesus is the Christ, the Son of God,
> and that believing you may have life in his
> name.

Naturally, there is overlapping among these categories, since in Johannine style many motifs are juxtaposed with many

others, to create an often intricate weave of christological
motifs, which contribute to the rich texture of the whole fab-
ric of the Fourth Gospel. Hence our categories are somewhat
arbitrary, but useful in demonstrating our thesis. Now to the
evidence.

A. THE ORIGIN OF THE BELIEVER

1. Those who believe are children of God and born of
    God: 1:12-13

Believers (τοῖς πιστεύουσιν) are explicitly identified as
τέκνα θεοῦ (*cf*. 1 John 3:2) in 1:12, and further designated as
ἐκ θεοῦ εγεννήθησαν in v. 13 following. Bultmann has adequately
given *Religionsgeschichtlich* background of this concept in his
commentary on John,[46] which need not be repeated here. What
may be noted for our purposes, however, is the *implication* of
perfection which lies within the notion of becoming children of
God. These children here were *adopted* (ἔδωκεν αὐτοῖς ἐξουσίαν
τέκνα θεοῦ γενέσθαι[47]) by the Logos himself after his own had
rejected him (1:11); such an adoption, resulting because of the
believers' reception of him (1:12a), definitely implies that
their act of faith (τοῖς πιστεύουσιν εἰσ τὸ ὄνομα αὐτοῦ), for
which adoption as children of God was a reward, was an indication of their perception of reality, when it appeared among
them as the true light (v. 9 τὸ φῶς τὸ ἀληθινόν). Such perception of reality implies a kind of perfection. This is only an
implication; there is nothing here which explicitly states that
the perceptive faith which results in adoption as children of
God is a sign of moral or spiritual perfection. (Indeed, in
1 John 3:2 the children of God have yet to become what they are
to be.) But the implication is strong, especially when this
motif of being born of God in 1:12-13 is seen in close relation
to the following examples of being born ἄνωθεν in chapter three
of the Gospel.

2. The believer is born ἄνωθεν (anew, from above)[48]
    3:3,7

Bultmann has given us a splendid interpretation of being
born from above in terms of receiving a new origin from God:[49]

> For rebirth means--and this is precisely the point
> made by Nicodemus' misunderstanding--something more
> than an improvement in man; it means that man receives
> a new *origin*, and this is manifestly something which
> he cannot give himself. For everything which it lies
> within his power to do is determined from the start by
> his old origin, which was the point of departure for
> his present life, and by the person he has always been.
> For it is one of the basic ideas of Johannine anthro-
> pology--as was hinted at already in 1.13--that man is
> determined by his origin, and determined in such a way
> that, as he now is, he has no control over his life,
> and that he cannot procure his salvation for himself,
> in the way that he is able to procure the things of
> this life. Moreover the goal of man's life corresponds
> to his origin. If his way is to lead to salvation, it
> must start from another point, and man must be able to
> reverse his origin, and to exchange the old origin for
> a new one. He must be "reborn"!

Certainly such a radical renewal of the believer through
the miracle of receiving a new origin implies the gift of at
least an incipient perfection. Jesus is from above (3:31) and
so, by adoption, is the believer. If they share the same divine origin[50] (Jesus intrinsically, the believer derivatively),
which is what our whole text here seems to be saying, it does
not seem too much to say that they share the same moral perfection. (Jesus' sinlessness is made rather clear in John 8:29b,
"For I always do what is pleasing to him", and quite explicit
in 1 John 3:5b, *cf*. Chapter Two, Note 12.) What goes for Jesus goes for the believer; he participates in his Master's perfection. This is a bold anthropology, to be sure, but line
after line of chapter three of John's Gospel seems to proclaim
just such a perfection as a *present* possibility, at least for
the man who believes in Jesus. What keeps this from being utter gnosticism is the emphatic Johannine insistence on being
born of God (from above) as completely a *gift* from God, not an
inherent right or possession of man.[51] Yet when this gift is
given the believer, he *becomes like*[52] his Master. The difference is, of course, that Jesus is the *eternal* Logos (1:1; 17:5),
he who is One-With-The-Father, and *inherently* perfect; the believer's perfection is derivative, but we would maintain, nonetheless real in his present existence.

3. The believer is born of the spirit and has received
   the spirit: 3:5-6:8; 7:39; 14:16-17; 19:30; 20:22b

The spirit is the means of new birth in 3:5-6, which means
that God himself, who is spirit (4:24), effects man's new origin. This in turn virtually means that God the spirit re-cre-
ates the believer into a perfect man.

In 3:8, he who has been born of the spirit (= born of God
= born from above) is like the spirit himself, especially here
in his utter freedom of self-determination; (he blows where he
wills). Such freedom may be called a factor in perfection.

Chapter 7, verse 39 is an editorial gloss referring to
the ultimate giving of the spirit to the believers. (οἱ πισ-
τεύσαντες, those who have once made the act of faith, as the
aorist here indicates.[53])

In 14:16-17, the first Paraklete saying,[54] this motif is
made explicit. If we may understand the indwelling of the
spirit in 14:17c (ὅτι παρ'ὑμῖν μένει καὶ ἐν ὑμῖν ἐστιν) as
equivalent to dwelling in Christ, as later expressed in 1 John
3:6, then the perfection of the believer is implied in 14:17c,
just as it is explicit in 1 John 3:6. The believer with whom
and in whom the spirit constantly dwells (note the present indicative of μένει[55]) could hardly be less than morally and spiritually perfect.

We list 19:30 here simply because it makes implicit, as
20:22b later makes explicit, that the spirit has been given
("handed over" παρέδωκεν) to the community.[56]

4. The believer is not of this world: 15:19b; 17:14c;
   17:16

The world here represents man's emnity toward God.[57] The
believer, like Jesus (note the καθὼς in 17:14c and 16), is di-
ametrically opposite the world. This implies that he, like Jesus, has *absolutely* no relationship with the world, and hence
does not participate in its evil. This, in turn, *implies*, at
least, moral perfection.

All the above citations, in the category (A) of the believer having his origin from God, present only implicit and
circumstantial evidence for his perfection. Yet when taken
with what follows, they add weight to the total evidence.

B. THE SECURITY AND SALVATION OF THE BELIEVER, AND HIS
    ASSURANCE OF ETERNAL LIFE.

1. The believer abides in Jesus, and he in him (mutual
    indwelling): 6:56; 12:26; 14:20,23; 15:4,5,7,9-10;
    17:21a, 26b

In 6:56 we find a eucharistic expression of the mutual indwelling of Jesus and the believer by means of eating and drink-
ing Jesus' flesh and blood.[58] The vividness[59] of the symbolism
here is probably due to the desire of the author[60] to emphasize
the reality of Christ's presence with the community via the
eucharist, and to identify that presence with the earthly, σάρξ
ἐγένετο presence of Jesus in an unbroken continuity. It is the
mutual indwelling, not the eucharist itself, which is important
here; the latter is only a means for the former to be realized.[61]

The figure of companionship, rather than that of mutual
indwelling, is denoted in 12:26, but the spiritual force is the
same: Christ is continually present with and in the believer.

In 14:20 and 17:21a, 26b, a parallel is drawn between the
eternal mutual indwelling of the Father and the Son and that
between the Son and the believer. (Cf. 14:2, 23, where the believers are the μοναί in which Jesus and the Father make their
dwelling.) To dwell in the Son is to dwell in the Father, and
more importantly, to have the Son in oneself is to have the
Father in oneself also. Here perfection is strongly implied;
to have the Father himself in one continually would necessarily
exclude sin and connote spiritual perfection.

Chapter 15, verses 1-10, provide the striking parable of
the vine and branches to illustrate this mutual indwelling, and
is the *locus classicus* for this motif. Any incipient gnosticism, which might be deduced from such statements as found in
14:20, 17:21a, 26b, is neutralized by the theology contained
in these verses. The believer has the divine life in him *only
as he remains in the community where the Son is continually
present*. This was vitally important to the self-understanding
of the Johannine community. Yet the moral perfection strongly
implicit in 14:20, 17:21a, 26b, is present here also, especially in the designation of the abiders as καθαροί, as we shall

see below.

    2. The believer is elect: 6:70; 13:18; 15:16,19;
17:2,6,10,12

In itself, election does not imply perfection. But in
John it is portrayed in typically strong dualistic tones, and
this can be seen as implicit of perfection. If the devil
(Judas) of 6:70, and Judas, who darkly lurks in the background
of 13:18, and the world of 15:19, represent the dualistically
contrasted side of evil, then the elect in these verses must
represent a good which is just as strong. This is again only
an implication, but not an unreasonable one. The divine initiative in this election, which implies divine favor, is explicitly stated in 15:16. The believers alone are elect; they
are dualistically contrasted with those who are of the world.

The verses above from chapter 17 do not use any form of
the verb ἐκλέγομαι, but rather have the motif of the disciples
being given (δίδωμι), *i.e.*, entrusted to the Son by the Father.
They are the Father's (17:10) as well as the Son's. This corroborates the election motif above, and adds weight to the implication of divine favor. For John, with his strong dualistic
view, it would be difficult to see how any persons less than
morally and spiritually perfect could receive such divine favor
and named God's own.

    3. Those who believe are τὰ ἴδια: 10:3-4; 13:1

Being specially God's own, the Good Shepherd's own sheep,
or Jesus' own true disciples, is a motif which fits in with
the previous one and reinforces it. It has the same theological meaning as the elect motif, and with it shares the same
implication toward perfection.

    4. The believer cannot perish, be cast out, lost or
        snatched away: 3:16, 6:37,39; 10:28-29; 17:12; 18:9

The terms ἀπόλλυμι (3:16; 6:39; 10:28; 17:12; 18:9), ἐκ-
βάλλω (6:37), ἁρπάζω (10:28-29, contrast the dualistic usage
in 10:12, where the sheep under the hireling are snatched
away), form a single motif which speaks of the utter security
of the believer. He is not only elect and the special posses-

sion of the Son, but forever secure. No Calvinist could hope
for better! His salvation is guaranteed. Of course, the all-
important qualification of abiding in the community where the
Son is present, is always in the background; but once the believer enters this community and *remains* in it (μένειν!) he can
rest assured of inevitable salvation. This does not necessarily imply moral perfection in the believer's present existence,
at least as he first enters the community. Perhaps a progressive growing toward perfection within the community is implied
here. However, the strong, pervasive dualism throughout the
Gospel of John suggests that those who are outside the community are totally evil, so those who are within it are already
good, *i.e.*, morally perfect.

    5. The believer is not judged: 3:18; 5:24

It is interesting to compare these verses with 1 John 4:17
where he who abides in love (and hence in God) may be bold at
the day of judgment. Another comparison may be made with Rev
20:4, where the special group of beheaded martyrs reign with
Christ during the millenium, and are called blessed and holy
(20:6) because they escape the second death, *i.e.*, the final
judgment (20:14b). In all these cases we find a specially
favored group who are apparently morally perfect enough not
to be required to appear at the final dreadful day. This is
strongly suggestive of moral perfection. In Rev 20 this honor
is given only to a certain group of martyrs, but in both the
Gospel and the First Epistle of John, it seems to be open to
all the believers who steadfastly remain within the community.

    6. The believer has a special place (τόπος): 12:26;
       14:2-3; 17:24

Like the former motifs, this one also denotes the special
favor the believer has with the Son. To these verses might be
added 13:23-25, where the Beloved Disciple, who is the prototype of the perfect disciple, has a special place of honor
nearest Jesus, ἐν τῷ κόλπῳ τοῦ Ἰησοῦ (*cf.* Luke 16:22[62] and
John 1:18), and ἐπὶ τὸ στῆθος τοῦ Ἰησοῦ. To have a special
place[63] with him who is divine is to enjoy the divine favor to
such an extent that definitely implies spiritual as well as

moral perfection.

Perhaps here we have the Johannine equivalent to the synoptic saying about the twelve disciples being seated on twelve thrones judging the twelve tribes of Israel. (Matt 19:28 and Luke 18:30). An even more majestic vision of the believer reigning in glory is found in Rev 4. All speak of an extraordinary privilege granted to the elect.

> 7. The believer is loved and honored by the Son and the Father: 13:1,34; 14:21,23b; 15:9,12; 16:27a (*cf.* 1 John 4:10,19)

This motif serves to corroborate all that has been said above about the privileges of those specially favored by God. To be sure, Paul does not see the love God has toward man as an indication of man's perfection; quite the contrary, as we read in Romans 5:5-9. But as we have already seen in the first part of this Chapter, in John there is no interest in any sin but that of unfaith. In most places in the Gospel of John, God's love is directed toward those with faith, and by implication, with a perfect moral life. The only exception to this is 3:16, where the world is the object of God's love.[64] (The world is most often representative of evil.) But taken in the context of the whole Gospel, being an object of God's love and honor implies having the faith and love in oneself which are in turn indicative of a perfect life.

> 8. The believer already enjoys the eschatological gifts of peace, joy and receiving what he asks for:
> a. Peace: 14:27; 16:33; 20:19,21,26
> b. Joy: 15:11, 16:6; 16:22a
> c. Receiving what is asked for: 14:13; 15:16c; 16:23-24 (*cf.* 1 John 5:14)

Peace and joy are eschatological gifts,[65] and for Paul they were two of the fruits of the spirit (Gal 5:22), already available to those who walk in the spirit. (The spirit is the ἀρραβών, the guarantee, of the eschaton in 2 Cor 1:22; 5:5; and Eph 1:14.) In a similar way, the Fourth Evangelist sees these eschatological gifts as presently available to the believer. Peace is paradoxically present with the disciples,

thrust into the strife-filled world of persecution. (*Cf.* 16:33)
It is an indication of inner perfection and harmony with God
and man, strong enough to overcome the inevitable strife of a
hostile world. Joy naturally accompanies it. Like peace, it
is paradoxically present with those enduring the λύπη (16:6,20)
of the end of the age; but their sorrow will be turned to joy,
indicating their steadfastness strongly akin to moral perfection.

The third reward, receiving what is asked for, may be the
Johannine equivalent of "Ask and you shall receive" in Matt 7:7
and Luke 11:9, which is also an eschatological characteristic.
Jesus' preaching of the imminence of the Kingdom of God included
his assurance that the long-desired prayers of those who awaited
the Kingdom were finally about to be realized. The same applies
here: since the disciples, according to John, are already enjoying the eschatological gifts of peace and joy, even in the
midst of strife and persecution', it is natural that their
prayers are being answered also. This is a definite sign of
the already self-realizing eschaton. Further, it is a sign of
moral perfection. James 5:16b, "The prayer of a righteous man
has great power in its effects" (RSV), comes to mind here; the
prayer of the righteous man is effective because of his righteousness. In the Johannine context much the same notion holds
true: the effective prayer of the faithful indicates their
righteousness, *i.e.*, their moral perfection. This is not to
say that the Gospel of John had knowledge of the tradition in
back of James 5:16b; Johannine thought moved in a different
world. Prayer in John must be understood within the total complex of the disciple/Jesus and Father relationship. In this
context it is simply a sign of the perfect peace and harmony
which reigns between the believer and his God. The believer
in John gets what he asks for from God because he cannot but
ask for what is pleasing to God. This points toward spiritual
as well as moral perfection.[66]

    9.   The believer is free; he is not a slave, but a friend:
        8:34-36; 15:13-15

In 8:34-36 δοῦλος and υἱός, and in 15:13-15 δοῦλοι and
φίλοι are dualistically contrasted. The slave in 8:34 is iden-

tified as "everyone who commits sin", with the implication that
being freed by the Son means being freed from sin. This is not
explicit, but the implication is logical. If it is true, then
sinlessness would be a characteristic of those who are "free
indeed" (8:36). However, Jesus here is addressing "the Jews
who had believed in him" (8:31), *i.e.*, Jewish-Christian members
of the Johannine community who had defected from it. Had they
remained in the teaching of Jesus (8:31), they would have been
his true disciples. But such was not the case; the Evangelist
is speaking only hypothetically. Yet this hypothetical talk
points to the implication of sinlessness of those who have indeed remained in the community's teaching. They are free--free
from sin.

As for the φίλοι, the opposite of the δοῦλοι in 15:13-15,
we perhaps have here a self-designation of the Johannine community: φίλοι. (Friends, or Beloved Ones.) C. K. Barrett, in
his commentary,[67] has an adequate discussion on the background
of this term in Philo and in Wisdom 7:27, where wisdom is said
to make men friends of God. He points out, however, that this
literature need not have influenced John; the concept of disciples as φίλοι is rather based on the φιλεῖν/ἀγαπᾶν motif.
Whatever its background, it certainly indicates that the community considered itself specially favored by God. As Barrett
points out, their friendship was based on having knowledge of
what God was doing, just as a friend, in contrast to a slave,
knows what the lord is up to. Barrett quotes Clement of Alexandria, Strom 7,11 (where the γνωστικός is τέλειος, φίλος and
υἱός), showing that the mystery religions equated knowledge
and friendship, which John's Gospel also seems to do here. Barrett does not consider John here to be gnostic, but the suspicion toward a gnosticizing tendency here remains, as far as the
notion of favoritism is concerned. It is hard to escape the
conclusion that Johannine Christians considered themselves specially enlightened,[68] and certainly such a self-understanding
is compatible with a perfectionist attitude.

10. The believer already possesses the life of the new
     aeon as a present reality: 3:15-16, 36 (*cf.* 1 John
     5:12); 5:12,24,26,40; 6:33,35,40a,47-48,53-54a,63,
     68; 7:38; 10:9-10,28a; 11:25a; 12:50; 14:6; 17:3;
     20:31

The eschatological orientation of all the verses quoted
above is toward the present. On the other hand, a future eschatological orientation may be discerned in 4:14,36; 5:25,28-
29; 6:27,40b,54b,57-58; 8:12; 11:24,25b; 12:25; 14:19b and
17:2. In these places the future tense of the main verb is
employed. (Other future-oriented eschatological motifs are
found in 6:39,40,44,54; and 12:48, where the oft-repeated re-
frain ἐν τῷ ἐσχάτῃ ἡμέρᾳ is found; also in 11:24, Martha's orthodox Jewish confession of faith in the final resurrection in
the future.)

It is not necessary here to resume the old debate, begun
by Bultmann, whether or not these future-oriented passages come
from the hand of an "ecclesiastical redactor." It is enough
simply to note that obviously two different eschatological orientations persist in the Johannine community, as reflected in
its Gospel, and they are not mutually incompatible. Their difference is only a matter of emphasis. The important fact to
acknowledge, however, is that the present-oriented eschatology
is *dominant*. It seems reasonable to assume that it represents
the distinctive Johannine thought, whereas the future-oriented
eschatology represents an older stratum of tradition, ultimately
going back to Jewish apocalyptic. There is nothing particularly Johannine or even Christian in 11:24; but 11:25a (with
the present tense Ἐγώ εἰμι) presents the eschaton as present
already in Jesus himself. The greatest of eschatological gifts,
eternal life, is now a possibility in the present existence of
everyone who comes to faith in Jesus. An even more radical
expression of this well-known Johannine eschatological shift
from the future to the present is found in 5:24, "Truly, truly
I say to you, he who hears my word and believes in him who sent
me, has (ἔχει, present tense) eternal life; he does not come into judgment, but has passed (μεταβέβηκεν, perfect tense) from
death to life." (RSV) All this is quite familiar to readers
of Johannine secondary literature.[69] What needs to be stressed

here as relevant to our thesis is that *the present-oriented eschatology carries within itself the definite implication of
moral and spiritual perfection*. This conclusion is based on
three observations:

(1) Those who enter the life of the new aeon (ἡ αἰώνιος
ζωή) are deemed *ipso facto* morally perfect. As we shall see
in the next chapter, this was an axiom underlying some Jewish
apocalyptic literature. The new aeon (or new age) was commonly understood as the righteous reign of God, into which only
the holy and perfect could enter. The sinless blessedness of
the martyrs in Rev 7:13-14, who have washed their robes white
in the blood of the lamb, is a Christian example of the same
apocalyptic conceptuality. Only the perfect and the sinless
may participate in the life of the world to come; this is affirmed commonly in both Jewish and Christian sources. (See
Chapter Four below.) The dualism in this concept is sharp:
only the perfect are admitted to the Kingdom of God, and the
wicked are excluded.[70]

(2) In the Gospel of John the new aeon has already arrived
in the person of Jesus,[71] who is the Son sent by the Father and
one with him; and *those who believe in him* have already entered
the life of this new aeon. Again, in 5:24 this is particularly
explicit: "death" (θάνατος) in this verse does not refer to
literal, physical death (as it does, for example, in 11:4),
but rather the spiritual[72] death which comes through sin. For
John, sin is the *unfaith* which leads to perishing (3:16). The
perfect tense of the verb μεταβαίνω (noted above) provides us
with another indication of the "already-ness" of the life of
the new aeon for the believer. "He has passed from death to
life" means that he, *in his present existence*, has *already*
passed out of the sin of unfaith into the perfect righteousness of the faith which alone brings life. He already enjoys
the sinless life of the new aeon.

Our case is not based on this one verse alone. A careful
examination of the rest of the verses cited at the beginning
of this section will reveal the same fact: the believer *possesses* (ἔχει, present tense, indicative mood) eternal life
(3:36; 5:24,26; 6:47,54); or the *possibility* of possessing it
is open to him in the present through faith (ἔχῃ, ἔχητε, ἔχωσιν,

74

present subjunctive, in 3:15,16; 5:40; 10:10; 20:31). In other
places the same thought is expressed in terms of being made
alive in the present (ζωοποιεῖ in 5:21 and 6:63); being given
life in the present (διδοὺς in 6:33); and τὰ ῥήματα imparting
life in the present (τὰ ῥήματα...ζωή ἐστιν in 6:63 and ῥήματα
ζωῆς αἰωνίου ἔχεις in 6:68). Besides these present-oriented
promises, there are the great Ἐγώ εἰμι sayings in 6:35,48;
11:25 and 14:6. All these examples taken together point con-
vincingly to the distinctive Johannine affirmation of the presence of the life of the new aeon in the believer.

What we have, therefore, in these first two observations
is a valid syllogism, which runs thus:

All who enter the life of the new aeon are *ipso facto*
perfect.

All Johannine Christians in their present existence have
entered the life of the new aeon.

Therefore, all Johannine Christians in their present existence are *ipso facto* perfect.

The syllogism is correct; only the major and minor prem-
ises need proving, which we have attempted to do by citing the
evidence above. Perhaps the second *all* in the minor premise
could be questioned: Did *all* Johannine Christians historically
claim such perfection? Perhaps not. But it remains evident
that the Gospel of John, in its preponderant viewpoint, claimed
such perfection for the believer.

Another way to put this argument is to say that Johannine
perfectionism is the result of the union of two major theological views, namely, "ethical dualism" and "realized eschatology."
This means that those who accept the truism derived from Jewish
apocalyptic, that at the eschaton all men will be dualistically
divided into the mutually exclusive camps of the righteous and
the wicked, and who *at the same time* affirm that the eschaton
has already occurred in the coming of Jesus the Revealer, are
most likely to be perfectionists. We are now anticipating the
conclusion of Chapter Four, where we shall show how Johannine
perfectionism resulted from the union of these two theological
affirmations. But now we must go on to our third observation:

(3) As we have seen earlier in this Chapter, there is no
sin but unfaith in the Gospel of John. Further, the absence in

John of the sort of paraenesis typical, for example, of Pauline and Matthean writings, indicates the seeming lack of concern over the moral problems which bothered other New Testament authors. Apparently the Johannine community did not feel it had any such moral problems. The unavoidable conclusions from these facts seems to be the corollary that if unfaith is sin, then faith is sinlessness. This cannot be made into a valid syllogism, but the implication is strong by an argument from silence. This argument, then, serves to corroborate the first two observations.

However, let us proceed with more evidence--albeit somewhat circumstantial--which will point to the validity of our thesis.

11. The believer is interceded for, glorified and
    sanctified: 17:9,20,17,19,10b,22a

Chapter 17 provides us with the Johannine characteristics of the believer *par excellence*. Verses 9 and 20 give us a motif which does not necessarily in its denote perfection; the heavenly intercession of Christ can also be found, for example, in Romans 8:34b, a context which hardly implies perfection in this present life (*cf*. Rom 7:14*ff*.). What marks these verses off as exhibiting a distinctive Johannine treatment of a common Christian doctrine[73] is the dualistic contrast in 17:9b, οὐ περὶ τοῦ κόσμου ἐρωτῶ... The strong suspicion arises again that the world is not interceded for because it is hopelessly lost in the sin of unfaith; the believing disciples, however, are the objects of the Son's intercession because of their faith. The implication follows that such faith is a sign of moral and spiritual perfection.

It is interesting to note that in 17:20 the "future" generation is being interceded for: περὶ τῶν πιστευόντων διὰ τοῦ λόγου αὐτῶν εἰς ἐμέ... We may take this group to be none other than the present generation of Johannine Christians for whom the Gospel was written. This means that all the characteristics of the believer in verses 20 through 26 were part of the self-understanding of the Johannine community at the time the Gospel was written.

Verses 17 and 19 deal with the sanctification of the disciples. In itself the term ἁγιάζω may denote virtual sinless-

ness,[74] but the implication is not strong here. It is notable,
however, that sanctification here comes through ἀλήθεια, which
in turn is equated with ὁλόγος ὁ σὸς (17:17b). (This will be
discussed below under Section D, dealing with orthodox belief
as a sign of perfection.)

Glorification is the concern in verses 17:10b and 22a. In
the former verse, Jesus is spoken of as glorified in the disciples, and in the latter verse the present generation is given
the glory the Father gave to the Son! Again, in itself, glorification need not imply sinlessness, but considering these
verses in light of the rest of chapter 17, not to mention all
the rest of the evidence adduced here so far, it would not be
too bold to suggest that a community whose self-understanding
included receiving the very same glory the Incarnate Son of God
had received from the Heavenly Father could also include the
notion of moral and spiritual perfection. It should be noted
also, that unlike the "eternal weight of glory", spoken of by
Paul in 2 Cor 5:17 as a *future* promise, the glory mentioned in
John 17:22a is *presently* given to the present generation of believers. (Κἀγὼ τὴν δόξαν ἣν δέδωκάς μοι δέδωκα αὐτοῖς... *i.e.*,
the perfect form of the verb here indicates that the giving of
glory to the present generation of Johannine Christians was a
fait accompli.) The motifs of sanctification and glorification
from the Father, through the Son to the community, provide
strong corroborating evidence for a perfectionist self-understanding in the Johannine community.

Now let us proceed to a third major category of characteristics of the Johannine believer, one which touches the concept
of perfection rather closely.

C. THE MORAL BEHAVIOR OF THE BELIEVER, HIS DISCIPLESHIP AND
   HIS MISSION

It is in this category where the anti-gnostic convictions
of the Evangelist are most evident. Without the moral theology
explicit in these verses, the Gospel of John would be even more
suspect of gnosticizing tendencies than it already is in some
quarters.[75]

1. The believer does the truth: 3:21a
"Doing the truth" (עשׂה אמת) is an ethical motif found in

sapiential literature, *e.g.*, Tobit 4:6; 13:6; and also in the
Qumran literature, *e.g.*, 1QS 1:5; 5:3; 8:9.[76] There is nothing
distinctively Johannine, or for that matter, Christian, in the
passage 3:20-21. (See above, Part One, B 9.) It is part of
John's Jewish-Christian heritage, as we have seen. If any Johannine stamp appears here, it would be in the sharpening of
the dualism, to the extent of becoming a real dichotomy based
on the decision for or against faith in Jesus as the One Sent
by the Father. *That* is distinctively Johannine. (Only in the
Qumran literature do we find a similar dichotomous attitude.[77])
Perfectionist implications, then, would be present here only to
the extent of the "johanninization" of a common Jewish ethic,
which in itself is not necessarily perfectionist. One could
hold a progressive view here: a person could gradually progress
toward doing the truth. This interpretation seems indicated in
verse 21 especially. The person who does the truth *comes to*
the light. Therefore, we must conclude that the basic theology
of this passage is not strictly perfectionist, but for that
matter, neither is it strictly Johannine. Only the sharpened
dualism here is Johannine, and it is not strong enough to provide any definite implication of perfectionism. All one may
say is that the whole passage is, however, compatible with Johannine perfectionism.

    2. The believer walks in the light: 3:21b; 8:12b (*cf.*
       1 John 2:5-8); 11:9-10; 12:26 (*cf.* Eph 5:8); 12:46

To "walk in the light" is another common ethical motif
with several New Testament parallels: Luke 11:35; 2 Cor 6:14;
Eph 5:8; 1 Thes 5:4; 1 Pet 2:9.[78] Its use in the Johannine examples above is also ethical, indicating the common ethical
concerns the Johannine community shared with the rest of Christianity and Judaism. Like the motif of "doing the truth", this
motif is juxtaposed with dualistic symbolism. ("Darkness" is
mentioned along with "light" in the context of all the examples
above, except 11:9, where "night", symbolizing the same thing,
is used instead of "darkness.") Similarly, this does not prove,
but only corroborates a perfectionist self-understanding in the
Johannine community.

3. The believer follows Jesus: 8:12b; 10:27-28; 12:26

The discipleship motif, indicated by the term ἀκολουθέω, appears in John as well as in the synoptic gospels and elsewhere in the New Testament[79] with the same ethical implications of loyalty and courage. It too, like the former two examples, appears in contexts where the "dualism of decision" predominates, suggesting that the true follower of Jesus either has attained, or is fast attaining, perfection. In 8:12b, for example, he who follows Jesus does not walk in darkness, *i.e.*, does not commit evil deeds. (*Cf.* 1 John 1:6-7 for the same perfectionist outlook.) In 10:27-28 and 12:26 the motif of following Jesus is juxtaposed and equated with other perfectionist motifs, discussed in this Chapter, *e.g.*, hearing Jesus' (the Good Shepherd's) voice, being known by him, being given eternal life, not perishing and not being snatched out of Jesus' hand (10:27-28). Similarly in 12:26 following Jesus means serving him, having a special place with Jesus, being honored by the Father. All this certainly suggests that the common Christian motif of discipleship, symbolized by the figure of following Jesus, has been transformed by all these Johannine juxtapositions in such a way as to strongly imply a perfectionist stance. However, *spiritual* perfection is not necessarily implied in the following motif--only moral perfection. Again, the evidence for a *complete* perfectionist self-understanding from the foregoing motif alone is lacking.

4. The believer does the work of God, and has been sent into the world (mission): 4:36; 14:12; 15:2,16; 17:18; 20:21

In three of these quotations, 4:36, 15:2 and 16, the motif of bearing fruit predominates, indicating that the disciples will continue the very work of Jesus himself, of bringing the life of the Father into the world. (In 12:24 Jesus' death is spoken of as bearing fruit, implying that the martyrdom of the followers will also have the same fruitful result.) This motif fits in well with the plenipotentiary motif found in 17:18 and 20:21 (note the καθὼς in both), where the disciples are empowered with the same saving power as the Son had! These in turn agree with 14:12, where the disciples are assured of even sur-

passing Jesus' earthly work! The disciples are effectively
continuing the mission of the eternal Son, with his same authority and power. In itself, this plenipotentiary concept of
mission does not necessitate an underlying perfectionism. However, when seen in the larger context of perfectionist motifs,
already explored above, it fits in well, especially with the
μένειν motif. Because the disciples *remain* in Jesus and he in
them, they are enabled to accomplish the mission he began. It
is the concept of *participation* in Jesus' ongoing life in the
community, which underlies this concept of mission, which carries within itself definite perfectionist implications.

5. The believer keeps the commandments, *i.e.*, remains in
   love with the Son and with his fellow believers: 13:34;
   14:15,21; 15:10,12

Just as the synoptic gospels have combined the texts of
Deut 6:4-5 and Lev 19:18 to make the "two great commandments"
in Mark 12:31, Matt 22:39 and Luke 10:27b, so the Johannine
tradition has juxtaposed the concepts of obeying God's commands
and loving one another.[80] Like Paul, John apparently sees love
as the fulfillment of all the commandments. (*Cf.* Rom 13:8.)
This juxtaposition of ἀγάπη and ἐντολή gives ἀγάπη moral content
and saves it from a gnosticizing indifference to human need.
(*Cf.* 1 John 3:17-18.) Likewise, it saves Johannine ethics from
degenerating into legalistic moralism. Although John does not
specify the content of his ethic here--he simply comprehends it
all under the title ἀγάπη--we may safely assume that the Johannine ethic was perfectionist, *i.e.*, it expected all the actions
and motivations of the Johannine community members to be ruled
by pure love, nothing else.

The measure of this love, however, is spelled out in 15:13
and it must be expressed even to the extent of giving up one's
life for his friends, *i.e.*, his brethren, just as Jesus did for
the community (the φίλοι, *cf.* 10:11). Just as there is "no
greater love than this", so probably there was no greater demand for perfection in the New Testament than in the ethic of
the Johannine community. And the demand is made in such a way
as to expect its fulfillment in fact by the members of the community. This certainly does point toward a perfectionist attitude.

6. The believer remains in unity and mutual love with his
   community:
   (a) Unity   10:16b; 17:11c,21a
   (b) Love   13:14,34-35; 15:12,14; 17:26

Mutual indwelling and unity are not merely mystical but
also ethical. In section B 1 the perfectionist implications of
it were brought out, and here they may be re-emphasized. The
disciples (= the believing members of the Johannine community)
not only dwell in Jesus, but also in each other, *i.e.*, in the
true unity which is not based superficially on similarities of
goals and aspirations, but ontologically on the fact that they
all have received a new origin and personhood from the Son --
ἄνωθεν! This has profound ethical implications, pointing certainly toward ethical perfectionism and a practical, mutual
concern among the members of the community for each other's
well-being. (*Cf.* 1 John 3:17-18, against the callous indifference of some.)

The same goes for the mutual love they are to have among
each other. 'Αγάπη is ontologically based; it has transformed
the community into a fellowship of perfect beings, perfect at
least in their self-understanding. Whether or not they remained
historically so loving among each other is, of course, quite
doubtful, especially in light of what we read in 1 John 3:11*ff*.
Nevertheless, mutual love is seen in the Fourth Gospel, as well
as in the First Epistle, as the crucial test of true discipleship (*cf*. John 13:35), and was apparently part of the Johannine
community's perfectionist self-understanding.

7. The believer is hated by the world: 15:18-16:4a (generally); 15:18-20; 16:2; 17:14-16

These verses do not prove the presence of perfectionism in
the community, but show an ethically dualistic attitude, similar to that found in the sectarian literature from Qumran.[81]
This attitude could well be expected of a community with a perfectionist self-understanding, and these verses are cited only
as corroborating evidence.

8. Those who believe are καθαροί (already): 13:10; 15:3

In 15:3 καθαροί may be translated "pruned" (as it is in

the Jerusalem Bible). But whether "pure" or "pruned",[82] perfection is implied. The ἤδη is crucial here for the perfectionist interpretation; *already*, in their present existence,
the disciples have achieved purity. (*Cf*. above, Section B 10.)
The reason for this achievement was τὸν λόγον ὃν λελάληκα ὑηῖν,
which we may take as the instruction the members of the Johannine community received when they were initiated into the
church.

In 13:10 there is probably a reference to the initiation
of baptism, at which time the new members of the community received the gift of purity, by being taken into a pure group,
one which claimed present union with Jesus, the imparter of
purity. All this need not imply a strict perfectionism; the
members could possibly fall away from their initial purity and
need some new means to receive forgiveness of their post-baptismal sins. We see in 1 John that this situation had arisen,
because of the presence of the doctrine of Christ's expiation
for sin, not only for the sin of the past, but also for any
present or future sinning on the part of community members (*cf*.
1 John 2:2). The system of casuistry in 5:16*ff*. also indicates
the decay of a thorough perfectionist self-understanding in the
Johannine community, as the conclusion to Chapter Two pointed
out. But in the Gospel we find none of this; this leads us to
conclude that the use of καθαροί in these verses cited above
indicates that a strict perfectionist attitude reigned in the
Johannine community at least at the time the sections which
contain these verses were written.

As has been noted before, the sharp ethical dichotomy between the believers and those outside, reflected in 13:10, where
Judas represents utter evil, points toward a perfectionist attitude. This attitude precludes paraenesis, which is notably
lacking throughout the Fourth Gospel, as also has been pointed
out above. The wicked are already lost (*cf*. 17:12 ὁ υἱός τῆς
ἀπωλείας) and the good are already pure (*cf*. 15:3). Hence moral
exhortation would be useless for the one and superfluous for
the other. The examples in this section do not generally provide positive proof of our thesis, but again, strong corroboration. The strongest evidence is the presence of the ethical
dualism in juxtaposition with many of these motifs. If the

judgment has *already* occurred (3:18), then the believer is already perfect.

D. THE ORTHODOXY OF THE BELIEVER.

Faith in the Gospel of John has rightly been described by Bultmann,[83] Dodd,[84] and Brown,[85] as a total, existential commitment of oneself to Jesus as the Son sent by the Father, and which results in the gift of eternal life. All fourteen uses of the term ὁ πιστεύων bear this out, and they are all tied in, in various ways, with the motif of ζωὴ αἰώνιος.[86] There are, however, some verses in John, listed below, in which faith (*i.e.*, the *act* of believing) is understood *to include as well* the concept of right belief (tacitly in contrast to wrong belief). In other words, *faith* in these following verses involves an emphasis upon *orthodoxy*: 4:23; 5:24; 6:60; 8:31,51; 14:23; 15:3,7, 20b; 17:6c,7-8,14a,17,20.

Chapter 4, verse 23 is in a class by itself. It describes the true worshippers as those who worship the Father in spirit and truth. This is genuine, real[87] worship, as opposed to the outmoded, unreal worship at either Jerusalem or Samaria. One is led to surmise that the Johannine Christians considered only themselves (at least in comparison with the Jews and Samaritans) as those who properly worshipped God. This is an attitude of orthopraxy rather than orthodoxy, but it is compatible with the orthodox "mind set."

In 5:24 we have what might be called an epexegetical juxtaposition of one motif with another: ὁ τὸν λόγον μου ἀκούων with πιστεύων τῷ πέμψαντί με. The one masculine article (ὁ) functions for both participles, which are joined by καί. The two motifs become mutually epexegetical,[88] each explaining the other in terms of the other. Actually they become equivalents here. To believe in him who sent Jesus means the same as hearing, *i.e.*, obeying (not merely listening to) the λόγος of Jesus, and vice versa.

Now there is reason to believe that the term λόγος in the following places (to be listed below) refers to the *teaching* of Jesus, or in some places, of the Father, which we may understand historically as the teaching of the community, *i.e.*, *what the Johannine community considered orthodox*. In several places,

of course, λόγος merely refers to a single "word" or saying,
quoted from the Old Testament, or from Jesus himself: 4:37,50;
7:36,40(pl.); 10:19(pl.),35; 12:38; 15"20a,25; 18:9,32; 19:8,
13.

But in the following verses it seems to mean *a whole set
of sayings*, altogether comprising a teaching: 5:24,38; 6:60;
8:31,37,43,51-52; 12:48; 14:23,24(twice); 15:3,20b; 17:6,14,
17b. In all these instances λόγος is indefinite, *i.e.*, it does
not refer immediately to a single saying or quotation in the
context. In 5:24 "hearing my word" could be taken as obediently
following [89] the right doctrine of the Johannine community. Its
juxtaposition with ὁ πιστεύων, then, means that *believing includes right belief*. (*Cf.* above, epexegetical juxtaposition.)
This is not to say that this is all faith means in John--obvi-
ously not. But by the time 1 John 5:1 was written, it becomes
evident that to have faith in Jesus *definitely* and *explicitly*
includes holding the right doctrines about him. We say that
this concern for orthodoxy is already implicit in the Gospel,
already apparent in these passages.

Our thesis here--that λόγος means orthodox teaching in same
places--is borne out by an examination of 6:60 in its context.
ὁ λόγος οὗτος must refer to the whole section 6:53-59; there is
no other referent for the οὗτος. This section comprises not
one mere saying, but a *complex* of sayings making up a unified
catechesis on the eucharist, the atonement and eschatology.
Verse 59 editorially refers to this section as what Jesus was
teaching in the synagogue at Capernaum. (Perhaps this is historically equivalent to what the Johannine community was teaching in some synagogue before it was "cast out", *cf.* 9:34.) Further, in verses 63 and 68 τὰ ῥήματα seem to refer to this section and be a synonym for λόγος.[90]

In the rest of these instances, showing λόγος as teaching,
the same phenomenon of referring to a whole complex of sayings
comprising a unified *catechesis*, may be noted. In 5:24 λόγος
refers to 5:19-23; in 5:38, the Father's word, to the Father's
witness to the Son, the subject of 5:31*ff.*; (6:60 has been discussed); 8:31,37,43 and 51-52, to 8:21-30; (8:43 perhaps to all
of Jesus' teaching, *i.e.*, the whole complex of Johannine doctrine). Chapter 12, verse 48 is part of a summary (12:44-50)

of the whole public ministry of Jesus narrated in the first half of the Gospel,[91] and hence could refer to everything Jesus (= the Johannine community) taught publically. In 14:23 λόγος refers to the whole discourse beginning at 14:1 (or 13:31); in 14:24 it is again the Father's teaching, *i.e.*, everything the Father has revealed in his Son, which is the content of Johannine doctrine. Λόγος in 15:3 refers to the whole Farewell Discourse; 15:20b likewise. In 17:6, 14 and 17b it refers to the Father's teaching; 17:17b is noteworthy in declaring the truth of the Father's word. This is much like the testimony of the final redactor in 21:24, about the veracity of the whole Gospel. Everything the Johannine community teaches is right and true.

Now let us return to our original list of sentences dealing with believing as orthodoxy. (The verses 5:24 and 6:60 have been discussed.) In those sentences λόγος is not only the life-imparting revelation of Jesus, but also *a specific content of doctrine about it.*

In 8:31 the Evangelist is apparently addressing lapsed Johannine Jewish-Christians. He exhorts them to remain in the teaching of Jesus (ἐν τῷ λόγῳ τῷ ἐμῷ), and consequently to be true disciples (ἀληθῶς μαθηταί). (ἀληθῶς here seems to acquire the connotation of being orthodox.) The concern for orthodoxy here is obvious. The lapsed "Jews who had believed in him" no longer hold the right Christology, which would liberate them. They are slaves, not only to sin, but also to false doctrine. They believe themselves to be Abraham's sons without the need of Jesus as the true Son from above, who alone can create truly free sons of God. (*Cf.* 8:33, 28).

In 8:51 this concern over right belief is carried out further. Here Jesus' opponents (= the opponents of the Johannine community) do not keep his word (τὸν ἐμὸν λόγον τηρήσῃ). The use of the verb τηρέω here itself indicates a concern for orthodoxy: to guard, to keep the right teaching. If they did keep it, they would never die! (θάνατον οὐ μὴ θεωρήσῃ εἰς τὸν αἰῶνα.) No wonder Jesus' opponents were sure he had a demon--or to put it historically, the opponents of the Johannine community must have thought them mad for stubbornly asserting with unshakable boldness that holding the correct doctrine about

Jesus guaranteed eternal life, with the ever-present, though unspoken,[92] corollary that wrong belief results in damnation. The Athanasian Creed is not more damnatory than this!

The motif of love is brought in with the concept of keeping the word in 14:23-24. This softens the impression, given in the preceding example, that concern for orthodoxy was harsh and dogmatic. (Yet love in John seems to be only for the brethren, *i.e.*, those *inside* the right-believing community, *cf.* Chapter Five, note 20, below.) For the Fourth Evangelist, with his totally dualistic, actually dichotomous outlook, love, right belief and obedience to the Father's commandments[93] all went naturally together. To be other meant being hateful, heretical and disobedient. Such was the way heretics were characterized in 1 John, the Pastorals, Jude and 2 Peter.[94] In fact, in the early centuries, through most Christian history, and sometimes even to this day, there has never been any such thing as a lovable heretic!

In 15:3 it is stated that the disciples *are* (ἐστε present tense) καθαροί already (ἤδη) because of (διὰ with the accusative) the word (λόγον, *i.e.*, teaching) that Jesus (= the Johannine community) has spoken to them. Here we find the decisive connection between orthodoxy and perfection. Right belief, *i.e.*, acceptance of λόγος imparted to those who joined the Johannine community, brought them the status of being καθαροί, which we have seen strongly implies ethical, if not spiritual, perfection. (The gnostic implications here are obvious. This makes the Johannine community look like a gnostic, or at least, a gnosticizing sect which imparted its own special teaching, alone considered to be true, and which was seen to impart life and perfection to the believer. This point will be taken up in the final chapter.)

In 15:7 the phrase τὰ ῥήματά μου appears to be a synonym for ὁ λόγος, and thus refer historically to the teaching of the Johannine community. The addition of the clause καὶ τὰ ῥήματά μου ἐν ὑμῖν μείνῃ to the initial clause ἐὰν μείνητε ἐν ἐμοὶ seems to indicate that the second clause is a further condition or qualification added to the first, in order to assure the desired result expressed in the final clause, receiving what one asks for. This juxtaposition also indicates that having Jesus' words

(= the community's teaching) abide in the believer is as important as the believer abiding in Jesus. Considering the usual
phrasing of the mutual indwelling motif--"abide in me and I in
you", *e.g.*, 14:20b; 17:26b--τὰ ῥήματά μου stand in the place of
Jesus himself! (*Cf.* 6:63b, 68b, where Jesus is said to have τὰ
ῥήματά which impart eternal life.) Jesus and his words are
one: both come from above and both are legitimized by the Father. For the Johannine community, Jesus' continuing presence
with them was through his words, *i.e.*, their teaching.

A good example of the dual use of the term λόγος is provided in 15:20. In the first part of the sentence it clearly
refers to the quotation which follows; but in the latter part
it has no definite referent, and seems to signify the whole of
Jesus' teaching. A legitimizing interest of the Johannine community seems to be operative in 20b: If they (the world) have
kept Jesus' teaching, they will keep the disciples'. Historically this must refer to the community's teaching; this teaching has been elevated to the same importance as that of Jesus.
Certainly the Johannine community believed that its doctrine
was equivalent to the teaching of Jesus, and could so esteem
it. (*Cf.* Chapter Five, on the "prophetism" of the Johannine
community; they believed they had the living Jesus speaking
viva voce to them.)

In chapter 17, verses 6c, 14a, and 17, the Evangelist
speaks of the *Father's* teaching, as he does also in 14:24b.
This may also be considered as stemming from a legitimizing
interest. The Johannine community teaches what Jesus taught,
and he taught nothing more nor less than what comes from the
Father himself. (*Cf.* 7:16b.) Such an interest in legitimacy
usually accompanies an interest in orthodoxy, especially an
orthodoxy engaged in polemic struggle with its rivals (as all
orthodoxy really is). The *Sitz-im-Leben* is, of course, a
struggle between one community, which claims to have the true
doctrine, over against its competitors. Such a community must
legitimize its teaching as *right*, *i.e.*, orthodox, by showing
that its origin is divine and has come from the Master himself,
through unimpeachable channels.

This concern for legitimate transmission is carried out in
17:7-8. Here the disciples (= the members of the community)

know that everything which the Father gave Jesus really comes from the Father (v.7). In verse 8 τὰ ῥήματα parallels πάντα in verse 7, and these words, which mean the true teaching of the community, come from the Father himself. The use of ὅτι with ἐπίστευσαν also indicates that the kind of faith being referred to here is primarily *right teaching*; they believed *that--i.e.*, they have accepted (a definite act in the past, note the aorist) as true the christological doctrine that the Father sent Jesus the Son, thus legitimizing him and his words, and in turn, the teaching of the Johannine community.

A further explication of the idea of an "apostolic succession" of teaching is found in 17:20. The present generation of the Johannine community is being referred to here by the phrase τῶν πιστευόντων and they come to faith by the λόγος of the disciples, which probably refers to the first generation, *i.e.*, the founders of the community. This λόγος, we hypothesize, was the authoritative teaching of the Fourth Evangelist and his disciples (*e.g.*, the redactor(s) of the Gospel), which was faithfully handed down to the second generation of the community. (Again, *cf*. 21:24.) In turn, the second generation (*e.g.*, the *final* redactor of the Fourth Gospel) caught in a polemic struggle with his opponents, emphasized the origin of this teaching in Jesus, and ultimately from the Father.

Now concern for orthodoxy in itself does not imply perfectionism, but it is certainly compatible with it. A community which considered itself morally perfect (on the chief ground that it believed it was already participating in the life of the new aeon), which dualistically associated right teaching with right living, and false teaching with immorality (in 1 John with the sin of hatred, *e.g.*, 1 John 3:12*ff*.), and which considered itself orthodox, would most likely possess a self-understanding which included both ethical and spiritual perfection.

E. THE GNOSIS OF THE BELIEVER

>   8:32; 10:14-15; 12:44; 14:4,6,9,17,20,26; 15:15b;
>   16:12,14-15; 17:3,7,25-26.

The term γνῶσις does not occur in the Gospel of John, but it is used here because the verses quoted above show the be-

liever as the one who possesses the true gnosis, the knowledge
of God himself. This gnosis brings eternal life (17:3). It is
not a static knowledge, but a lively, dynamic knowing of the
Father in a personal, existential way. Chapter 17, verse 3 is
rooted in the Old Testament concept of knowing God, as found in
Jeremiah 31:34 and in numerous places in Ezekiel; it is not
basically gnostic, although the language may be gnosticizing.
John avoided the nouns πίστις and γνῶσις but emphasized their
cognate verbs; this well-known fact points to a dynamic and
biblical concept of believing and knowing, instead of a static
and gnostic one of possessing special secrets about God. However, in John, the action of believing and knowing results in
a special status for the believer: the status of perfection.

In 8:32 knowing the truth means knowing reality itself,
and thus achieving perfect freedom. Certainly this is compatible with moral perfection; or to put it the other way around,
imperfection, sin, could hardly be expected to be found in such
a free, enlightened believer. This latter way of saying it does
not, of course, prove its corollary, but it shows its strong
probability.

In 10:14 Jesus' own sheep know him, *just as* (καθὼς) the
Son and the Father know each other, *i.e.*, eternally and perfectly. Such perfect knowledge is said to exist among the
sheep, *i.e.*, among the true believers of the Johannine community. It is most likely that such perfect knowledge would exclude any kind of imperfection, including moral imperfection.

The disciples' possession of this knowledge of Jesus and
who he is, especially as the revelation of the Father himself,
is emphasized in 14:4,6 and 9b. In verses 17 and 20 (within
the first Paraklete saying, 16-20), and in verse 26 (in the
second Paraklete saying), the Paraklete guarantees perfect
knowledge: the disciples know the spirit of truth, and it remains with them (verse 17); they will know the highest secret
of the universe, namely, the mutual indwelling of the Father
and the Son (verse 20). The Paraklete, who is now identified
with the Holy Spirit (verse 26), will teach them *all things*
(πάντα!), and remind them of all (πάντα again) Jesus told them.
Certainly this is perfect knowledge *par excellence*; there is
nothing more than knowing πάντα!

The familiar legitimizing interest is present in v. 26b. The community, guided by the Spirit, properly remembers *all* the tradition going back to Jesus himself. What the Johannine community taught was deemed absolutely sufficient. (This implies that what it may have known in the synoptic tradition, but did not pass on, was considered doctrinally unnecessary.) The Fourth Evangelist asserts that everything needed for eternal life can be found within the pages of his gospel. (*Cf.* 20:30-31; 21:25.)

In 15:15b the disciples (*i.e.*, the friends) are again assured that they possess all (πάντα) which Jesus has heard from none other than the Father himself.

The fourth Paraklete saying, 16:12-15, reiterates this guarantee of the possession of perfect knowledge. The community will be guided into *all* truth (16:12). A note of progressivism is present here, and in v. 12: the disciples cannot yet bear total knowledge, but will understand it later. The same idea-- that it took time for the disciples to understand everything-- occurs in 2:21-22. Perhaps all this reflects an actual historical situation: the early Johannine community did not yet come into the mature theology reflected in the final redaction of its gospel. Thus 16:12-13 are a later apologia from the second generation of Johannine Christians, explaining the slowness of the first generation to understand and *know* what came to be apparent.

The *locus classicus* for the motif of eternal life through knowledge of the Father, plus knowledge of the correct christology that Jesus Christ was sent by the Father, is found in 17:3. In 17:7 it is explicitly stated that the disciples *now* know all which comes from the Father. Historically this probably indicated that, in spite of the imperfect knowledge (*i.e.*, real depth of understanding) of the first generation of the community (referred to in 16:12), the present community now possesses perfect and complete knowledge. In v. 25 the disciples' knowledge of the true christology is again mentioned, dualistically contrasted with the world's ignorance. In v. 26 they have received knowledge of the Father's *name*, which possibly implies knowing God's essential being.

In summary, all these verses depict the believer as the genuine gnostic who belongs to the community which has the guar-

antee of knowing all anyone need know about God, and which cannot deviate from the truth (provided, of course, it remain in
the Son). This characteristic fits in well with the characteristic of orthodoxy, discussed above. In turn, to be perfect in
doctrine and perfect in knowledge--the knowledge which brings
the life of the new aeon to the believer as a present reality--
most likely means to be perfect in moral conduct and spiritual
life. Conduct, spirituality, orthodoxy and gnosis cannot be
separated in the genuine believer, according to the Gospel of
John.

At this point it would be well to evaluate the relative
merits of the foregoing arguments for perfectionism in John.
As we have seen, Sections A and C provided mostly only circumstantial or corroborating evidence, showing the compatibility
of the idea of the believer originating in God and behaving
morally with the concept of complete moral and spiritual perfection. Only C 8, on being *already* καθαροί, pointed decisive-
ly to complete perfectionism. Sections D and E go together to
demonstrate the self-understanding that the Johannine community
had involved the possession of the right doctrine about Christ
and the complete and perfect knowledge of God. As we have seen,
this is strongly suggestive of perfectionism.

But it is Section B, especially subsection 10, which dem-
onstrates that the Gospel of John considered the believer already to have entered the life of the new aeon; it is this which
most definitely shows a total moral and spiritual perfectionist
self-understanding to have existed in the Johannine community
at the time its gospel was written. Of course, as we saw at
the end of Chapter Two, by the time the First Epistle was written, this self-understanding underwent substantial changes, to
the point of disappearing in its strict sense. The dynamics of
this, as well as the implications for the evaluation of the Johannine community as a "sect", will be discussed in the final
chapter.

Now to summarize: The believer in the Gospel of John is
the child of God, born from above (ἄνωθεν), born of the spirit,
possessing the spirit, and is not of this world; he abides in
Jesus and Jesus in him; he is elect, God's own (τὰ ἴδια), not
subject to judgment; he has a special place with the Son, and

is loved and honored by him and by the Father; he presently enjoys the eschatological rewards of peace, joy and having his
prayers answered; he is Jesus' friend, not his slave, and already possesses the life of the new aeon in his present existence; he is interceded for by the Son himself, beloved by the
Father himself, glorified and sanctified; he does the truth,
walks in the light, follows Jesus, does God's work, fulfilling
and surpassing Jesus' own mission; he keeps the commandments,
and remains in unity and mutual love with his community; he is
hated by the world, but declared already pure by the doctrine
he has been taught; finally, he is orthodox and in possession
of the true gnosis of the Father himself. In short, he is perfect.

At this point we may safely conclude that the origin of
the orthodox perfectionism found in 1 John (notably in 3:6,9)
is rooted exclusively in the Gospel of John itself. No addi-
tional hypothesis need be constructed to account for its origin.
However, three questions now arise:

1. What are the origins of the *heretical* type of perfectionism alluded to in 1 John?
2. What are the origins of Johannine perfectionism
   itself?
3. How are these two types related to each other?

We might be tempted to answer the first question prema-
turely and state that the heretical perfectionism also originated from the Gospel of John, but suffered from a later gnosticizing perversion, perhaps from the gnosticizing tendencies
already within the Johannine community. But it is too soon to
jump to that conclusion, if, indeed, it is true at all. Instead
we must now explore rather far afield among various types of
pre-Johannine literature, which may show evidences of perfectionist tendencies. There we hope to find the source of the
original perfectionism of the Gospel of John, and some clues
of how and why it bifurcated into orthodox and heretical types
by the time the First Epistle was written.

PERFECTIONIST TENDENCIES IN PRE-JOHANNINE LITERATURE

Introductory Remarks

In our quest for the origins of the perfectionism in the Gospel of John, we shall survey various literary sources which possibly could have influenced the Johannine community. In doing so, no implication is made as to the probability of any literary dependence on the part of the Gospel of John on any of these sources. Rather, similarity in thought and obvious parallels between them and the Johannine corpus will be explored.

A. Hebrew/Jewish Literature

    1. The Old Testament and the Apocrypha

      (a) In the Pentateuch

Perfectionism as defined in this study (*Cf.* Chapter One) is not found explicitly in the Old Testament nor in the Apocrypha, but the legends, oracles and wisdom sayings about great and holy men found in them come close to perfectionist thought. In the Pentateuch we have the legends about Enoch in Gen 5:22, 24; Noah in 6:9:17; Abraham in 17:1; and Moses in Deut 34:10. In all these cases these men are regarded as exceptionally great and holy: "Enoch walked with God" (Gen 5:22). The *hithpa'el* of the verb *hlk* here indicates that Enoch had a close and constant fellowship with God, *i.e.*, he walked about regularly with God,[1] and was rewarded for his righteousness by being directly assumed into heaven, a privilege given to only two other blameless men in the Old Testament: Elijah (2 Kgs 2:11) and, by tradition, Moses (The Assumption of Moses[2]).

"Noah was a righteous man, blameless in his generation; Noah walked with God." (Gen 6:9b, RSV.) The same comment about walking with God is made about Noah, as was made about Enoch,

94

with the addition of two important adjectives, "righteous"
(צדיק) and "blameless" (תמים), which describe his moral character. The juxtaposition of these two adjectives provide us with
strong evidence for a perfectionist tendency in the Old Testament. Their application to Noah indicate his virtual sinlessness, and consequently make him worthy to be God's chosen man
for the creation of a new race after the Flood.

Abram is exhorted, "I am God Almighty; walk before me and
be blameless" (תמים). Here again we find one of the same adjectives, indicating Abram's moral uprightness with his God.
Like Noah he is the subject of an elective covenant.

The Deuteronomic editor who affixed verses 10-12 to the
end of the final chapter of Deuteronomy (34), and hence to the
whole Pentateuch, gave the pious readers of the Torah a climac-
tic encomium on the moral character of Moses:

> And there has not arisen a prophet since in Israel
> like Moses, whom the Lord knew face to face, none
> like him for all the signs and the wonders which the
> Lord sent him to do in the land of Egypt, to Pharoah
> and to all his servants and to all his land, and for
> all the mighty power and all the great and terrible
> deeds which Moses wrought in the sight of all Israel.
> (RSV)

This is indeed extraordinary praise. Moses enjoyed the
closest fellowship possible with God (*cf.* Num 12:6-8), and as
the Lawgiver of Israel received the highest praise of any man
in the Pentateuch, if not in the whole of Hebrew scripture and
tradition.[3]

All these men were more than mighty heroes, such as Gideon
and Samson, or David's mighty men; they were renowned for their
basic holiness. In the apocalyptic literature of a later time,
Enoch and Moses become the pseudonymous protagonists of the
works which bear their names, and Noah and Abraham also figure
importantly in some apocalyptic literature.[4] The choice of
these men was not at all accidental; like Daniel (*cf.* Ezek 14:
14,20; 28:3), they had become for the apocalyptic writers proto-
types of righteous conduct among men and holy fellowship with
God.

Besides these legends about the holiness of great men, the
Pentateuch provides some other notable examples of perfectionist thinking. In Deut 18:13 we come across the adjective תמים

again, now as part of an exhortation to all Israel:

You shall be blameless (תמים) before the Lord your God.

Indeed the whole book of Deuteronomy could be regarded as an exhortation to perfection--not merely ritual or legalistic perfection, but to a deep, moral and spiritual perfection. Chapter 30, verses 15-20 (on the two ways set before Israel, life and death), and 32:47 (which equates the keeping of the Torah with life), are notable examples of such earnest moral concern. The Deuteronomic passage in Joshua 24:14ff. (Joshua's charge to Israel to serve Yahweh "in sincerity and in faithfullness"-- בתמים ובאמת), is another such example. We know from Paul's own testimony in Phil 3:6b (κατὰ δικαιοσύνην τὴν ἐν νόμῳ γενόμενος ἄμεμπτος), that the Deuteronomic exhortations to virtual sinlessness were not only taken seriously by the many generations of pious Jews who followed, but were instrumental in their actual achievement of perfection in the observance of the Torah. In the synoptic gospels the Pharisees are never chided for breaking the Torah.

Finally in Leviticus, תמים is used innumerable times to indicate ritual purity;[5] yet it would be a mistake if one supposed that the Priestly writers had reduced that splendid moral term, as found in Deuteronomy, from ethical concern to a concern for mere ritual purity.[6] In Lev 19:2 the call to holiness, "You shall be holy; for I the Lord your God am holy", has definite ethical content, reaching its climax in v. 18b, "You shall love your neighbor as yourself: I am the Lord." Here Yahweh lays upon Israel the demand that it participate in his own moral perfection; to be an Israelite means to be a son of God who is expected to live righteously and blamelessly in all his relationships to God and his fellow man. To be sure, the Old Testament makes it abundantly and repetitively clear that the people of God did not generally meet such a high moral expectation and hence there is no real perfectionism, strictly speaking, in the sense of holding out to the average Israelite the possibility of achieving actual sinlessness in his present existence. Only the great men of God in the Pentateuch, mentioned above, seem to come close to perfection. Yet they are not the only such great ethical heroes; the second section of Hebrew scripture, the Former and Latter Prophets, provide us with other examples of perfection.

(b) In the Prophets

The hagiography of 1 Kings 17 through 2 Kings 13, concerning Elijah and Elisha, present us with the legends of extraordinary, holy, wonder-working men, who are often called "Men of God" (*e.g.*, 1 Kgs 17:18). It is not necessary here to rehearse their amazing feats. However, the demise of each of them bears notice: Elijah is miraculously delivered from the common fate of men by his spectacular assumption alive into heaven (2 Kgs 2:11); while Elisha, though dying a natural death (2 Kgs 13:20), retained his holiness and wonder-working power effectively in his bones, which caused a corpse brought into contact with them to spring immediately into life! (2 Kgs 13:21, *cf* Sir 48:14-15) The implication throughout all this highly legendary and even fantastic hagiography is clear: Elijah and Elisha were virtually sinless and ethically perfect as extraordinary men of God. But the average man of Israel could not hope to achieve their perfection; and since such a possibility was closed to him, the hagiography of 1-2 Kings cannot be classified as strictly perfectionist.

Two more examples from the prophets will suffice. In Jeremiah 31:31-34 (significantly quoted in that pro-perfectionist writing, the Epistle to the Hebrews, 8:7) we have the famous prophecy of the creation of a new human nature. In Jeremiah it is only a promise; yet this prophet, in spite of his general pessimism, seemed here to hold out the *eschatological* possibility of ethical perfection for man.

In Ezekiel 18:5-9, we have this prophet's exact description of the morally perfect man:

> If a man is righteous and does what is lawful and right--if he does not eat upon the mountains or lift up his eyes to the idols of the house of Israel, does not defile his neighbor's wife or approach a woman in her time of impurity, does not oppress anyone, but restores to the debtor his pledge, commits no robbery, gives his bread to the hungry and covers the naked with a garment, does not lend at interest or take any increase, withholds his hand from iniquity, executes true justice between man and man, walks in my statutes, and is careful to observe my ordinances--he is righteous (צדיק), he shall surely live, says the Lord God.
> (RSV)

Here we have a curious mixture of ritual, cultic and ethical

perfection, all of which Ezekiel apparently expected his hear-
ers to keep. This would make him more of a perfectionist than
Jeremiah, inasmuch as Ezekiel saw such perfection as a viable
possibility for man in his *present* life, not merely in the eschatological future (*cf.* Jer 31:31, "Behold the days are coming..."). However, with Ezekiel also, prophetic expectation
most often fell short of actual realization.

> (c) In the Writings--Wisdom Literature of the Old
> Testament

Perfectionist thought can be found in some of the Psalms of
the wisdom/didactic class.[7] In Psalm 1, "Blessed is the man
who walks not in the counsel of the wicked" (RSV), it occurs
only by implication. There is no evidence that the psalmist
expected moral perfection from the blessed man; but his abhor-
rence of the sinful life and "his delight in the law of the
Lord" indicate a perfectionist tendency. A similar line of
thought is found in Psalm 15.

Psalm 34:12-14 also describes the moral attributes of the
man who strives after some measure of perfection:

> What man is there who desires life,
>   and covets many days, that he may enjoy good?
>
> Keep your tongue from evil,
>   and your lips from speaking deceit.
>
> Depart from evil, and do good;
>   seek peace and pursue it.   (RSV)

Again, there is nothing here to prove an affirmation of strict
perfectionism; nevertheless, the psalmist apparently expects
persons to be capable of the moral activity he describes here,
and in the wisdom tradition, believes that such behavior con-
tributes to the perfect and wise life characterized by that one
word *shalom*.

In Psalm 37, "Fret not yourself because of the wicked," we
read in verse 18:

> The Lord knows the days of the blameless, תמימים
>   and their heritage will abide forever;   (RSV)

This whole psalm is a complaint against the temporary prosper-
ity of the wicked and the temporary suffering of the righteous,
with the hopeful affirmation of the temporary nature of both
situations. The author considers himself one of the blameless,

but there is not enough evidence to tell whether he is a thoroughgoing perfectionist.

Psalm 91, especially verses 7-8, expresses a similar thought
to that verse quoted above from Psalm 37. In both the idea of
God's special providence and care for his elect, in contrast to
his rejection of the wicked, is stressed. Moral dualism is
present, but this alone does not necessarily imply perfectionism.

Psalm 101:1-4 is worthy of note:

> I will sing of loyalty and justice;
> to thee, O Lord, I will sing.
>
> I will give heed to the way that is blameless;
> Oh when wilt thou come to me?
>
> I will walk with integrity of heart
> within my house;
>
> I will not set before my eyes
> anything that is base.
>
> I hate the work of those who fall away;
> it shall not cleave to me.
>
> Perverseness of heart shall be far from me;
> I will know nothing of evil.   RSV)

The same protestations of innocence can be found in Psalms
26 and 139:19-24. This comes very close to perfectionism, especially if the verbs in the Hebrew imperfect could be translated by a simple English present tense, e.g., "I give heed"
(אשכילה) "to know the way that is blameless" (בדרך תמים); or,
"I know (אדע) nothing of evil." In this case, an expression
of habitual moral goodness would be evident.

Psalm 112, like Psalm 1, describes the blessedness of the
man who fears Yahweh and does what is right; Psalm 128 is of
the same type. Each begins with the initial word אשרי , and
goes on to describe the special blessings of the man who is
wise enough to follow in the ways of Yahweh. There are, however, no explicit statements of blamelessness or sinlessness,
as we virtually have in Psalm 101.

Finally, Psalm 119:1, 3 and 80:

> (1) Blessed (אשרי) are those whose way is blameless,
> (תמימי־דרך)
> who walk in the way of the Lord!
>
> (3) who also do no wrong,
> but walk in his ways!

(80)May my heart be blameless (חמים) in thy statutes,
that I may not be put to shame!   (RSV)

In the LXX 118:80 reads, γενηθήτω ἡ καρδία μου ἄμωμος ἐν
τοῖς δικαιώμασίν σου. The word ἄμωμος is used to translate
חמים, bringing to mind the similar word ἄμεμπτος, used by Paul
in describing his blamelessness in the law in Phil 3:6. The
author of Psalm 119 was a pious scribe who had been influenced
by the wisdom tradition, and like Ben Sira, equated wisdom and
Torah(cf. Sir 24:23). If he was speaking of attaining blamelessness by keeping the Torah in the same way Paul was speaking of his blamelessness in the law, then it is not likely that
the scribe of Psalm 119 was a perfectionist. In other words,
both he and Paul apparently did not equate blamelessness in the
Torah with utter sinlessness. Yet the absence of a strict perfectionism here does not mean that the tendency toward it is
not strong. In conclusion, it may be said that even in those
Psalms which contain no explicit perfectionism, the tendency
toward it is present because of the moral dualism inherent in
them.

Some passages in the Book of Proverbs contain sentiments
which betray a perfectionist tendency. Proverbs 1:2-7, the editorial introduction, which explains the theology of proverbial
wisdom, seems to imply that the keeping of the wise precepts in
this book can lead to a blameless life:

> That men may know wisdom and instruction,
>   understand words of insight,
> receive instruction in wise dealing,
>   righteousness, justice and equity;   (RSV)

In verse 7 wisdom is equated with the worship of Yahweh,
in the well-known formula: "The fear of the Lord is the beginning of knowledge..." Thus it could not be said that the col-
lector of these proverbs, the final redactor of the Book of
Proverbs, believed that wisdom itself could inculcate sinlessness into the life of the practitioner of wisdom; only the fear
of Yahweh was sufficient for that. Wisdom without the Yahwist
religion, the keeping of the Torah, plus the proper worship of
Yahweh, was deemed inadequate to help the Israelite achieve the
blameless life. Yet wisdom, in the form of proverbs, was certainly considered a help toward righteousness.

In 2:2-21 we come close to the same sort of perfectionist tendency found in the wisdom psalms:

> So you will walk in the way of good men
> and keep to the paths of the righteous.
> For the upright will inhabit the land,
> and men of integrity will remain in it;
> (RSV)

The famous call of wisdom in chapter 8 expresses the author's reverence for the wisdom tradition in guiding Israel toward a righteous life; yet, like the other material in Proverbs and in the Psalms, it falls short of being explicitly perfectionist. Finally, as a *caveat* concerning the attempt to detect perfectionism in Hebrew wisdom literature, we must quote Proverbs 20:9,

> Who can say, "I have made my heart clean;
> I am pure from my sin"?
> (RSV)

Here it is apparent that the wisdom tradition in Israel was not perfectionist in the strict sense that sinlessness was a viable possibility for man in his historical existence. Wisdom, to be sure, might help man achieve the righteous life and even blamelessness in keeping the Torah. But a certain skepticism concerning the *inner heart* of man is betrayed by Proverbs 20:9. The authors of Hebrew wisdom literature may have felt much as Paul did, when he expressed his personal dissatisfaction with his blamelessness in keeping the Torah in the famous autobiographical passage in Phil 3:3-12. Verse 12 was quoted at the beginning of Chapter One of this study, and it is appropriate to call it to mind now. Paul and his forebears in Hebrew wisdom did not expect to achieve total *inward* purity of heart, utter sinlessness, in the sense of union with God, by mere external perfection, or blamelessness in keeping the Torah. However, the wisdom writers in Israel did apparently believe that the practice of wisdom, coupled with the fear of Yahweh, could lead men to *near* perfection, in the sense of being צַדִּיק, *i.e.*, being in a right relationship with one's neighbor and one's Creator. Here Paul and the wisdom writers are not too far apart.

One more example of near-perfectionism can be found in the prologue of Job, 1:1-5,8:

> There was a man in the land of Uz, whose
> name was Job; and that man was blameless

and upright (חם וְיָשָׁר), one who feared God,
and turned away from evil.
(RSV)

Job's blamelessness (*cf*., also his apologia in chapter 29)
is crucial to the theme of the book; yet all his perfection
does not help him with his relationship to God, and certainly
not to his "miserable comforters":

"Oh, that I knew where I might find him,
that I might come even to his seat!"

(23:3 RSV)

This is the agonized cry of a man who seeks to *know* God,
in the intimate sense of Jeremiah 31:31. All his perfection
has not given him what he really yearns for. His is only a
one-sided perfection: an ethical blamelessness without a full-
filling spiritual union with God. Here in Job we find a beau-
tiful and classic expression of both the hope and despair of
the wisdom tradition in Israel: hope, because through wisdom
one could attain righteousness--a view well expounded by Eliphaz, Bildad and Zophar; and despair, because wisdom could not
make man capable of achieving spiritual union with God. The
despairing cries of Job are echoed by Paul in Romans 7. Wisdom
could take man only so far, but could not fulfil his deepest
spiritual needs.

Hence it may be said that the wisdom tradition in Israel
had only certain tendencies toward perfectionism, in the negative sense of achieving some measure of blamelessness in the
practice of the Torah, but was not strictly perfectionist in
the sense we find in 1 John 1:3 (fellowship with God), or in
3:6,9 (being born of God and abiding in Christ). There is no
kind of "mysticism" in Hebrew wisdom, although Job comes close
to it.[8] There only the overwhelming revelation of God in the
whirlwind, not human wisdom, restores to the suffering and
yearning Job his longed-for fellowship with God.

(d) In the Apocrypha--Hebrew Wisdom

Tobit 1:3 ("I, Tobit, walked in the ways of truth and
righteousness all the days of my life, and I performed many
acts of charity to my brethren and countrymen who went with me
into the land of the Assyrians, to Nineveh.") represents Tobit
as the epitome of the wise, righteous and pious Israelite in
the tradition of the wisdom psalms, the Proverbs and the theol-

ogy of Eliphaz and company. No new thought can be detected
here. The same applies to the stirring chapters 44-50 of Sirach, the praise of famous men. All these men are renowned for
their wisdom, righteousness and virtue, but no real perfectionism can be found in Sirach's description of them. The author
seems to be following the tradition we find in the Pentateuch
about Noah and Enoch, or even the tradition of David's mighty
men in 2 Sam 23:9-39. The famous men are mentioned as examples
of repentance (Enoch, Sir 44:16), righteousness (Noah, 44:17),
faithfulness (Abraham, 44:19-20), faithfulness and meekness
(Moses 45:4), holiness (Aaron, 45:6), zeal (Phinehas, 45:23),
wisdom and sound judgment (David, 45:26), etc. All these men
were examples of laudable moral attributes to be emulated by
the people of Israel, but no claim was made for their perfection in any sense. Hence Sirach belongs to the older tradition
of wisdom in Israel, which simply did not deal with the question of perfection. His most significant contribution (as we
pointed out in connection with the author of Psalm 119) is his
equation of wisdom and Torah, in Sir 24:23:

> All this [the instruction of wisdom] is the book
> of the covenant of the Most High God, the law
> which Moses commanded us as an inheritance for
> the congregations of Jacob.
> (RSV)

The Deuteronomic tradition of obedience to the Torah and
the wisdom tradition of achieving the good life through the
study of wisdom and prudent actions, are married together by
Sirach, as well as by the editor of the Proverbs and some of
the Psalmists. Nevertheless, neither tradition, either together or separately, brings the literature of the Hebrew people
into the perfectionist camp, strictly speaking. All that can
be said is that Hebrew wisdom could have been one of several
factors which led to a type of perfectionist thought which turns
up among the Jewish apocalypticists, the Hellenistic Jews and
the sectarians of Qumran. To these groups we must now direct
our attention.

(e) In the Apocrypha--Hellenistic-Jewish Wisdom

James M. Reese, in his excellent study, *Hellenistic Influence on the Book of Wisdom and Its Consequences*, has shown tha
the anthropology of the Book of Wisdom (*i.e.*, The Wisdom of

Solomon) is based on the Hellenistic Kingly Ideal, rather than on biblical tradition.[9] Thus the Wisdom of Solomon needs to be considered separately from the rest of Hebrew wisdom tradition.

According to Reese, human nature for the author of Wisdom is inherently weak (*cf.* Wis 9:14-16), and only by the gift of wisdom can it grow in virtue (*cf.* 7:7-14).[10] King Solomon is pseudonymously made to exemplify the just man and the virtuous ruler; this example, in turn, is held up to all men to emulate.

In 9:6 we find an explicit statement concerning human perfection:

> for even if one is perfect (τέλειος) among the
> sons of men,
> yet without the wisdom that comes from thee he
> will be regarded as nothing.   (RSV)

This statement indicates the presence of the same sort of skepticism we found in Job and elsewhere in Hebrew wisdom literature. Blamelessness or sinlessness are at best only negative virtues, and cannot by themselves effect union with God. That comes, if at all, only through wisdom, which here is obviously a divine gift, present with God from creation. (*Cf.* especially the Book of Wisdom Proper, 6:12-16 + 6:21-10:21.)

Further, the author of the Wisdom of Solomon goes on to say that moral virtue (blamelessness) is worthless without God's gift of wisdom. Yet even with this gift of wisdom, no where is it stated in the Wisdom of Solomon that the wise man can achieve *spiritual* perfection, *i.e.*, union with God in his present existence. Therefore, it may be concluded that the Wisdom of Solomon, for all its Hellenistic influences, actually brought the Hebrew wisdom tradition no closer to strict perfectionism than its predecessors in the Hebrew wisdom literature. Following them, and following the Hellenistic Kingly Ideal, the Wisdom of Solomon was able to hold before the eyes of Israel the *ideal* of the virtuous and just life.

We can add, however, that even though the Wisdom of Solomon did not further perfectionist thought, it did enable Christians to develop the doctrine of grace through Jesus Christ by finding in wisdom, as God's gift, a model for understanding Jesus as God's pre-existent gift of grace to man. Hence wisdom in this book provides the later Christians more with a christological than an ethical model.

104

2. In the Pseudepigrapha--Jewish Apocalyptic

(a) 1 Enoch (Ethiopic)

Finally, in the whole realm of Jewish literature, we come to an explicit statement of perfectionism in the strict sense, found in some of the apocalyptic writings. Our first example is 1 Enoch 5:8-9:

> And then there shall be bestowed upon the elect
>   wisdom,
> And they shall all live and never again sin,
> Either through ungodliness or through pride:
> But they who are wise shall be humble.
>
> (Charles, Vol. II, p. 190)

Here we have a complete perfectionism: negatively, in the sense of sinlessness, and positively, in the sense of humility, which seems to denote a spiritual closeness to God. "Ungodliness" probably refers to breaking the Torah, by the pro-Hellenistic Jews during the Maccabean period, and "pride" to the self-righteousness of the strictly observant. The author here is critical of both the "publican" and the "pharisee" of his day.[11]

Chapters 1-5 comprise the editorial introduction, probably written by the final redactor. Here we find the eschatological background of this passage, *e.g.*, 1:1, "The words of the blessing of Enoch, wherewith he blessed the elect and the righteous, who will be living in the day of tribulation, when all the wicked and godless are to be removed." Here also we find an important characteristic of all apocalyptic literature: in the end time there will be a total separation of the righteous from the wicked, and the ethical dualism which characterized their radical differences will finally become an absolute ethical dichotomy. This is seen in the unrelenting and merciless condemnation of the wicked in 1 Enoch 1:9 and 5:4-6, and the unreserved praise of the righteous in 1:8 and 5:7-9. Other apocalyptic examples of this final and utter separation of the good from the evil can be found in several diverse New Testament passages. There, the sheep and the goats are divided (Matt 25:32b); the wheat goes into the barn and the tares into eternal fire (Matt 13:30), the great gulf is fixed (Luke 16:26), the door is shut (Matt 25:10b), the righteous celebrate the wedding feast while the wicked outside wail and gnash their teeth (Matt 22:13, *cf.* 25:11-12), and finally in Rev 22:11, the wicked are considered

too far gone to bother with. This absolute dichotomy of the
good from the bad is already found in 1 Enoch; it is a sign of
the end time.

Hence we can now make a general observation, which is important in our discussion of the origin of perfectionism in the
Gospel of John, namely, *In Jewish apocalyptic literature, perfection is one of God's eschatological gifts to the elect*. With
the eschaton, and not before, comes the possibility that the
righteous man may go on to achieve total perfection, both in
the ethical sense of blamelessness, and in observance of the
Torah, and in the spiritual sense of a holy union with God.

Two more examples of Jewish apocalyptic perfectionism may
be cited:

> (b) Jubilees 5:12
>
> And he made for all his works a new and righteous
> nature, so that they should not sin in their whole
> nature for ever, but should be all righteous each
> in his kind always.
>
> (Charles, Vol. II, p.20)

> (c) Testament of Levi 18:9
>
> And in his priesthood the Gentiles shall be multi-
>   plied in knowledge upon the earth,
> And enlightened through the grace of the Lord:
>
> In his priesthood shall sin come to an end,
> And the lawless shall cease to do evil.
>
> (Charles, Vol. II, p.315)

These passages also bear out the apocalyptic expectation
of eschatological perfection, to be realized at least among the
Levites (*cf*. Mal 3:3, for a similar expectation), or among the
pious few in Jerusalem. (A dualism is inherent here, as it is
in Johannine literature.) The perfectionism here is obviously
indicative of the concept of blamelessness in the keeping of
the Torah; but its implications go even further to indicate a
spiritual state of holiness which excludes sin. All this, of
course, is set in the apocalyptic conceptuality, which looks
for the imminent end of the old evil world (or age), and the
establishment of God's righteous reign. The perfect in Jerusalem are *already* experiencing the eschatological blessedness of
ethical and spiritual perfection, just as the sinners of the
land are wallowing in their wickedness. The end is soon expected, when the hateful presence of the wicked will be utterly

106

removed, and God's saints will finally reign on earth.

It may be said, therefore, that in all Jewish literature, it is not until the Maccabean period and after, that a genuine, full-blown perfectionism appears; and it appears only in the type of literature which was the most prominent of that period --apocalyptic. It certainly had its forbears in the holy legends of the Pentateuch and the Former Prophets, in the eschatological hopes of Jeremiah and Ezekiel and in the wisdom tradition. There, however, only mere blamelessness in the observance of the Torah could be hoped for; and a certain pessimism about human nature is evident in some of the wisdom writings. But when the *hasidim* of Israel--those pious scribes of the Maccabean/Hasmonean period--penned their apocalyptic literature out of their hope for an imminent eschaton, perfectionism finally appeared in Israel. It seems to have been the logical extension of an ever-widening ethical dualism, which must reflect the sociological cleavage within Jewish society in the second century B.C., between the pious Jews and the ungodly Hellenists. In the eyes of the apocalyptic writers, the approach of the end time makes each group more extreme, driving the ungodly to utter degradation (actually, "acute Hellenization", *cf*. 1 Mac 1:11-15) and the pious to utter perfection, both ethically and spiritually. *Ethical dichotomization coupled with the hope for the imminent end* (cast in stark apocalyptic imagery) seem to be the parents of the perfectionism which appeared in some Jewish apocalyptic writings. *When these two factors are present, genuine perfectionism may arise.* The parallels here to the rise of perfectionism in the Johannine community are obvious, and will be dealt with at the close of this chapter.

3. In the Sectarian Literature of Qumran

Matthew Black, in his book, *The Scrolls and Christian Origins*,[12] states:

The element of "perfectionism" in this secretly revealed legalism of Qumran is not only to be seen in the prominence of the description of the sectarians and their religion as "the perfect" or "perfection of way", but also in the absolute and total demands which are made on their obedience to "the whole Law" as thus secretly divulged by its priestly interpreters. It is difficult, indeed, to avoid the impression that I QS is not just the statement of an ideal, and not as it is usually taken to be, a "Manual of

Discipline". The sectarians are to be obedient and
perfect in *all* that is revealed to them (*cf.* I QS i.
8-9; v.9; vii.1,15; ix.13,19), in "everything which
He has commanded" (i.17; v.1,8; ix.24), to keep "*all*
the words of God" (i.14; iii.11), to "depart from
all evil (i.4,7; ii.3; v.1), "every perversity" (v.15;
vii.18; ix 21).[1]

This ideal of a "legalistic perfection", secretly
imparted, no doubt owes much to the unreal world of
apocalyptic fantasy in which the sect lived. We may
partly, no doubt, account for it as a reaction, in
the direction of a priestly ascetic type of life,
from the corruption of the age, but it is only to
be understood fully in the context of the other revealed "mysteries" of the Sect--in its "prophetism"
and apocalypticism. The Age was an evil one moving
to its end when it would fall under the catastrophic
judgment of the Wrath of God. It was all the more
necessary and urgent that this Remnant should keep
the whole Law with perfect obedience.

[1]*Cf.* H. Braun, *Spätjüdisch-häretischer und frühchrist-
licher Radikalismus, Beiträge zur historischen Theo-
logie*, Tübingen, 1957, I, p.28.

Undoubtedly the Manual of Discipline presents us with a
kind of perfectionism. But in no way is it like that which we
find in the Johannine literature, or even in Jewish apocalyptic. It is a perfection of *constant striving*, not of eschatological achievement. The confession of sin in I QS 1:24-26,
mandatory for all who enter the Sect, and the strictures and
punishments in I QS 6:24-7:25, admit the *continued* presence of
sin in the community. A. R. C. Leaney,[13] commenting on I QS
1:17 ("all that he has commanded"), agrees with Black's observations about the "element of perfectionism" in Qumran, but
goes on to say that "This ideal of legal perfection must not
be confused with the inner qualitative perfection which is the
ideal of the Christian ethic." According to Leaney, the sectarian literature of Qumran offers us no more than a legalistic
perfectionism in the sense only of blamelessness in the keeping
of the Torah (and of a great deal more regulations!). Perhaps
the paucity of genuine spiritual concern for union with God and
the absence of a thoroughgoing apocalyptic outlook prevented
the Qumran covenanters from achieving a genuine perfectionist
ethic. Their view of the eschaton was not strictly apocalyptic because they believed that it would come not from heaven
but from the literal physical force of their own arms--warfare
on earth, not from heaven. Thus the ethic of Qumran takes us

no further toward perfectionism than that of the canonical Old
Testament (including the Apocrypha), and in a sense, less so,
because of its lack of a true eschatological hope based on God's
extra-historical intervention at the end time. (*Cf.* The War
Scroll.) Perfection, along with all the other characteristics
of the eschaton, can only be a total gift from God. Without
such an eschatological hope the members of the Qumran community
could not develop a genuine perfectionism; rather, only an ob-
sessive striving toward a perfection never to be completely
achieved, was open to them.

Therefore, in spite of the remarkable similarities between
I QS and 1 John, especially in the light/darkness symbolism
used in both writings, to denote ethical dualism,[14] the literature of Qumran does not provide us with a probable source for
Johannine perfectionism.

In conclusion to this section on Hebrew/Jewish literature,
we may state that only in some writings of Jewish apocalyptic
can we find a perfectionism like that found in the Johannine
corpus. It was an ethical and spiritual perfectionism born out
of the *conjunction* of eschatological hope with ethical dualism
within the beleaguered and small ranks of second century B.C.
Jewish pietism. Unless both elements--imminent eschatological
hope and strict ethical dichotomization--are present, no genuine and complete perfectionism arises.

B. Christian Literature--The New Testament and the Apostolic
    Fathers

Introductory Remarks

The burden of this section of this chapter is to show that
the perfectionism we meet in 1 John 3:6,9, which was rooted in
the Gospel of John, is unique in the New Testament. A brief
survey of other New Testament theological traditions will make
this thesis clear.

1. The Pauline and Deutero-Pauline Corpus.

In Romans 1:18-2:29 and 7:7-25 we meet the opposite pole
of perfectionist thought. Here Paul presents the pessimistic
view of man's inherent sinfulness. However, in 8:13-14 he more
optimistically proclaims the possibility of becoming sons of
God by being led by the Spirit. This good news of being adopted

as sons of God may be compared to the declaration in 1 John 3:2,
"We are God's children now..." (RSV). Both Paul and the author
of 1 John acknowledge the common early Christian confession
(probably originating in baptism) that a Christian was *already*
the child or son of God. That self-understanding, however, does
not imply a perfectionist stance. Rather, as 1 John 3:2 goes
on to say, "it does not yet appear what we shall be..." (RSV),
perfection lies in the future.

The same concept of *future* perfection is found in Romans
8:22-24, where we read of Paul's vision of all creation, including man, groaning in the eschatological expectation of being finally adopted as sons of God. With Paul the tension between the already and the not yet is never broken; nor is it
broken in 1 John 3:2. Hence neither passage can be called perfectionist, *i.e.*, where the already has finally overtaken the
not yet, as, for example, in John 5:24. For Paul, salvation,
i.e., the final realization of the incipiency of being a son of
God, comes only by hope (v. 24), only in the *future*, not in the
present.

Paul's ethic in Romans 12:1-2 and 13:8-10, the "law of
love", is unsurpassed in nobility, but cannot be called strictly
perfectionist. The imperatives are *not yet* indicatives.[15] The
implications of gradualism, of striving after an ethical goal,
are ever-present in Paul's ethical instructions.

Romans 13:11-14 confronts the reader with the eschatological demand for purity. Because the final hour is nearer than
when formerly believed (v. 11), the time to awake from one's
ethical slumbers has arrived. No doubt the common assumption
of Jewish apocalyptic is operating in Paul's mind in this passage: when the eschaton draws near the dichotomy between the
good and the wicked grows greater, and the demand for perfection becomes more insistent. This is the closest Paul ever
gets to genuine perfectionism; yet, in the main, he remains a
gradualist.

In 1 Cor 2:6, Paul speaks of the "mature" (RSV)--τοῖς τε-
λείοις--among the Corinthians, to whom he can address wisdom.
But there is no evidence in the rest of the letter that these
persons comprise a group of perfected Christians; they are mature in their Christian *growth* and relative to the "babes in

Christ" of 3:1-4--who seem to comprise the greater portion of the Corinthian congregation--they have a greater capacity for understanding what true wisdom is.

In 3:16-17 (*cf*. 6:19) Paul declares the believer to be the temple of God where the Holy Spirit dwells. Yet the tension between holiness and sin is still seen to exist among the Corinthians, a fact evident by Paul's need to correct them.

In 4:8 the pretentiousness of Paul's opponents is sarcastically attacked. Paul deflates their claim to be already filled and already reigning. Schmithals, commenting on this passage, attributes this boast to *gnostic* opponents:[16]

> The basic feeling of the Gnostic, who boasts of his salvation as a sure possession and basically expects nothing more of the future, is expressed with equal clarity in both cases.

Here we may have an equivalent to the gnostic perfectionism condemned in 1 John 1:8*ff*., although there is no suggestion here of any connection between the alleged gnosticism in Corinth around 52 A.D. and that which existed wherever 1 John was written many years later. Paul's opposition to his opponents' perfectionist presumptions clearly shows his own anti-perfectionist attitude, as expressed in its *locus classicus* in Phil 3:12-14. (*Cf*. Chapter One of this study.)

1 Cor 6:11 gives us a neat summary of Paul's view of the dynamics of conversion:

> Καὶ ταῦτά τινες ἦτε. ἀλλὰ ἀπελούσασθε, ἀλλὰ ἡγιάσθητε, ἀλλὰ ἐδικαιώθητε ἐν τῷ ὀνόματι τοῦ κυρίου Ἰησοῦ Χριστοῦ καὶ ἐν τῷ πνεύματι τοῦ θεοῦ ἡμῶν.

Washed, sanctified and rightwised. But not yet perfected. Paul's ethic never goes to the extreme of John's.

The anaology of running the race, in 9:24-27, bears out Paul's gradualism. The stern exhortations against sin in 10:1-13 could not have been addressed to a group of the perfect. Love (ἀγάπη) is to be pursued (Διώκετε, imperative, not indicative, in 14:1).

In 2 Cor 1:9 Paul movingly states his reliance on God who raises the dead, and goes on in 3:5*ff*. to declare that his sufficiency (ἡ ἱκανότης) is from God. This is not the talk of a perfectionist. In 3:18-19 the note of gradual progress is struck with the concept of being transformed from glory to

glory. Life is *at work* (ἐνεργεῖται) in the Corinthians (2 Cor
4:12b), but not perfected. In 5:1-5, reminiscent of Rom 8:23,
we find the motif of groaning (στενάζομεν) to be clothed in the
heavenly οἰκία. Perfection lies in the eschatological future
only.

In Galatians 5:16-25 we encounter the famous ethical passage on the fruits of the spirit, ending with the challenging
exhortation in v. 25: εἰ ζῶμεν πνεύματι, πνεύματι καὶ στοιχῶ-
μεν.

Bultmann[17] is correct in observing here Paul's insistence
that the indicative and the imperative are to be united in the
lives of the believers. This is Paul's ethical *goal*. But the
very fact of it being a goal and not a realization--as we can
tell by Paul's constant need to correct his readers--excludes
Paul's ethic from the perfectionist camp.

Philippians 3:12-14 has already been cited several times,
but may be listed here as an excellent paradigm of the Pauline
gradualist ethic.

Finally we may cite Ephesians 3:16-19 and 4:13-16, together with Colossians 3:14 and 4:12 as splendid examples of the
ringing exhortations to maturity in Christ typical of this Deutero-Pauline literature. However, here also perfection is seen
only as a goal.

2. Matthew

The term τέλειος is found twice in Matthew, 5:48 and 19:21,
in both cases as a predicate adjective applied to human beings.
However in neither case can it be interpreted in the strictly
perfectionist sense as found in 1 John 3:6,9, but rather in the
Matthean sense of being a mature and whole-hearted,[18] sincere
and true[19] disciple.

Matthew 5:17-20 sets forth the demand for this quality of
discipleship in terms of a righteousness (δικαιοσύνη) which is
to exceed that of the Pharisees. This section interprets all
the dicta that follow in chapter 5; 5:48 can be seen as the
summary statement which forms an *inclusio* with the 5:17-20 section.[20] Τέλειος in 5:48, therefore, must be interpreted in
light of all the demands made in chapter 5, and in line with
the leading ethical rubric of 5:17-20. It is obvious that no
perfection in the sense of utter sinlessness is demanded here;

112

yet a *totality* of devoted discipleship, which goes beyond the over-scrupulosity[21] of the Pharisees, is expected.

The same can be said of the demand Jesus makes of the rich young man in 19:21. He is asked to *go beyond* the mere legality of keeping the commandments (which even the Pharisees do so scrupulously), and give away his riches to the poor, before coming to follow Jesus. This cannot be construed as a demand for perfection in the absolute ethical or spiritual sense, but rather as the requirement of whole-heartedness in discipleship.

Further evidence that Matthew is not strictly perfection- ist can be found in the community regulations in 18:15-20, and in the following parable in 21-35 about the necessity of for- giving the brother who sins against one. Such regulations are *prima facie* evidence of a disciplinary system in the Matthean community which, like that in Qumran, or in the later period of the Johannine community, when 1 John 5:16*ff*. was written, ex- pected its members to sin occasionally, in spite of their ex- pectation of total discipleship.

Hence we may conclude that no perfectionism such as found in the Johannine literature exists in Matthew.

3. Hebrews

For all its use of the verb τελειόω and its related forms throughout its length,[22] the Epistle to the Hebrews has no per- fectionism in it like that in the Johannine literature. As A. Wikgren has expressed it:[23]

> These terms, it is true, may not in themselves connote
> progressive, spiritual growth, but may refer--as is
> often suggested--to the once-for-all (ἐφαπαξ) exper-
> ience of conversion to the Christian faith. Yet there
> can be little doubt about the Epistle's depiction of
> the Christian life and faith as involving progress to-
> ward an end or goal, as in the figure of the wilderness
> journey of the people of God, a central feature of the
> author's typology. The various terms to which we have
> referred are philologically related to the form τέλος
> and develop from its basic significance of "end" or
> "goal."[5]
>
> [5]*Cf*. Aristotle, Metaphysics iv. 1021b.

Other characteristics in Hebrews also indicate its basi- cally gradualistic ethic, in spite of its well-known severity in its attitude toward post-baptismal sin (*cf*. 6:4). The exhor- tations to hold fast one's confidence, *e.g*., in 3:14 and 12:12

indicate the need for the congregation receiving this letter to
strengthen its faith and endurance. The magnificent recital of
the faith of the heroes and saints of the past in 11:1-12:2
functions in the same way.

Evidence that sin still exists within the community addressed can be found in 3:12; 4:15; 6:12; 9:26-28. In these
passages the implications are present that the members of the
community have already, or are in danger of so doing, fallen
into the sin of unfaith. They already have probably committed
some sin, although the author does not imply that they have
gone too far into the unforgivable sin of apostasy, referred
to in 6:4 and 10:26, where no forgiveness is provided for any
who have sinned deliberately ('Εκουσίως).

Thus we must discount the Epistle to the Hebrews as having
any possible influence on Johannine perfectionism.

4. Later Writings

There are some passages in 1 Peter which hint at a perfectionist attitude. This letter is addressed to those who "have
been born anew to a living hope through the resurrection of Jesus Christ from the dead" (RSV), and who are further characterized as "newborn babes" who need to "grow up" (αύξηθῆτε) to
"salvation" (2:2 RSV). This obviously indicates the addressed
group as newly baptized Christians who have not yet reached
spiritual maturity. A gradualist ethic, therefore, is present
here.

The recipients of 1 Peter are also exhorted to bear up in
the midst of persecution (3:13-17), and by so doing will be
able to cease from sin (4:1). This plainly shows the presence
of sin still among the faithful, although they are expected,
through suffering, to overcome it.

In Revelation 7:13-17 much the same concept of winning sinlessness through suffering can be found. In 14:1-5 an exceptional group of the perfect are described (παρθένοι, v. 4; per-
servering in discipleship, v. 4; first fruits, v. 4; without
lying and spotless, v. 5). They are probably the same group of
martyrs referred to in 6:9 and 7:13ff. But here perfection
comes only after a martyr's death and exaltation into heaven,
not in one's present existence. The Book of Revelation, rooted,
of course, in the tradition of Jewish apocalyptic, did not de-

rive a perfectionist ethic from it as the Johannine literature did; rather, it retained only a futuristic eschatology, which prevented the development of a realized eschatology, a necessary factor for the development of a genuine perfectionism.

Finally, a quotation from Ignatius' Letter to the Ephesians, 14:2, is appropriate here:

οὐδεὶς πίστιν ἐπαγγελλόμενος ἁμαρτάνει,
οὐδὲ ἀγάπην κεκτημένος μισεῖ.

This seems to reflect 1 John 3:6,9, although no definite connection can be established; and, of course, this could have no bearing on the Johannine corpus, which came earlier. What this does show is that some dim reflections of true perfectionism live on after the Johannine period, and show up here in Ignatius, although, in general, his ethic could not be characterized as strictly perfectionist.

In conclusion, then, it must be admitted that Johannine perfectionism is *sui generis* in the New Testament. The only forbear it seems to have is in the selections from Jewish apocalyptic quoted above. The similarity in thought is due, as has been pointed out, to the similarity in eschatological orientation and ethical dualism.

C. Gnostic Literature

Introductory Remarks

One of the chief problems in speaking of the relationship between Johannine literature and that literature commonly designated as "gnostic" is the problem of dating. Many scholars who have been critical of Bultmann's important thesis that the Mandean writings can be used to recover an underlying pre-Christian gnosis common to both John's Gospel and the Mandean writings themselves, have more recently accepted the probability of a pre-Christian gnosis. The discovery of *The Apocalypse of Adam* alone has established this probability to an almost certainty.[24] Even acknowledging, however, the wide circulation of highly syncretistic gnostic thought in the early centuries of the Christian era, it is still problematical that the Gospel of John was dependent on any one particular gnostic system which may have antedated it. It is safer to assume that John came out of the same world of thought, and in its use of obviously

gnosticizing language, it was operating in a naive or unself-
conscious fashion. (16:28 will suffice as an example of this
naive, gnosticizing language.)

Therefore, in listing below a few examples of gnostic or
gnosticizing literature as coming from the same milieu from
which the Johannine literature also sprang, no intention is
made to establish any causal relationships between them. The
problem that now remains is not the origin of the *orthodox* perfectionism found in 1 John; that, as we have seen, originated
from its parent Gospel, which in turn owed its perfectionism to
its ethical dualism and realized eschatology, rooted in a *Sitz-
im-Leben* not too different from that of Jewish apocalyptic.
(The basic difference between the Johannine community and the
communities which produced 1 Enoch, Jubilees and the Testament
of the Twelve Patriarchs, is that the former saw the eschaton
as imminent, whereas the latter saw it, in a very real sense,
as already present. But both, like Qumran, were severely ethically dualistic.) No, the question which remains now is the
origin of the heretical perfectionism evident in the opponents
in 1 John. Is it simply an abnormal, pathological outgrowth
from perfectionist tendencies already inherent in the Gospel of
John? Or has it been influenced by gnostic thought basically
foreign to the world of the Johannine community? Or are both
factors operating: a Johannine *Tendenz* coupled with *outside*
gnostic influence? In order to deal with this question we must
now review comments made by some scholars on the perfectionism
found in some gnostic writings, and then go on to examine some
relevant speciments of gnostic literature.

1. Some Observations about Gnostic Perfectionism

In Chapter Two we characterized the heretical perfectionism found in 1 John as "gnostic" inasmuch as it was based on a
gnostic anthropology, radically different from any to be found
in all biblical literature. Hans Jonas has given us a concise
and excellent summary of the anthropology common to nearly all
gnostic systems:[25]

> Man, the main object of these vast dispositions, is
> composed of flesh, soul, and spirit. But reduced
> to ultimate principles, his origin is twofold: mun-
> dane and extra-mundane. Not only the body but also
> the "soul" is a product of the cosmic powers, which

shaped the body in the image of the divine Primal (or
Archetypal) Man and animated it with their own psychi-
cal forces: these are the appetites and passions of
natural man, each of which stems from and corresponds
to one of the cosmic spheres and all of which together
make up the astral soul of man, his "psyche." Through
his body and his soul man is a part of the world and
subjected to the *heimarmene*. Enclosed in the soul is
the spirit, or "pneuma" (called also the "spark"), a
portion of the divine substance from beyond which has
fallen into the world; and the Archons created man for
the express purpose of keeping it captive there. Thus,
as in the macrocosm man is enclosed by the seven spheres,
so in the human microcosm again the pneuma is enclosed
by the seven soul-vestments originating from them. In
its unredeemed state the pneuma thus immersed in soul
and flesh is unconscious of itself, benumbed, asleep,
or intoxicated by the poison of the world: in brief,
it is "ignorant." Its awakening and liberation is effected through "knowledge."

It was logically inevitable that such a view of man would
include a denial of the reality of sin, and hence a type of
perfectionism. W. C. van Unnik, in commenting on the Valentinian document, The Gospel of Truth, observes:[26]

Although one does find in the New Testament expressions
such as "ignorance", "error" and the like to indicate a
falling away from God, the primary cause of this falling away, from the New Testament standpoint, is sin--
and in this "gospel"--or whatever you choose to call it
--sin is not even mentioned!

H. E. W. Turner, speaking of the Gospel of Thomas,
states:[27]

There is no sense of sin. Those who come to our Lord
and find rest for themselves are not described as the
weary and heavy-laden (Saying 90). There is, it seems,
a passage from death to life, but it has nothing to do
with sin; it is the way of purgation from transcience
and materiality.

("A passage from death to life" is, of course, reminiscent
of John 5:24, but no connection is thereby proved. This is
simply another instance where Johannine language resembles that
found in various gnostic documents; the intention in John's
Gospel, however, is not gnostic, in the sense of imparting secret knowledge. Rather, it is part of the familiar Johannine
motif of attaining eternal life through faith in Jesus.)

G. Van Groningen refers to these latter two authors when
he says:[28]

Various scholars have stressed the fact that the Gnostics never speak of sin. Sin is a spiritual and moral

concept. It has no place in a scientistic framework
which can only speak of having sufficient quantity
or being of the proper quality of material.

There seems to be, therefore, a general consensus among
scholars that perfectionism is inherent in gnosticism. A few
examples from gnostic or gnosticizing literature will suffice
to show this.

2. The Odes of Solomon

Let us turn first to the 13th Ode of Solomon, quoted here
in its entirety, from the Harris and Mingana edition and translation:[29]

> 1. Behold! the Lord is our mirror;
>   Open your eyes and see them in Him.
> 2. And learn the manner of your face;
>   And tell forth praises to His Spirit:
> 3. And wipe off the filth from your face;
>   And love His holiness and clothe yourself
>   therewith:
> 4. And you will be without stain at all times
>   with Him.
>   Hallelujah.

Without doubt this is perfectionist. Here the believer
sees himself for what he is in the mirror of Christ--a beauti-
ful metaphor--and compatible with the motif of confronting Jesus as the *krisis* of the world in the Gospel of John. This
confrontation in Ode 13 leads the beholder to faith: he does
away with his sins (perhaps the phrase "wipe off the filth from
your face" refers to some kind of initiatory penance, along
with baptism), and he enters into a life of holiness with God,
which results in a life "without stain", *i.e.*, a life of spiritual and ethical perfection. There is nothing intrinsically
gnostic in this Ode; it could well have been part of the devo-
tions of any sincere Johannine Christian. The problem here is,
of course, the question of the relationship between the Odes
of Solomon and the Gospel of John. Robert Grant contends that
"the Fourth Gospel and the Odes of Solomon come from the same
environment."[30] His arguments are convincing, yet this does
not answer our question. The Odes and John could well have developed totally independently of each other, out of the same

spiritual/conceptual milieu; or the Odes could have been influenced by the Gospel. There is no positive way to establish any
causal connection between the two. Further, as it has been often noted, the Odes are more gnosticizing than gnostic, so that
we cannot entertain the hypothesis that the heretical perfectionism found in 1 John was derived from the Odes or from the
historical community which produced them. All we can say is
that perfectionism is quite unsurprisingly found in other places
than in the Johannine corpus, and that the traditions behind
both the Odes of Solomon and the Johannine literature are similar in respect to the concept of perfection.

3. *Excerpta ex Theodoto*

Now let us look at an oft-quoted excerpt from the *Excerpta
ex Theodoto*, 78:2:[31]

ἔστιν δὲ οὐ τὸ λουτρὸν μόνον τὸ ἐλευθεροῦν, ἀλλὰ καὶ
ἡ γνῶσις, τίνες ἦμεν, τί γεγόναμεν· ποῦ ἦμεν, ἡ ποῦ
ἐνεβλήθημεν· ποῦ σπεύδομεν, πόθεν λυτρούμεθα· τί
γέννησις, τί ἀναγέννησις.

Here we find an anthropology which fits the heretical,
gnostic anthropology which apparently lies behind the heretical
perfectionism condemned in 1 John 1:8,10. But again we run into the problem of dating. Theodotus was a member of the Orien-
tal school of Valentinus,[32] and his works cannot be earlier
than the latter part of the second century,[33] making the above
excerpt too late to have influenced the Johannine community before 1 John was written. Of course, the above excerpt may very
well reflect a much older tradition. In this case, then, we
have found corroborating evidence that such a heretical perfectionism, based on a gnostic anthropology, flourished, probably
quite early and quite wide-spread. In other words, the Valen-
tinians may have been teaching in the late second century a
form of perfectionism, based on their gnostic anthropology,
which had been long before in general circulation, and which,
in this case, could have exercised a definite influence on some
members of the Johannine community before 1 John was written
"to set them straight."

4. Valentinian Perfectionism According to Irenaeus

Irenaeus provides us with ample evidence of perfectionism

in the Valentinian system; we quote here from *Adv. Haer.* 1, 6, 4:[34]

> ...they highly exalt themselves and claim to be perfect
> and the elect seed... (cf. 1 John 3:9) ...On this ac-
> count, they tell us that it is necessary for us whom
> they call animal men, and describe as being of the
> world, to practice continence and good works, that by
> this means we may attain at length to the intermediate
> habitation, but that to them who are called "the spir-
> itual and perfect" (πνευματικοί) such a course of con-
> duct is not at all necessary. For it is not conduct
> of any kind which leads into the Pleroma but the seed
> sent forth thence in a feeble, immature state and here
> brought to perfection.

Here is further evidence of a definite match between the Valentinian perfectionists of whom Irenaeus complains and the opponents of the author of 1 John. In 1 John 1:6-10, we noted in Chapter Two that the author is complaining against the hypoc-risy of his opponents: they claim to be in the light but actu-ally walk in darkness, etc. This matches Irenaeus' complaint above. Both groups of opponents seem to be licentious gnostics who make no connection between their spiritual state and their outward, physical behavior. Both are morally indifferent.

D. Conclusions and Further Questions

Thus we seem to have here in Irenaeus basically the same conflict, almost a century later, which we discerned in 1 John --between the gnostic perfectionists and an orthodox, semi-per-fectionist gradualist. (*Cf. Adv. Haer.* 4, 38, 3 for Irenaeus' gradualist ethic.[35]) It would be easy to conclude, therefore, that the heretical perfectionism found in 1 John owed its ori-gin to a precursor of Valentinianism. The gnostic evidence we have quoted here is all later than 1 John, but it would not be unreasonable, as we have already inferred, to hypothesize that it had earlier forbears which could have inspired the perfec-tionist heretics of 1 John. There can be no direct proof of this, but it is possible, and because of the close match be-tween the Valentinian evidence and 1 John, even probable that some hypothetical early gnostics were responsible for the he-retical perfectionism condemned in 1 John.

However, another possibility must be explored. Perhaps the heretical perfectionists of 1 John derived their perfec-tionism chiefly, or even solely, from the same source the or-

thodox perfectionists derived theirs, namely, from the Gospel
of John. In this case, heretical perfectionism would be seen
as merely a logical extension of a *Tendenz* already found in
John's Gospel. This, in turn, would imply that the Gospel of
John contains doctrine, when pushed too far, that becomes what
is later declared as heresy.

The chief *caveat* of that hypothesis is this: if our grammatical analysis in Chapter Two of 1 John 1:8 and 10 is correct,
then the perfectionism being condemned there was based on a radically different anthropology--such as exhibited in the gnostic
samples above--than found in John, and furthermore, *totally*
alien not only to the Johannine, but to the whole biblical tradition! Hence it would not be accurate to say that the heretical perfectionism found in 1 John was merely an exaggeration of
that found already in John's Gospel; it could not have been
merely Johannine perfectionism pushed to its logical extreme.
The anthropologies underlying each type are too different to
allow one type to shift easily into another. The basically
biblical anthropology found in John--that man is the creature
of God, not a "spark"[37] from the eternal, divine flame--makes
it impossible for the perfectionism in John ever to shift over
to a heretical type. Rather, Johannine perfectionism shifted
because the *anthropology* underlying it shifted. Move the earth
beneath and all on top of it moves. To put it another way, Johannine perfectionism, originating in the Gospel and echoed in
the First Epistle, in its orthodox form in 3:6,9, was radically
perverted by an alien anthropology.

Our hypothesis would now run thus: The orthodox perfectionism found in 1 John was derived solely from the Gospel of John,
as was concluded at the end of Chapter Three. It had been modified by the introduction of the doctrine of expiation and the
construction of a casuistic system, which distinguished between
mortal and non-mortal sins, thus reducing it to the status of
an old doctrine held onto out of respect for the Johannine tradition, but not really followed any longer by the author of
1 John, who in reality had become a gradualist. This we saw at
the end of Chapter Two.

Heretical perfectionism, on the other hand, was derived
ultimately also from the Gospel of John only insofar as its ex-

ponents had been members of the Johannine community, and would
naturally have inherited this teaching. But we hypothesize
that they had been converted (or perverted, from the standpoint
of the author of 1 John) to a gnostic anthropology, and hence
contaminated their inherited perfectionism with an alien, gnostic view of man. Once a gnostic anthropology had been substi-
tuted for the common biblical one, then all other doctrines became gnosticized. The leaven of gnosticism spread to all parts.
Or to change the analogy, if the foundation is crooked, the
building and all its parts will be out of line.

From the standpoint of 1 John, the heretical perfectionists, by their gnostic view of man, made all perfectionism thoroughly repulsive. The author of 1 John had the task of repudi-
ating his gnostic opponents and trying to save Johannine perfectionism in its original state. This, as we have seen, he
accomplished only imperfectly, and in the end perfectionism
disappeared from the Johannine community.

In conclusion, it may be said that Johannine perfectionism
in itself, before it bifurcated into orthodox and heretical
types by the time 1 John was written, was the result of two
powerful theological movements, which profoundly shaped the Johannine community and its literature: ethical dualism and realized eschatology. The Gospel of John obviously represents the
flowering of these two theological orientations.

In ethical dualism the whole world was sharply divided
into the good and the bad, defined in John solely in terms of
those who either confess or deny Jesus as the One From Above.
The ultimate parent of this dualism, which in John becomes an
absolute dichotomy, is Jewish apocalyptic. It is there, as we
have seen, that the concept of the absolute dichotomy between
the righteous and the wicked is emphasized in light of the imminent eschaton.

As for realized eschatology, no doubt the delay of the
parousia forced the Johannine community to rethink its eschatology, as it did the rest of the church. For John the problem
was solved by such verses as John 5:24 and 11:25. In Jesus the
eschatological event had already occurred.[38] Perhaps we may
attribute the origin of this insight to the theological genius
of the author of the Gospel of John himself; or perhaps we can

the author felt called upon to exhort his faithful followers in
such a way. The best hypothesis is that the opponents continued to have influence on the community, as 2 John alone demon-
strates. Much like the author(s) of the Pastoral Epistles, the
author-pastor of 1-3 John shows a protective attitude toward
his flock. We cannot tell the extent of his opponents' influence, nor can we be sure that any of the members of the community had become "heterodox", whatever that term might mean. All
we may say is that groups 6, 7, 8 and 10 consisted of basically
faithful members of the Johannine community whom the author believed (rightly or wrongly--we cannot tell) needed protection
against false teachers, or needed the sort of encouragement or
gentle correction in doctrine which any pastor would normally
give his congregations.

Now let us turn to the real opponents in 1 John.

We may begin with two groups of explicitly identified and
characterized opponents: the ἀντίχριστοι and the ψευδοπροφῆται
(Groups 1 and 2). As Bultmann has pointed out,[4] the author has
historicized the old antichrist myth and applied it to a specific group of persons, many in number (2:18), who have "gone
out" from the Johannine community (ἐξ ἡμῶν ἐξῆλθαν, 2:19).
Nauck[5] has rightly observed that the wording here indicates
that they were once true members of the Johannine community,
but left the community because of a clash in doctrine with the
author-pastor of the First Epistle and his followers. Were
they excommunicated? There is no positive evidence for this,
since no hint of any excommunication system in the Johannine
community can be found in the Johannine letters.[6] The author
claims that "they were not of us", *i.e.*, they never were true
members of the community, else they would have remained. This
is typical Johannine determinism, such as we find in John 10:26
--they were never part of the true flock which hears Jesus'
voice. (*Cf*. also 8:35, 43.) Historically, it is more likely
that the ἀντίχριστοι here had once been full-fledged members of
the Johannine community, but had adopted a gnostic christology
(probably of a Cerinthian type[7]), and who then *went out as mis-*
sionaries, or itinerant teachers, in the name of the community
to spread their teaching. This would give the phrase ἐξ ἡμῶν
ἐξῆλθαν a rather different meaning from its usual interpreta-

CHAPTER FIVE

HISTORICAL RECONSTRUCTION

A. The Opponents in 1 John - A Survey

In order to identify exactly who the heretical perfectionists of 1 John were, and in what way they and their teaching
were related to the rest of the members of the Johannine community, both orthodox and heretical, it would be well to make a
survey of all the apparent oponents of the author of 1 John.
This will be done not only by citing those sections in the
First Epistle which obviously refer to opponents by some specific designation of the author (e.g., ἀντίχριστοι πολλοί in
2:18 and πολλοὶ ψευδοπροφῆται in 4:1), but also by "reading between the lines" throughout the Epistle in order to discern the
controversial background of the author's statements.

Here is an outline of the opponents, put into ten identi-
fiable categories. We shall see how these groups are related
to each other and whether we may identify some of them with
each other.

1. ᾿Αντίχριστοι

   2:18 Last days: the antichrist; ἀντίχριστοι πολλοί

     19 They have gone out from the community. (Cf. 4:1b.)

     20 They apparently claim to have a χρῖσμα not shared by
        the rest of the community, which seems to be a special
        knowing of all things (οἴδατε πάντες). (Cf. v. 27.)

     22 The ἀντιχριστοι are defined as docetists; apparent quo-
        tation: "᾿Ιησοῦς οὔκ ἔστιν ὁ Χριστός."

     26 They are deceivers of the community. (Cf. 3:7.)

     27 They have a special teaching or χρῖσμα. (Cf. v. 20.)

     28 It is implied that they do remain in the community.

   (It should be noted that these opponents, described in 2:18-
27, receive no accusations from the author of immoral behavior)

124

2. ψευδοπροφῆται
   4:1a They have charismatic gifts;
      b they have gone out (*cf*. 2:19) from the community;
      2 They are docetists (*cf*. 2:22 and 2 John 7).
      3b They are identified as ἀντίχριστοι. (*Cf*. 2:18).
      5 They are apparently successful missionaries.

3. *Libertines*
   1:6 They claim fellowship with God, but walk in darkness
       (= immoral behavior, *cf*. ch. 2).
   2:4 They claim to know God, but do not keep his command-
       ments.
     6 They claim to abide in God, but apparently do not walk
       (*i.e.*, behave) as they should.
    15-17 They love the world, the lust of the flesh, greed of
       eyes, boastfulness of life.
   3:4*ff*. Sin is ἀνομία; they apparently are indifferent to
       their outward, *sarkic*, behavior and hence can be desig-
       nated *antinomians*.
     7 They are deceivers. (*Cf*. 2:26.)
    10 They are called sons of the devil; they hate the breth-
       ren. (*Cf*. category #4.)
   (3:23 and 5:1 are both summary sentences which summarize the
   two major themes of the First Epistle, and were written with
   these opponents, and others, in mind: believe the right
   christology and love the brethren.)

4. *Haters of the Brethren*
   2:9 They claim to be in the light but hate the brethren.
    11 He who hates his brother is in the darkness and walks in
       it. (*Cf*. ch. 9 of John.)
   3:12 They are likened to Cain; their works are evil. (Lib-
       ertines also?)
    13 They are identified with ὁ κόσμος. (*Cf*. 1 John 2:15-
       17; also John 7:7; 8:23,39; 9:39; 12:31; 14:17,19,22,27,
       30; 15:18-19; 16:8,11,20,33; 17:6,9,11,14,16,25;18:36.
       In these places the world is the enemy of Jesus and the
       disciples.[1])
    14b They abide in death.
    15 They are murderers. (*Cf*. v. 12.)
    17-18 They are callously indifferent to the needs of their

brethren; they are hypocritical (*cf*. 1:6; 2:4).

4:8 They do not love and therefore do not know God, who is love.

20a Hypocrisy: they are apparently quoted as saying "Ἀγαπῶ τὸν θεόν", but actually they hate their brethren; they are liars. (*Cf*. 1 John 1:10; 2:4,22; 5:10 for others called ψεύστης.)

b They are callous (*cf*. 3:17-18).

5. *Heretical Perfectionists*

1:8 "We have no sin." (*Cf*. Chapter Two.)

10 "We have not sinned." (*Cf*. Chapter Two.)

6. *The Faint-Hearted*. (Not opponents, but members of the community who need bolstering up.)

2:28 (Addressed as τεκνία) They will be ashamed of themselves at the parousia.

3:1-3 (τεκνία, 2:28; Ἀγαπητοί, 3:2) They apparently need to be reassured about God's love and the hope for ultimate perfection. (*Cf*. 3:2.)

19-22 (Ἀγαπητοί, v. 21) Their hearts accuse them; they need to have παρρησία (*cf*. 2:28; 4:17; 5:14).

4:17-18 (Addressed as Ἀγαπητοί in 4:17,11) They lack παρρησία at the day of judgment; they have fear, therefore they are not perfect in love.

5:3b They apparently consider the commandments burdensome.

14 They need παρρησία to ask for what they need. (Note the important qualification here, κατὰ τὸ θέλημα αὐτοῦ, which is not found in the Gospel of John.)

7. *Some Claim the Initiative in Loving God*

4:10 (Addressed as Ἀγαπητοί in v. 7, therefore not opponents, but members who need correcting) "ἡμεῖς ἠγαπή-καμεν τὸν θεόν" could be an apparent quotation.

19 Re-affirms 4:10.

8. *Ἀγαπητοί who were Influenced by the Callous*

4:11 They need to be exhorted to love the brethren, although they are not accused of hating them, as group #4.

12 Their love is apparently not yet perfected. (*Cf*. v.18.)

9. *Those who Deny that Jesus Christ came by Blood*

5:6-11 (Called liars in v. 11) They apparently accept the

baptism of Christ as his divine anointing, but not his
death upon the cross as his expiation for sin. (*Cf.* 1:7b.)[2]

10. *Idolators?*

   5:21 (Addressed as τεκνία, not opponents) The author warns
his congregation against idolators. Probably no special
group of opponents is being referred to here; rather the
author is characterizing all his opponents generally by
this opprobrious appellation.[3]

   Before we examine the groups of definite opponents listed
above, it would be well to dispose briefly of groups 6, 7, 8
and 10, who are obviously not opponents outside the community,
but community members in need of pastoral exhortation, as the
addresses ἀγαπητοί and τεκνία in each case indicate. It seems
that in groups 8 and 10 the author-pastor is concerned about
the possibility of deleterious influence from the heretical opponents. We might go so far as to say that the community members he lovingly addresses are either "heterodox" or in danger
of becoming so. Certainly in the case of groups 6 and 7 there
are indications that the author feels the need to correct his
readers' theology. Somehow some persons within the community
got the idea that they should be fearful about the impending
day of judgment--not a surprising fact, in view of the dreadful
literature of Jewish apocalyptic on that subject, not to mention the stern Christian traditions on judgment day, such as
found in Rev 20, which may well have been familiar by oral tradition to the members of the Johannine community. Such apocalyptic concepts of judgment day were in common circulation.
This would explain the need for the author to reassure his
flock in group 6, the "faint-hearted", of the Johannine teaching of confidence, such as we explored in Chapter 3, Section B.

   How the persons in group 7 got the notion that loving God
was man's initiative is unknown. It does not seem to be con-
nected with any known gnostic heresy, although it would be compatible with gnostic thinking. Most likely the author has in
mind the opponents referred to in 4:20a, hypocrites who claim
to love God, but who hate their brethren. These opponents
might have had a bad influence on some of the faithful.

   We are involved in mere speculation here, since there is
little positive evidence to enable us to give exact reasons why

say that the gnosticizing tendencies evident in him accounted for his re-oriented eschatological perspective. This is a moot point. What we may say is that *the parents of Johannine perfectionism were ethical dualism and realized eschatology.*

All of the questions at the end of Chapter Three have now been answered: the origin of heretical perfectionism (from the perversion of Johannine perfectionism by an alien, gnostic anthropology); the origin of Johannine perfectionism itself (from the conjunction of ethical dualism and realized eschatology); and the question of their relationship to each other (they were related only by the historical accident of co-existing in the same community, but theologically they were disparate).

These questions now remain:

Who were all the opponents against whom the author of 1 John wrote?

How were the heretical perfectionists related to the rest of the heretics in 1 John?

Are there one or many groups of opponents?

To this task the final chapter is directed.

The outcome of this investigation, together with the material from Chapter Three on the *sui generis* perfectionism of the Gospel of John, will enable us to deal with the final problem of this study: Was the Johannine community "sectarian"?

tion: "They went out as itinerant teachers in our name spreading heresy!"

Chapter 2, verses 20 and 27 imply that these teachers have a special χρῖσμα which they impart to their pupils. This was probably some form of secret, gnostic teaching.[8] The author protests that the community does not need this, since they have already received all the instruction they need before they were baptized.[9]

Plain evidence that they were docetists, who proclaimed "'Ιησοῦς οὐκ ἔστιν ὁ Χριστός" is found in 2:22. Such teachers are denounced further as also denying the Father as well (v. 22b). Verses 23-24 give the official Johannine teaching that to deny the Son is to deny the Father also. (Cf. John 5:23; 15:23.) The author probably has this same group in mind in the epigram of 5:12. Of course, the πολλοὶ πλάνοι of 2 John 7 are also called the antichrist; they explicitly deny that Jesus Christ has come in the flesh, and *they have gone out into the world* (ἐξῆλθον εἰς τὸν κόσμον). No doubt they are all the same group of itinerant docetists of a Cerinthian type. (The bathhouse legend in Irenaeus *Adv. Haer*. 3,3,4[10] identifies Cerinthus as one of the Elder's opponents, and although the story is probably apocryphal, there is no good reason to doubt that there may well have been some historical connection between the Cerinthians and the Johannine community.)

The author implies in 2:22-24 that his opponents claim a special relationship to the Father without having to confess the orthodox Johannine christology, which the author reminds his readers in verses 24-25, they have received "from the beginning."[11] (The same implication can be discerned in 2 John 9b.) Further, they are called deceivers, an accusation echoed in 2 John 7. Hence it is safe to conclude that the ἀντίχριστοι of 1 John 2:18-27 and the similar opponents referred to in 2 John 7-11 are the same group. We may go further than this, however, and tie this group to others who turn up in 1 John.

The second group explicitly identified in 1 John are the ψευδοπροφῆται of 4:1 (Group 2). They too have "gone out" into the world. In 4:2 they are identified as docetists also, such as those of 2:22 and 2 John 7. Then in 4:3b they are also called the antichrist. The author commends his readers in 4:4,

much as the special groups in 2:12-14 were commended, for over-
coming the evil influence of these worldly (*cf*. 4:5) men. Apparently these itinerant false prophets had considerable success in the world to which they went out, as 4:5b implies. From
this evidence we may go on to identify these ψευδοπροφῆται of
1 John 4:1-6 with the ἀντίχριστοι of 1 John 2:18-27 and 2 John
7-11. (Groups 1 and 2 form the same group.)

An objection to this conclusion may here be anticipated:
it does not logically follow automatically that two groups with
some similar characteristics are the same. The term ἀντίχριστοι could be the pejorative appellation commonly given by the
author to various different groups of opponents. However, there
are enough similarities between the two groups of 2:18-27 and
4:1-6, plus the corroborating evidence of 2 John 7-11, to make
the identification probable. On this working hypothesis we
shall proceed to delineate the nature of the opponents in 1
John.

So far we have a group of former Johannine Christians who
have become (or perhaps always were) docetists, who are also
ecstatic prophets, gone out into the world to teach their special χρῖσμα with a great measure of success. What more can we
find out about them? They claim to have special access to the
Father without the Son (2:22-24). This sounds exactly like the
opponents described in 1 John 1:6, 2:4,6, delineated above in
Chapter Two of this study. From the standpoint of the author,
they are hypocrites; fellowship with God should be accompanied
by proper moral behavior, which they lack. Now this group of
opponents, referred to in 1:6; 2:4,6, could well be libertines
(Group 3), such as referred to in 1 John 2:15-17. In this latter group of verses, which comprise a separate paraenetic subsection of the first ethical section (1:5-2:17, *cf*. Chapter One
on structure), we meet, "between the lines", a group of worldly
persons who are morally indifferent, *i.e.*, libertines. The author must have considered their influence morally detrimental
to the community, since only here in the Johannine corpus do we
find a type of moralistic paraenesis against the worldly vices:
"the lust of the flesh, and the lust of the eyes and the pride
of life" (v. 16 AV), such as we find in 2 Cor 6:14-7:1 or 1
Cor 10:1-14. We may assume that these opponents were libertine

gnostics, whose worldly behavior was justified in their own
eyes, because they believed that the actions of the *sarx* and
the *psyche* had no influence on the *pneuma*.[12] These libertines
show up again in 3:4 (part of the second ethical section, 2:28-
3:24), where the author identifies sin with lawlessness. He is
saying to his congregation in effect, "If you live like these
gnostic libertines, you sin, and your sinning makes you law-
less, like they are." The term ἀνομία here reflects the anti-
nomian stance of the libertines; as pneumatics they were above
the law. Again, their influence upon members of the Johannine
community must have been strong enough to warrant the author's
rather unJohannine identification of sin with lawlessness. No
such notion could have occurred to the Fourth Evangelist. Thus
the danger of libertine gnosticism was such as to force the
leadership of the Johannine community to adopt a view of sin
quite different from that of its Gospel. Times had changed and
so had the ethic; as most commentators have noted, in John's
Gospel there is no indication of any problem concerning law
and justification, and the ethic which this problem assumes.
Now, however, we find this concern behind 2:15-17 and 3:4.

In 3:7 the author warns against deceivers. Who were
they? Persons who scoffed at doing δικαιοσύνην, who believed
that one could be δίκαιος (*i.e.*, πνευματικός) without doing
δικαιοσύνην. In verse 8 the author condemns them as being of
the devil. Such was the intensity of his reaction, which
again indicates the strength and influence of his libertine
opponents.

Then in 3:10a they are called τέκνα τοῦ διαβόλου (*cf*.John
8:44), and identified further as those who hate. This in turn
opens up a fourth category of opponents: the haters (Group 4),
referred to often, *viz.*, 2:9-11; 3:12 (like Cain), 13,14,15
(murderers!), 17-18 (callously indifferent to human need); 4:8
(they do not love, hence do not know God), and 20 (they claim
to love God, but hate their brothers). It appears, then, that
the libertines and the haters are the same group, which in turn
are identified with the ἀντίχριστοι and the ψευδοπροφῆται; all
four groups (1 through 4) delineated so far seem to comprise
one and the same group. This means that the chief opponents
of the author of 1 John were docetist, libertine, charismatic

prophets and itinerant teachers, treasuring a secret χρῖσμα,
which they gladly imparted to a listening world. They had been
members of the Johannine community, and perhaps still considered themselves to be so. (2 John indicates that they persisted
in visiting some of the churches in the community.) They continued to exercize influence over the members of the Johannine
community, though they themselves became separated from it. 2
John suggests that they were still being entertained in the
homes of Johannine community members. Hence the author had to
warn his flock against them.

Now how do the heretical perfectionists (Group 5) fit in
here? They seem at first glance at the text to form a group by
themselves. It is interesting to note, however, that the author's orthodox version of perfectionism occurs within the context of a stern warning against the libertines (3:4-10), which
in turn continues over into the next subsection on love (3:11-
18). These subsections overlap because it was probably the
same group the author was speaking against: libertine haters of
their brethren, callous hypocrites. Although the heretical
perfectionists discerned in 1:8,10 need not necessarily be identified with our main group of heretics, there is every indication that the identification should be made. However, before
we proceed with our proof, it would be well to anticipate two
objections.

First, there is no evidence in any of the texts relating
the teachings of Cerinthus (Irenaeus, Hippolytus and Eusebius[13])
that he or his followers were perfectionists. Since the chief
group of heretics is most often identified as Cerinthian, it
would be expected that, if the perfectionist heretics belonged
to that group, their teaching would have been reflected in the
teaching of Cerinthus. However, this need not be the case, and
nothing can be proved from an argument from silence alone. Further, as we have seen, perfectionism of the heretical type is
quite conducive to Valentinian thought. The chief group of
heretics in 1 John may well have been "proto-Valentinians", as
we suggested in Chapter Four. Besides, gnosticism is well-known
for its syncretistic tendencies, and almost any combination of
gnostic doctrines could exist in the late first, early second
century, in a variety of possible combinations. This is to say

that we cannot precisely label the heretics of 1 John by the
labels of the later heretical groups, either Cerinthian or Valentinian. All we may say is that Cerinthian and Valentinian
gnostic characteristics may be found among the opponents of 1
John; but they may have been combined in a different way, not
as we find them in the later systems we know about from the
Church Fathers and the Nag Hammadi documents.

Secondly, it has been noted that there is no moral condemnation of the heretics described in 2:18-27. They were obviously docetists, but not necessarily libertines; the possibility exists, then, that Groups 1 and 2 (the ἀντίχριστοι/ψευδο-
προφῆται) may have constituted a quite separate entity from the
libertines. After all, the author speaks of many (πολλοί) anti-
christs; this is ambiguous: does he mean many groups, or a large
number in one group? We cannot tell yet whether the author is
fighting on one front or several. But now let us proceed with
some evidence which points to there being only *one* chief group
of heretical opponents.

First, to review, the heretical perfectionists were seen
(in Chapter Two) to have espoused an alien, gnostic anthropology. Such also seems to be the anthropology underlying both
the docetist ἀντίχριστοι/ψευδοπροφῆται and the libertines. It
is an anthropology which is consistent with the theology of the
former group and the behavior of the latter.

Second, hatred of the brethren (which may well have been
mutual between the orthodox and the heretics!) may well have
been nothing much more than the callous indifference of the opponents in 3:17-18, which so upset the author. The attitude of
indifference is consonant with libertinism.

Third, separation from the community would have exacerbated
this mutual hatred. Groups 1 and 2 "went out", and by implication Group 3 (the libertines) also left. We would not expect
the libertines to have remained welcome within the community
(*cf.* 2 John!).

Fourth, docetic teaching would also lead to mutual hatred,
rivalry and alienation (again, witness 2 John!), considering,
as we have seen in Chapter Three of this study, the vital importance of *right belief* in the Johannine community, even at
the time the Gospel was written.

All of this, of course, is only circumstantial evidence;
but putting it all together, it would not be groundless to hypothesize that the heretical perfectionists can be legitimately
identified with *both* the docetists (Groups 1 and 2) *and* the
libertines (Group 3), and in turn, these latter two may be identified with each other. It is not valid, of course, to state:
"All perfectionists were docetists/All perfectionists were lib-
ertines/therefore, All docetists were libertines." Nevertheless, in the absence of any contrary evidence, demonstrating
that each of these groups was separate from each other, our
thesis will stand that they all comprised the same group, and
therefore the author of 1 John fought on only one front--(dis-
counting his pastoral admonitions to the faint-hearted, etc.
within his community).

Before we go on to delineate the heretical-perfectionist-
docetist-libertine-charismatic-prophetic-itinerant-teachers--
the opponents of 1 John--we must deal finally with Group 9,
those who denied that Jesus came by blood. Most likely they
were one and the same with our main group. They may with reasonable certainty be identified with the same opponents the author had in mind when he wrote (or someone else later interpo-
lated) 1:7b, on expiation. The heretical perfectionists, considering themselves perfectly good Johannine Christians, in the
tradition of *their* Gospel, would have had nothing to do with
this primitive doctrine. Further, as docetists, they could not
have allowed Christ to have been identified with the Jesus who
bled and died on the cross.[14]

The opponents had been Johannine Christians. The vital
question now is: Was there something *inherent* in Johannine theology which *naturally led in a straight line development* to this
heretical perfectionism, which in turn was a part of a larger
gnostic complex, including docetist-libertine prophetism? We
answer no, for these reasons:

1. If we say that a perfectionist Johannine Christian has
a "mind set" which could easily lead to gnosticism, then we are
psychologizing without firm evidence. We have no definite evidence which allows us to speculate whether Johannine Christians,
because of their perfectionism, were naturally vulnerable to
gnostic thinking. They may or may not have been. We possess

no spiritual autobiographies from any Johannine community members. Not even the authors and redactors of the Johannine literature tell us their "inmost thoughts." If we are to trace influences and countercurrents we must use the only evidence we have on hand, namely, the *texts*, and not what we imagine could have gone on *in the minds* of some rather remote first and second century Christians.

2. Thus we must look at the perfectionist *theology* found in the Gospel of John and ask, Is heretical perfectionism *inherent* here? Did it develop *naturally* out of it? No, because the theology (*i.e.*, the doctrine of God and creation), anthropology and soteriology underlying the Gospel of John are not gnostic. In some places it is gnosticizing, *i.e.*, it employs gnostic myth and language; but it remains consonant with biblical faith. To be more specific, nowhere in John is it suggested that the Father is not the creator of the world--1:3 makes this explicit. The God of the Gospel of John was not the "unknown Father" of gnosticism.[15] He is known through the Son, Jesus, who is apprehended not by gnosis but by faith. The God of John's Gospel is the same God of the Old Testament. Thus in the doctrine of God and creation the Gospel of John is antignostic.

The same goes, as was made clear in Chapter Two, for anthropology. Man in John is a sinner in need of redemption; he is in the dark world and must come to the Light of the world. Of course, once he comes to faith in Jesus, he enters already into the perfect life of the new aeon. But this is a *gift*, not an inherent right.

Finally, in soteriology, man in John is saved through faith, not by gnosis, although this faith involves knowing (17:3), which in turn involves right belief. Although John's Gospel knows nothing of the common, primitive doctrine of Christ's expiation for sin, its peculiar and novel doctrine of the atonement, in terms of Jesus freely laying down his life for his sheep (and only for his sheep--10:11,18), is not outside the bounds of soteriological orthodoxy.

It is mainly in the areas of *christology* and *ecclesiology* that the Gospel of John exhibits definite gnosticizing tendencies. (See below, our discussion of Käsemann's view of this.) Therefore, whenever anyone asks, To what extent is the Gospel

of John gnosticizing?, he ought to make certain distinctions:
Is it the theology (doctrine of God and creation), anthropology, soteriology, eschatology, christology or ecclesiology
which are gnosticizing? Which areas and to what extent? The
question of gnosis in John is much more complex than has often
been inferred.

Now we would reconstruct the history of perfectionism in
the Johannine community, its origin, bifurcation and final disappearance, as follows:

Perfectionism originated in the community before or by the
time the Gospel was written as a natural and direct result of
the interplay of ethical dualism and realized eschatology,
stressed by the Evangelist. In turn, Jewish apocalyptic provided the ultimate background for both these eschatological
perspectives.

By the time 1 John was written, some Johannine Christians
had become gnostics. Again, it would be unwarranted psychologizing to attempt to say how and why they did. Of course, Johannine perfectionism, not to mention the gnosticizing language
of the Gospel, made gnosticism "attractive" to the Johannine
mind set. But we cannot tell, by the evidence available, exactly *how* these Johannine community members became gnostics.
Perhaps they always were gnostics, *i.e.*, perhaps the Johannine
community suffered an influx of pro-gnostic gentiles who had
never accepted the basic biblical doctrines of God and man.
Certainly without an Old Testament background of belief in God
as the creator and man as his creature, an alien, gnostic theology and anthropology could easily have developed among some
within the community. We cannot tell. The point here is that
when these opponents espoused their heretical opinions, they
were radically rejecting the basic theology and anthropology of
the Gospel of John, and adopting gnostic and alien views on
these subjects. (Their christology also apparently turned from
a "naive" to an explicit docetism.) In other words, their perfectionism was *perverted*; it was syncretistically subsumed into
the libertine-docetist prophetism present around the Johannine
community at the time. These gnostics continued to exercise
influence within the community, and continued to do so even
after their exit.

In reaction to this, the author wrote his First Epistle, denouncing the heretics, restating the original Johannine perfectionism in 3:6,10, with its two vital qualifications of abiding in Christ and being born of God, and also by introducing the doctrine of Christ's expiation for sin, as well as a casuistic system to differentiate between mortal and non-mortal sins. This latter move spelled the end of Johannine perfectionism within the community. In a sense it survived only among the heretics, who must have thought of themselves as perfectly good Johannine Christians, the true descendents of the original Evangelist. We note, for example, that in 1 John 2:27, the author has to defend *his* teaching as not false. His opponents must have claimed to have had the true Johannine teaching.

How justified was their claim? Outwardly they did carry on perfectionism. But their actual behavior, if we can take the author's word for it, betrayed their insincerity; and the gnostic theology and anthropology they adopted actually destroyed any genuine tie they might have claimed to have with Johannine Christianity.

Thus we would say that the Gospel of John does *not* contain within itself the seeds of gnostic heresy, or even that its gnosticizing tendencies could have naturally developed into any full-fledged gnostic system. No, it had to be radically perverted into gnosticism. The chief reason 1 John was written was to fight this perversion, to keep the weak-minded and the faint-hearted from being seduced by it, and finally, to legitimize the author and his followers as the true heirs of the teaching of the Gospel of John.

Although the orthodox perfectionism in the Johannine community was not inherently gnostic, it was *sui generis* in the New Testament and somewhat out of the main stream of Christian ethics. Its *sociological* effect contributed to the peculiarity of Johannine Christianity. At this point we raise our last question:

B. Was the Johannine Community "Sectarian"?

For Ernst Käsemann the Johannine community was "a conventicle with gnosticizing tendencies."[16] He speaks often of the "naive docetism" of the Fourth Evangelist.[17] His case is strong in regard to the christology of John's gospel; in it Jesus seems hardly human. We remarked in Chapter Two about his cool collectedness during the "passion." Not only there, but all through the Gospel, Jesus appears as the One From Above, whom only the faithful can understand. As Käsemann so aptly put it, "He does not really change himself, but only his place."[18] Further, Käsemann contends that the "Incarnation in John does not mean complete, total entry into the earth, into human existence, but rather the encounter between the heavenly and the earthly."[19] The clause in John 1:14 καὶ ὁ λόγος σάρξ ἐγένετο, for Käsemann is to be interpreted in terms of the following clause in the same verse, καὶ ἐσκήνωσεν ἐν ἡμῖν. "Flesh" in John is nothing more than the tent (σκήνη) in which God meets with his elect (the believers) in the wilderness (the alien world).[20]

We must admit that the christology of John's Gospel is gnosticizing, but not, of course, gnostic. Käsemann calls it "naive" because the Evangelist was not aware of any "gnostic heresy" at the time he was writing. (This awareness comes only later, at the time of 1 and 2 John.) Also we admit, with Dodd, that the soteriology in John is unique to the New Testament, and quite unlike that which we find in 1 John. Here, then, is the evidence of the peculiar nature of the Johannine community. However, peculiar christology and soteriology alone do not make a community "sectarian", in the sense of being *at odds* with the rest of Christianity and with the world around it. Further, we have seen that the First Epistle modified the Gospel in both these areas: the christology became explicitly antidocetic and the soteriology explicitly expiationist. If the Johannine community was "sectarian" when the Gospel was written, only because of these two doctrines, then it certainly ceased being so by the time the First Epistle was written. Can we find any other Johannine peculiarities?

Wayne Meeks, in his recent article, "The Man From Heaven in Johannine Sectarianism",[21] comments:

> Thus, despite the absence of "ecclesiology" from the Fourth Gospel, this book could be called an etiology of the Johannine group. In telling the story of the Son of Man who came down from heaven and then re-ascended after choosing a few of his own out of the world, the book defines and vindicates the existence of the community that evidently sees itself as unique, alien

from its world, under attack, misunderstood, but living in unity with Christ and through him with God. It could hardly be regarded as a missionary tract, for we may imagine that only a very rare outsider would get past the barrier of its closed metaphorical system. It is a book for insiders, for if one already belonged to the Johannine community, then we may presume that the manifold bits of tradition that have taken distinctive form in the Johannine circle would be familiar, the "cross-references" in the book--so frequently anachronistic within the fictional sequence of events--would be immediately recognizable, the double entendre which produces mystified and stupid questions from the fictional dialogue partners (and from many modern commentators) would be acknowledged by a knowing and superior smile. One of the primary functions of the book, therefore, must have been to provide a reinforcement for the community's social identity, which appears to have been largely negative. It provided a symbolic universe which gave religious legitimacy, a theodicy, to the group's actual isolation from the larger society.

Here we come to the nub of the issue. What made and *kept* the Johannine community sectarian--in the sense of its being both peculiar in doctrine *vis à vis* the rest of the church, and defensive and alienated *vis à vis* the world around it--was *its perfectionist self-understanding*, not merely its doctrine. The evidence we have adduced from Chapter Three corroborates both Käsemann's and Meeks' views of the Johannine community:

1. Johannine Christians considered themselves not of this world (John 15:19b; 17:14c,16).

2. They considered themselves elect (6:70; 13:18; 15:16, 19; 17:2,6,10a,12) and God's own (10:3-4; 13:1).

3. They had passed beyond judgment (3:18; 5:24).

4. They had a special place (τόπος) with God (12:26; 14:2-3; 17:24).

5. They believed themselves hated by "the world" (their hostile environment of non-believers and former believers, 8:31, *cf*. 15:18-16:4a; 17:14-16).

6. They considered themselves καθαροί (13:10; 15:3), orthodox, possessing the true gnosis and above all, already living the perfect life of the new aeon (*cf*. Chapter Three, *ad loc.*).

And all this in strict dualistic contrast to *everyone*

around them! In short, their perfectionist self-understanding, born of their peculiar eschatological perspective, contributed greatly to their sectarian self-understanding, to which Käsemann and Meeks refer.

Another factor points toward their being sociologically an in-group. This is their prophetism. The Evangelist appears all through the pages of his Gospel as a Christian prophet who continues to speak *viva voce* the words of the Living Jesus, the One From Above who continues to abide in his believers. They too have the words of eternal life (*cf.* 6:68). As Dodd has pointed out, the Fourth Gospel exhibits a unique doctrine of the spirit, different from any other in the New Testament, including 1 John. The First Epistle also modifies the prophetism of the Gospel, *viz.*, in 4:1, where spirits must be tested. Certainly the prophetic movement was very much alive in the early church, as the Acts of the Apostles, 1 Corinthians and the Didache attest.[22] A prophetic church always exists in contrast with an ordered church, although both can co-exist.[23] In any case, it is unusual and sectarian. (*Cf*, 3 John: perhaps Diotrephes was suspicious of the Elder's and his followers' prophetic utterances.)

Thus we would argue that the perfectionist self-understanding in the Johannine community was a major contributor, if not the chief contributor, to its sectarianism. Further, the Epistles testify that this sectarian spirit persisted. Although 1 John brings the christology and soteriology of the Gospel completely into the orthodox camp of main-stream Christianity, corrects its perfectionism (to the point of obliterating it), limits its prophetism, it *confirms* its stand against the world. By the time 1 John was written, the Johannine community had become more like the rest of Christianity, but more alienated from the rest of the world. Love, in 1 John as well as in the Gospel, is still only for the brethren.[24] The world is hostile and is to be utterly despised and avoided.

In 2 John the author (the Elder) denies even common, courteous hospitality to heretics, and in 3 John he complains that Diotrephes (probably a monarchial, orthodox bishop) is treating him the same way, considering *him* suspect![25] All this adds up to sectarianism. The bathhouse anecdote about the Elder is quite believable!

One final question remains. If the Johannine community
was really so sectarian, how is it that we possess its writings
in our canon of scripture? We need not go into all the history
of the canon here; the answer to this question is already at
hand: *The First Epistle of John made it possible*. The First
Epistle marked the transition of the Johannine community from
its original situation of being a peculiar, gnosticizing group
(in some areas), with unusual theological emphases, and with an
extraordinary perfectionist self-understanding, alienated from
the world about it, and even removed from the main-stream[26] of
Christianity, to a community within orthodox Christianity. It
remained alienated from the world and therefore sectarian in
that sense; but from the standpoint of Jews and pagans in the
early centuries of our era, *all* Christians were sectarians! The
sectarian nature it had in relationship to the rest of the
Church (which it exhibited notably in its Gospel), probably
disappeared, over a period of time. Only 3 John indicates that
the Elder of the community was not wholly acceptable to every
Christian Church. (Possibly because of his prophetism rather
than his teaching as such.) But 1 John must have made the teaching of the Johannine community, especially its somewhat suspect
Gospel, more palatable to the rest of the Church. When it was
written, the split between the orthodox and the heretics had
finally come. The former remained in the community and became
more like their fellow Christians; the latter disappeared into
the myriad, syncretistic groups of gnosticism, possibly to show
up later in the traditions underlying the teaching of Heracleon
or the Acts of John.[27]

Johannine perfectionism was, then, a transitory phenomenon
in the early church. Because it was perverted by gnostic influence and taken up into a heretical gnostic system (probably
of a Valentinian or Cerinthian type), it provoked an orthodox
reaction, which effectively removed it from the Johannine community. This means that this community in the period before
the writing of 1 John was a theological Camelot: "for one,
brief, shining moment" there was a place where men were perfect. (At least *they* considered themselves so.)

Because the leader of the Johannine community wrote his

epistles to bring his followers squarely into the main stream of orthodox Christian thought, we may say that he greatly helped preserve the Gospel of John for its later inclusion in the canon, and hence, for posterity. For this alone we owe him our thanks. In fact, we may say that the First Epistle of John helped the Gospel of John become the Fourth Gospel.

SUMMARY CONCLUSION

Our odyssey has taken us far. We began with the attempt
to solve the exegetical puzzle in 1 John concerning the apparent contradiction between the author's condemnation of perfectionist claims in 1:8,10 and his affirmation of similar ones in
3:6,9. Our solution was the initial hypothesis (in Chapter
Two) that there were two disparate types of perfectionism in
the Johannine community by the time 1 John was written: the
heretical type, based on a thoroughly gnostic theology and anthropology (condemned in 1:8,10), and the orthodox type, based
on the common biblical view of God and man (affirmed in 3:6,9).

Our second hypothesis (in Chapter Two) was that the author
of 1 John, in order to combat the heretical type, reintroduced
(from an older stratum of common Christian tradition) into the
Johannine community the doctrine of Christ's expiation for sin
(1:7b-2:2) and a system of casuistry, which distinguished between mortal and non-mortal sins (5:16-17). This turned out,
however, to be a theological "overkill", and effectively weakened the orthodox type of perfectionism also, so that the Johannine community, after the departure of the heretical perfectionists (2:19), finally evolved a gradualist ethic, in place
of its originally held perfectionist one.

The third--and very important--hypothesis (in Chapter
Three) was that orthodox perfectionism originated within the
Johannine community and can be found totally within the Gospel
of John itself, its sole source. We saw that in the Gospel of
John there is no sin but unfaith, and that he who believes in
Jesus as the One From Above is assured of salvation, already
enjoys the life of the new aeon, and is already pure in his
conduct, orthodox in his doctrine and perfect in his gnosis of
the Father. In short, he has a complete perfectionist self-
understanding.

The fourth hypothesis (in Chapter Four) was that a perfectionist self-understanding can occur in history when two *sine-qua-non* elements co-exist in the same community at the same time: ethical dualism and imminent eschatological hope. We found that a genuine perfectionism existed only in the apocalyptic Jewish community which produced 1 Enoch, Jubilees and the Testament of the Twelve Patriarchs, and in the Johannine community at the time its Gospel was written. The ethic in each of these communities was dualistic, and even though their respective eschatological viewpoints differed greatly--the former futuristic, the latter realized--yet each shared the same vivid awareness of the imminence of the eschaton. (This hypothesis does not imply that any causal relationship existed between these two communities.) Hence ethical dualism and realized eschatology were the parents of Johannine perfectionism.

The fifth hypothesis (in Chapter Four) was that, although orthodox Johannine perfectionism stemmed solely from the Gospel of John, the heretical type was a perversion of it by outside and definitely alien gnostic influences. It did not "evolve naturally" or "in a straight-line development" from the orthodox type.

The sixth hypothesis (in Chapter Five) was that the heretical perfectionists were only part of a larger group of heretics referred to in 1 John, all of whom comprised only one front of opposition to the author. They were gnostics of the docetist-libertine type and also charismatic, itinerant prophet-teachers, who had gone out from the Johannine community to spread what they considered was the true and right version of the Johannine traditions.

The seventh and final hypothesis (in Chapter Five) was, in agreement with Käsemann and Meeks, that the Johannine community was indeed sectarian and out of the main stream of early Christianity. However, when 1 John was written, Johannine theology was made safe for orthodoxy, and its perfectionism became a memory of an ephemeral past.

By now some theological implications from this study of perfectionism may begin to form in our minds. We cannot take the time and space here to develop them--let us leave that task for the theologians. Yet one thought on all this comes to mind:

Johannine perfectionism is both attractive and repulsive to us.
Certainly we are rightly repulsed by its implicit ethical and
spiritual arrogance, its ingrown self-understanding and its
sectarian sociological stance. And yet there is something attractive about it. Ethically, it optimistically expects the
believer to achieve a good, wholesome and mature life. Its
ethic of love is unmatched in the Christian tradition--although
we would want to expand it to embrace the whole human race, and
not keep it confined to our like-minded friends. Spiritually,
perfectionism implies a vivid, joyful and fulfilled life with
God in the present. Its aspect of the *already* is irresistible.
Certainly if the Christian life is to mean more to us than just
promises to be realized only in the future--"somewhere over the
rainbow"--then it must be possible for us to live out the reality of love for God and man in all our present moments.

Therefore we conclude that Johannine perfectionism need
not remain an ethical/spiritual museum-piece. It is theologically and ethically viable today. Although it came out of a
community which must remain strange to us, it still calls us
to rethink all the dimensions and possibilities of our human
existence.

146

NOTES

NOTES ON CHAPTER ONE

1. See the discussion on perfection and sinlessness in R.
    Newton Flew, *The Idea of Perfection in Christian Theology*,
    p. xii*ff*. *Cf*. also the article on "Perfection", *Interpre-*
    ter's Dictionary of the Bible, Vol. 3 (K-Q), 730.

2. For various purification rituals, *cf*. Lev 12-15, Num 19 and
    IQS 3:3-9.

3. *Cf*. Chapter 17 of John: union with God is achieved by be-
    lieving in Jesus as him whom the father has sent; v. 21
    provides the most explicit expression of the mutual indwell-
    ing of the believer with the Father and the Son: "that they
    all may be one; even as thou, Father, art in me, and I in
    thee, that they also may be in us..."

4. It will be shown that 1 John, although it contains perfec-
    tionist teaching, is ultimately not perfectionist in the
    absolute sense, since the author anticipates temporary
    lapses into sin, even among the faithful. *Cf*. 1 John 1:
    7b-2:2 and 5:16-17.

5. *Cf*. Deut 32:47; Aboth 2:8.

6. See Chapter Four, Section C 2 of this study.

7. *Cf*. 1 John 3:6,9; also John 5:24 and the whole discussion
    in Part Two of Chapter Three of this study.

8. *Cf*. Walter Bauer, *Orthodoxy and Heresy in Earliest Chris-*
    tianity (ET), xxii. His use of these terms seems a bit im-
    precise.

9. *Cf*. 1 Tim 1:3; 4:1-8; 6:3-6,21; 2 Tim 2:14-18, 23-24; Tit
    1:10-16; 2 Pet 2:1-3; 3:3-7,16; Jude 5-16.

10. *Cf*. Raymond Brown's discussion of ecclesiology and sacra-
    mentalism in John in *The Gospel According to John*, Vol. 29,
    The Anchor Bible, CV-CXIV. *Cf*. also Eduard Schweizer, "The

Concept of the Church in the Gospel and Epistles of St. John", in *New Testament Essays in Memory of T. W. Manson*, ed. by A. J. B. Higgins, 230-45.

11. E. Käsemann, *The Testament of Jesus* (ET), 73.

12. *Cf*. Wayne Meeks, "The Man from Heaven in Johannine Sectarianism", *JBL*, Vol. 91, No. 1 (March 1972), 44-72.

13. *Cf*. R. Bultmann, *The Theology of the New Testament* (ET), Vol. II, 91:

    ἐκκλησία...does not mean "Church" but "a church"...

14. *Cf*. R. Bultmann's articles, *Die Bedeutung der neuerschlossenen mandäischen und manichäischen Quellen für das Verständnis des Johannesevangeliums*, ZNW 24 (1925), 100-46. This was the first fruits of Bultmann's investigations into possible sources for a pre-Christian gnosis, which was followed later by the full harvest of his commentary on John, *Das Evangelium des Johannes*, published in 1941.

15. *Cf*. W. C. van Unnik, *Newly Discovered Gnostic Writings* (ET), in Studies in Biblical Theology, No. 30, 1960, 16-17, for a complete catalogue of the Nag Hammadi find.

16. Walter Schmithals, in his book, *Gnosticism in Corinth* (ET), 29, states that gnosticism "is exhibited as a religious phenomenon *sui generis*, for which two essential features are characteristic and distinctive: a pronounced understanding of the world and of self, and a distinctive mythology as the expression of that understanding... Only where the two coincide may one speak of genuine Gnosticism." Schmithals here is in harmony with the general consensus of scholarly usage of the terms "gnosis" and "gnosticism" (see Note 17, below). Certainly the use of gnostic mythology *alone*, common in Paul and John, does not warrant the terming of their works as "gnostic."

17. Ugo Bianchi (ed.), *Le Origini dello Gnosticismo*, Colloquio di Messina, 13-18 aprile 1966, XXVI (the beginning of the English text of the Proposal "for a terminological and conceptual agreement with regard to the theme of the Colloquium.").

18. Walter Schmithals, in his books *Gnosticism in Corinth* (ET),

and *Paul and the Gnostics* (ET), maintains that Paul's opponents were genuine gnostics, and uses the Pauline corpus as the means to reconstruct their teachings. Dieter Georgi effected a reconstruction of Paul's opponents in 2 Cor by much the same basic method--of using Paul's text as a primary source for reconstructing his opponents' teaching--in his *Die Gegner des Paulus im zweiten Korintherbrief.*

19. R. Bultmann, *Die drei Johannesbriefe, passim.*

20. *Cf.* A. Deissmann, *Licht vom Osten*, 194-95, for the marks of a letter (*Brief*), and an epistle (*Epistel*). Of the former he says, "Der Brief ist etwas Unliterarisches: er dient dem Verkehr der Getrennten." Of the latter, "Die Epistel ist eine literarische Kunstform, eine Gattung der Literatur, wie zum Beispiel, Dialog, Rede, Drama."

21. B. F. Westcott, *The Epistles of St. John*, XXIX.

22. *Ibid.*, XXX.

23. H. Windisch, *Die Katholischen Briefe*, 107.

24. C. H. Dodd, *The Johannine Epistles*, XXI.

25. R. Schnackenburg, *Die Johannesbriefe*, 1-2.

26. *Ibid.*, 2.

27. *Cf. Neutestamentliche Studien für Rudolf Bultmann* (1954), in Beihefte zur ZNW, ed. by Walter Eltester. Beiheft 21 (1957), 194-201.

28. H. Conzelmann, "Was von Anfang war", in *Neutestamentliche Studien für Rudolf Bultmann* (1954), Beihefte zur ZNW, ed. by Walter Eltester, Beiheft 21 (1957), 201:

Für das vorgeschlagene Verständnis des Briefes besteht ein weiteres Argument: in der Verwendung der anderen johanneischen Grundbegriffe ist eine analoge Verscheibung zu bemerken. Das Auslassen bestimmter Vorstellungen, die Modifikation der rezipierten und die Ergänzung durch neue scheinen ein in sich geschlossenes Bild zu ergeben. Die nächste Analogie bildet die Übertragung des paulinischen, eschatologischen Aspekts in die Denkweise kirchlicher Tradition durch die Pastoralbriefe; trotz aller Unterschiede liesse sich angesichts dieser Entsprechung der 1 Johannesbrief als ein "johanneischer Pastoralbrief" bezeichnen.

29. W. Marxsen, *Introduction to the New Testament* (ET), 261.

30. Feine-Behm-Kummel, *Introduction to the New Testament*, 307-9.

31. R. Bultmann, *Die drei Johannesbriefe*, 87.

32. M. Shepherd, Article on 1 John in *The Interpreter's One-Volume Commentary on the Bible*, 935.

33. P. Parker, "Two Editions of John", *JBL* 75 (1956), 303.

34. A. Wilder, Introduction and Exegesis of the Epistles of John in *The Interpreter's Bible*, Vol. 12, 210.

35. T. Haering, *Gedankengang und Grundgedanke des ersten Johannesbriefes*, reproduced in Brooke, see Note 37.

36. Westcott, *op. cit.*, xlvi-vii.

37. A. E. Brooke, *The Johannine Epistles*, ICC, xxxiv-viii.

38. C. H. Dodd, *op. cit.*, xxii.

39. R. Schnackenburg, *op. cit.*, ix-x. *Cf.* his table of contents which gives the editorial titles he assigns to the various sections.

40. A. Wilder, *op. cit.*, 211.

41. R. Bultmann, *op. cit.* One must look throughout his commentary on 1 John for his editorial headings in order to discern his outline.

42. M. Shepherd, *op. cit.*, 936-38.

43. *The Jerusalem Bible*, *ad loc.*, 1 John, gives these major divisions:

Introduction	1:1-4
Walk in Light	1:5-2:29
Live as God's Children	3:1-4:6
Love and Faith	4:7-5:13
Ending	5:14-21

44. R. Brown, *New Testament Reading Guide, The Gospel of St. John and the Johannine Epistles*, 103. *Cf.* A. Feuillet (in Bibliography, p. 188).

45. Dobschütz' *Grundsätze* are conveniently reproduced in W. Nauck, *Die Tradition und der Charakter des ersten Johannes-*

briefes, 1, with a commentary on them by Nauck.

46. R. Bultmann, *op. cit.*, 23-24.

47. C. H. Dodd, *The Interpretation of the Fourth Gospel*, 290.

48. *Cf.* R. Brown, *The Gospel According to John*, Vol. 29, The Anchor Bible, XXXIV-IX, for his theory on the five stages in the composition of John's Gospel.

49. *NTS* VII (1960-61), 56-65. Reprinted in *Twelve New Testament Studies*, 126-38.

50. C. H. Dodd, "The First Epistle of John and the Fourth Gospel", *BJRL*, Vol. 21, No. 1 (April 1937), 129-56. *Cf.* also his commentary, *The Johannine Epistles*, liii-lv.

51. For a cogent argument for this commonly held assumption, see Dodd, *op. cit.*, lxvii-viii. Conzelmann's article, "Was von Anfang war", discussed above, under genre, gives the most decisive reasons for the priority of the Gospel, and the reasons for the First Epistle as a pastoral dealing with the proper interpretation of the traditions of the Gospel.

52. *Cf.* E. Käsemann, "Ketzer und Zeuge", *ZThK* 48 (1951), 306.

53. E. Schweizer, "The Concept of the Church in the Gospels and Epistles of St. John", *op. cit.*, 240.

54. In spite of the well-known observation that 1 John is the only book in the New Testament which fails to quote the Old Testament, the reference to Cain in 3:12 can hardly have arisen from an author ignorant of the Old Testament scriptures. His obvious dependence on the Fourth Gospel, full of Old Testament quotations, corroborates this.

55. R. Bultmann, *op. cit.*, 26.

56. R. Fortna, *The Gospel of Signs*, 15-17.

NOTES ON CHAPTER TWO

1. Dobschütz, Bultmann and O'Neill (see Bibliography) all have done studies on the *Grundlage* of 1 John, but to my knowledge, no one has undertaken an analysis of these six sentences as has been done here in this study.

2. For the use of ὅτι to introduce a quotation, see Blass and Debrunner, *A Greek Grammar of the New Testament and Early Christian Literature*, par. 397 (5), 205.

3. The first person singular conjectured here matches the third person singular of the ὁ λέγων form.

4. *Cf*. B. Noack's short study, "On I John ii. 12-14", in *NTS* 6 (1959-60), 236-41. Here another six sentences of striking similarity, yet with two forms of the opening formula (γράφω and ἔγραψα) are discussed. The situation Noack is dealing with is different from our situation at hand, but the methodological principles of investigation are basically the same, namely, exegesis must determine whether variations in formulae are due merely to "stylistic mannerism and nothing else" (Noack, 241), or due to a real difference in intended meaning. In Noack's case, he opts for the variation being a reflection of a real difference; but in our case here, we choose to see the two forms of the verb λέγω as stylistic only. However, there is merit in Noack's view that the variation here may serve to reiterate what the author has said in the past many times. In Noack's words: "What I have just written [= what I have said] I repeat. Yes, indeed, I have written it and I do stick to it." (p. 241)

5. R. Bultmann, *Die drei Johannesbriefe*, 18, note 1:
   > Von dem "Wir" in οἴδαμεν (3:2,14), in dem sich der Verfasser mit dem Leser zusammenfasst wie in 4:14, 16, sind die Wir-Satze zu unterscheiden, die mahnenden Charakter haben und das Kriterium des echten Glaubens angeben wie z.B. 4:6; 5:2. Doch ist der Unterschied fliessend wie etwa 4:6--Wiederum anders ist das "Wir" zu verstehen in 1:6-10, das den Sinn von "man" order "jemand" hat; s.u. S. 15f., 17,1.

   See also *Ibid.*, 24, note 1.

6. *Cf*. I Cor 15:35 or 2 Pet 3:4 for two examples of character-

155

izations of opponents' views, which probably reflect with
reasonable accuracy what in essence the opponents actually
said, without claiming to be precise quotations.

7. This sharp dualism is especially evident in the concluding
    clause, which describes the present spiritual state of the
    opponents (element *d*). Of the six sentences under discus-
    sion, all but 2:6 and 9 have this concluding clause, which
    is cast in the form of a *parallelismus membrorum*:

    1:6b ψευδόμεθα
          καὶ οὐ ποιοῦμεν τὴν ἀλήθειαν·

    1:8b ἑαυτοὺς πλανῶμεν
          καὶ ἡ ἀλήθεια οὐκ ἔστιν ἐν ἡμῖν.

    1:10b ψεύστην ποιοῦμεν αὐτὸν
          καὶ ὁ λόγος αὐτοῦ οὐκ ἔστιν ἐν ἡμῖν.

    2:4b ψεύστης ἐστίν,
          καὶ ἐν τούτῳ ἡ ἀλήθεια οὐκ ἔστιν·

The καὶ connects the two parallel lines in every case. The
second line repeats the thought of the first line exactly,
only in different terms, much like Hebrew poetry. An antithetical parallelism is implied here, since, if we remove
the negative οὐ/οὐκ, line b would then describe the good
Christian of the true faith. This stark dualistic contrast
is typical of the Fourth Gospel, *e.g.*, on lying, 8:44,55,
cf. 1 John 1:6,10 and 2:4. (In 1 John 2:22 the liar is the
one who denies that Jesus is the Christ, *i.e.*, a heretic;
cf. John 4:20 and 5:10.) It is interesting to note the
parallelism also between the ἀλήθεια in 1:8 and the λόγος
in 1:10, each set in line b with exactly the same words;
hence we may take these two terms as interchangeable for
the author of 1 John. The term λόγος here, as well as in
1 John 2:5,7, seems to designate orthodox teaching.

8. R. Bultmann, *op.cit.*, 21, comments thus on the sentence ὁ
    θεὸς φῶς ἐστιν:

        Dieser Satz gibt ebensowenig wie das ὁ θεὸς
        ἀγάπη ἐστίν 4:8,16, and das πνεῦμα ὁ θεὸς
        Joh 4:24 eine Definition des Wesens Gottes,
        wie Gott an sich ist. Er besagt vielmehr,
        was Gott für den Menschen bedeutet.

Bultmann goes on to point out how the light as a symbol of eschatological salvation includes the demand for moral behavior; this salvation is not a possession of the believer, rather believer is always "on his way."

9. For references to περιπατεῖν used in a metaphorical sense to denote either moral or immoral behavior, cf. Matt 7:5; John 8:12 (walking in darkness); 12:35 (walking in light); Acts 21:21; Rom 6:4 (walking in newness of life; 8:4 (walking κατὰ σάρκα); 13:13; 14:15; 1 Cor 3:3; 7:17; 2 Cor 4:2; 5:7; 10:2-3; 12:18; Gal 5:16; Eph 2:2,10; 4:1,17; 5:2,8,15; Phil 3:17,18; Col 1:10; 2:6; 3:7; 4:5; 1 Thess 2:12; 4:1,12; 2 Thess 3:6,11; Heb 13:19; 1 Pet 5:8; 1 John 1:6,7; 2:6,11; 2 John 4:6; 3 John 3,4; Rev 21:24. Besides all these references in every major tradition within the New Testament, there are many more examples of it to be found in the Old Testament, e.g.., Deut 5:33, where the verb halak is used in the same metaphorical sense as περιπατεῖν. Hence this ubiquitous metaphor in the N.T. has its roots in a common O.T. usage. Cf. Bultmann, op. cit., p 26, note 1.

10. See note 7. 2:9 does not have the same form in its concluding clause as do 1:6,8,10 and 2-4--the parallelismus membrorum--but it still describes, as do the others, the final spiritual state of the unbelievers and heretics.

11. ἐκεῖνος in 2:6 refers to Christ, as it does elsewhere in 1 John. Cf.Bultmann, op. cit., 32.

12. The sinlessness of Jesus is found not only in 1 John 3:5b καὶ ἀμαρτία ἐν αὐτῷ οὐκ ἔστιν, and implied in 3:3b καθὼς ἐκεῖνος ἀγνός ἐστιν·--but explicitly also in 2 Cor 5:21 and Heb 4:15, and implicitly in Matt 3:14-15, Luke 23:25 and John 8:29b.

13. (a) Having fellowship with God (1:6) is found also in 1 John 1:3,6. The term κοινωνία is not found in the Fourth Gospel, but the motif of fellowship with God is strongly implied in the whole 17th chapter of John, as well as in John 15:1ff. Cf. Schnackenburg, Die Johannesbriefe, 57f., his important Exkurs 2, Gemeinschaft mit Gott.
(b) To know God (2:4) finds its classical parallel in the famous definition sentence in John 17:3, "This is eternal

life, to know thee, the only true God...", *cf*. 8:55 and 17:
25, where Jesus states that though the world has not known
the Father, he has, and his disciples know that the Father
has sent him. Here the disciples' correct knowledge of Jesus' true origin seems to be the first step in knowing the
Father as Jesus knows him, and hence obtaining eternal life.
A kind of perfectionism is implied here: the disciples will
eventually become like Jesus, *cf*. 1 John 3:2b, "We know
that when he is manifested we shall be like him..."
(c) Dwelling in Christ (2:6) is one of the most important
motifs in Johannine literature. John 15:1*ff*., and all the
places the verb μένω appears testify to it. *Cf*. R. Brown,
The Gospel According to John, Anchor Bible, Vol. 29, 510,
on the frequency and meaning of μένειν.
(d) Being in the light (2:9) has parallels in 1 John 1:7
and John 8:12*f*.; 9:5; 12:35-36.

14. Blass and Debrunner, *op. cit.* (note 5), 166, par. 318 (2)
cites the durative force of the present indicative.

15. Bultmann, *op. cit.*, 22-23, speaks of "die Behauptung gnos-
tisierender Irrlehrer, in Lichte zu sein..."

16. Blass and Debrunner, *op. cit.*, 175, par. 340.

17. *Cf*. Irenaeus, *Adv. Haer.*, 1, 24, 1-2. (Anti-Nicene Library
Vol. 1, 348-9.) Speaking of the anthropology of Saturninus
Irenaeus reports:

Man, too, was the workmanship of angels, a shining
image bursting forth below from the presence of the
supreme power; and when they could not, he says,
keep hold of this, because it immediately darted
upwards again, they exhorted each other, saying,
"Let us make man after our image and likeness."
(Gen 1. 26.) He was accordingly formed, yet was
unable to stand erect, through the inability of
the angels to convey to him that power, but wrig-
gled (on the ground) like a worm. Then the power
above taking pity upon him, since he was made after
his likeness, sent forth a spark of life, which
gave man erect posture... He declares, therefore,
that this spark of life, after the death of a man,
returns to those things which are of the same nature with itself...

(2)...Christ came to destroy the God of the Jews,
but to save such as believe in him; that is, those
who possess the spark of his life.

Cf. also 2, 19, 3 on the "truly spiritual" (πνευματικοί)

men, who have "a certain particle of the Father of the universe...deposited in their souls."

Cf. also Gospel of Thomas 50, on those who originate from the light. Finally, *cf.* W. Schmithals' succinct comment in his *Gnosticism in Corinth*, 149, "Thus Gnosis does not *bestow* divine nature upon the Gnostic—this occurs in the mystery cults through some sort of magical act, for which the designation Gnosis cannot possibly have been the original—but it causes him to *recognize* his divine nature and the way to his, and that means to its, redemption."

18. This use of the term "gnostic" to describe the view (set forth above in note 17) that man's soul is essentially divine and hence *intrinsically* sinless, is well explicated in the work of Hans Jonas, *The Gnostic Religion*, 44-47, where he quotes from the *Excerpta ex Theodoto*, 78, 2, as a typical example of this gnostic notion:

> What liberates is the knowledge of who we were, what we became; where we were, whereinto we have been thrown; whereto we speed, wherefrom we are redeemed; what birth is, and what rebirth.

(*Cf.* Chapter Four below, p. 118, for the Greek text of this famous quotation.)

The Hymn of the Pearl, found in the Acts of Thomas (Hennecke Schneemelcher, *New Testament Apocrypha*, Volume Two, 425-531, and quoted in Jonas, *op. cit.*, 113-16, is a classical expression of this gnostic teaching.

Cf. also The Gospel of Truth 21:5; 22:1,5,10,15; 25:10,15; 34:1*ff*.

19. For "expiation" as a proper translation of ἱλασμός, see Dodd, *The Johannine Epistles*, 25. Also see Leon Morris, "The Meaning of HILASTERION in Romans iii.25", *NTS* 11, 33-43.

20. On παράκλητος applied to Jesus and meaning an advocate or intercessor on behalf of man before God, *cf.* Bultmann, *op. cit.*, 29, "Er [Jesus] wird παράκλητος genannt als der Fürsprecher [deprecator] bei Gott." Note 4 on the bottom of p. 29 gives a full list of references to the use of this term. Dodd, *op. cit.*, 24-25, also has an excellent discussion of the background and use of this term. The remarkable

thing about 1 John 2:1 is, of course, its use of παράκλητος
to refer to Jesus, not to the Holy Spirit, as in the Gospel
of John. Dodd, however (p. 25), points out that in John 14:
16 the Spirit is called *another* Paraklete, implying that
Jesus was the first Paraklete. If this is so, then the use
of the term to apply to Jesus was already present in the
Johannine community during the writing of the Gospel, but
was submerged by its more frequent use in the Gospel to refer to the Spirit; it emerges again here in 1 John 2:1. *Cf.*
also R. Brown, *op. cit.*, 711-17, on the Paraklete's activity.

21. Bultmann, in his *Theology of the New Testament*, Vol. 1, 46,
locates this doctrine in the "Kerygma of the Earliest
Church":

> In the tradition that had come down to Paul, do not
> both "according to the scriptures" κατὰ τὰς γραφάς
> and "for our sins" ὑπὲρ τῶν ἁμαρτιῶν ἡμῶν go back
> to the earliest Church? Then Jesus' death would
> already have been conceived as an expiatory sacri-
> fice in the earliest Church!

22. *Cf.* Dodd, "The First Epistle of John and the Fourth Gospel",
BJRL 21 (1937), 145:

> In the Fourth Gospel the death of Christ is first
> and foremost that by which Christ is "glorified"
> or "exalted" (xx. 23, 32-33, xiii. 31), and by
> virtue of which He "draws" all men into the sphere
> of eternal life (xii. 32, xi. 52). It is the
> means by which the virtue and power of His own
> being--His flesh and blood--are released for the
> sustenance of eternal life in mankind (vi. 51).
> His death is a sacrifice, on the one hand as be-
> ing self-dedication (ἁγιάζω ἐμαυτόν xvii. 19), and
> on the other hand, as an expression of His "love
> to the end" for His own (xiii. 1), as a man will
> lay down his life for a friend (xv. 13), or a shep-
> herd for his flock threatened by the wolf (x. 15).
> It is not a sacrifice for the expiation of sin.

Here Dodd has correctly demonstrated the vital difference
between the doctrines of the atonement found in the Gospel
and First Epistle of John.

23. *Cf.* R. Brown, *op. cit.*, 411:

> Jesus proclaims that he is the one who has truly
> been consecrated by God. This seems to be an in-
> stance of the Johannine theme that Jesus is the new
> Tabernacle (i 14) and the new Temple (ii 21).

160

24. Dodd, *op. cit.*, 145*ff*.

25. Raymond Brown's theory of the five stages of the editing of
John's Gospel, found, *op. cit.*, XXXIV-IX, comes in handy
here to account for the different strata of theological
traditions found in John. "Stage Four, Secondary edition
by the evangelist" (p. XXXVI) assumes that the evangelist
himself re-edited his own work in his own lifetime, introducing material hitherto unused, but nonetheless current in
the Johannine community. Hence an old tradition can be introduced later in either the Gospel or the Epistles.

26. *Cf*. Bultmann, *Die drei Johannesbriefe*, 26: "Er hebt sich
nicht nur durch seine Prosa vom poetischen Stil der Umgebung ab, sondern er stört auch sachlich."
"Sachlich" differences are important and essential *theological* differences, not mere differences in style.
Robert Fortna,in his book, *The Gospel of Signs*, 15, speaks
of various criteria for source analysis, and among them
names the *ideological* criterion, about which he comments:

> I use this term, as a rough equivalent for the some-
> what more general German *sachlich*, to indicate cri-
> teria which have to do with the material content,
> and very often the theological substance, of a pas-
> sage.

Our use of the term *sachlich* will be the same; however, we
prefer the term "theological" to "ideological."

27. A. E. Brooke, *A Critical and Exegetical Commentary on the
Johannine Epistles*, I.C.C., 1912, 86.

28. C. H. Dodd, *The Johannine Epistles*, 78-81.

29. *Ibid.*, 78.

30. *Ibid.*, 80.

31. *Ibid.*

32. *Ibid.*, 21.

33. *Ibid.*, 80.

34. In *ZTK* 48, 1951, 262-91.

35. *Ibid.*, 276.

36. *Ibid.*, 277.

37. *Ibid.*, 279.

38. *Ibid.*, 280.

39. See notes 17 and 18 above for a listing of the sources of this gnostic teaching, especially The Hymn of the Pearl, on the themes of "remembering" and "waking from sleep."

40. R. Schnackenburg, *Die Johannesbriefe*, Band XIII: Faszikel 3 of Herders Theologischer Kommentar zum Neuen Testament.

41. *Ibid.*, 256.

42. *Cf.* 1 John 2:19 and 4:1 about the ἀντίχριστοι and the ψευδο-προφῆται who went out from the Johannine community. These groups will be discussed and identified in Chapter Five.

43. *Cf.* Bultmann, *The Gospel of John* (ET), 137. (See Chapter Three, note 49.)

44. See note 18 above for the quotation from the *Excerpta ex Theodoto* 78, 2. (Quoted in Greek on p. 118, below.) *Cf.* the Corpus Hermeticum XIII, *Peri Paliggenesis*, for another important witness to the gnostic doctrine of rebirth.

45. W. Nauck, *Die Tradition und der Charakter des ersten Johannesbriefes*, 1957.

46. *Ibid.*, 122.

47. Nauck see 1 John as a *reditus ad baptismum, Ibid.*, 123: "Der 1 Joh bekommt dadurch den Charakter einer Scheidungs-proklamation und zugleich eines reditus ad baptismum."

48. Blass and Debrunner, *op. cit.*, 171, par. 331. The ingressive (inceptive) aorist. It denotes "a gradual becoming.."

49. N. Turner, *Grammatical Insights into the New Testament*, 151.

50. Bultmann, *Die drei Johannesbriefe*, 28.

51. *Ibid.*, 56. *Cf.* also Bultmann's *Theology of the New Testament* (ET), Vol. II, 79-80, on John's concept of freedom from sin.

52. M. Shepherd, Article on 1 John in *The Interpreter's One Volume Commentary on the Bible*, 1971, 938.

NOTES ON CHAPTER THREE

1. Bultmann, *The Gospel of John* (ET), 551. On p. 563, com-
    menting on 16:9, he reiterates this insight:

    > The meaning of sin is expounded in the sense of
    > 15.21-25; it is unbelief vis-à-vis the Revealer.
    > The world reacts to Jesus by clinging on to it-
    > self, by μένειν ἐν τῇ σκοτίᾳ (12.46; cp. 9.41;
    > 3.36), and precisely this is sin. Sin therefore
    > is not any single ghastly action, even if that
    > action be the crucifixion of Jesus; sin is not
    > moral failure as such, but unbelief and the bear-
    > ing that springs from it, i.e. the world's con-
    > duct determined by unbelief and taken as a whole.
    > From now on that is "sin."

2. References to the paschal lamb in the Old Testament are
    found chiefly in Exodus 12, Leviticus 23:5*ff*., Numbers 9
    and Deuteronomy 16. In John 19:14 we find the paschal sym-
    bolism connected with Jesus' death; *cf*. especially 19:36,
    alluding to Numbers 9:12, on not breaking the bones of the
    paschal victim.

3. See above, Chapter Two, p. 35, for the New Testament refer-
    ences to Christ as the expiatory sacrifice for sin.

4. *NTS* 1 (1954-55), 217.

5. Lambs do not take away sin, nor do any other sacrifices in
    the Old Testament. *Cf*. Leviticus 4:2 on the provision of
    sacrifices only for "unwitting sin"; *cf*. also Hebrews 10:11
    on the impossibility of any Old Testament sacrifice to take
    away deliberate sin.

6. *Cf*. Dodd, *The Interpretation of the Fourth Gospel*, 238.

7. C. K. Barrett, "The Lamb of God", *NTS* 1 (1954-55), 210.

8. The paschal lamb is a symbol of deliverance, not of expia-
    tion for sin. (It is the only sacrifice in the Old Testa-
    ment to be conducted within the family unit at home.) The
    two motifs of the paschal lamb as deliverance from Egypt
    and of the various sacrifices as offerings to God are al-
    ways kept separate in the Old Testament.

9. For references to the sin offering (חטאת) *cf*. Lev 4:3*ff*. (a
    bull without blemish); 5:6*ff*. (a female sheep or goat); 5:
    16*ff*. (a ram).

10. *Cf.* Isaiah 53:6b, "The Lord laid on him the iniquity of us all"; 10, "Thou shalt make his soul an offering for sin"; 12, "He bare the sins of many..." Also *cf.* John 11:50, "that one man die for the people..." and 2 Cor 5:14, "one died for all." The same concept—of one man dying on behalf of all the people of Israel—is commonly found in all these passages.

11. Sin in John's normative usage (see below, Part Two of Chapter Three) is really equivalent to the unforgivable sin of Mark 3:28-29; par. Matt 12:31-32; Luke 12:10.

12. Barrett, *op. cit.*, 210-11. *Cf.* the paschal allusions in John 19:31,36. In John, Jesus dies on the 14th of Nisan, the day the paschal lambs are slain in preparation for the Passover on the next day.

13. R. Fortna, *The Gospel of Signs*, 53; *cf.* p. 240 for the text of the reconstructed source.

14. Barrett, *op. cit.*, 213.

15. The sentence in John 5:8, Ἔγειρε ἆρον τὸν κράβαττόν σου καὶ περιπάτει, is remarkably close to Mark 2:11, particularly in the use of the unusual word κράβαττόν. *Cf.* C. K. Barrett, *The Gospel According to St. John*, 212. The similarity between John and Mark here argues for some kind of causal relationship between the two: either John knew Mark or was acquainted with a similar oral tradition. Because of the use of this unusual word, the former alternative is preferable, *contra* Barrett.

16. 3:19b-20 speaks of evil deeds. This is moralistic and "un-Johannine", as are the two other examples given in this section. See below, 59-61 of this study.

17. R. Brown, *op. cit.*, 1039. (Vol. 29A.)

18. *Cf.* W. Bauer, W. F. Arndt, F. W. Gingrich, *A Greek English Lexicon of the New Testament and Other Early Christian Literature*, 392: καθώς: "1. indicating a comparison, *just as* ..." *Cf.* Blass and Debrunner, *op. cit.*, 236, par. 453.

19. Bultmann, *op. cit.*, 347, note 5.

20. See Wayne Meek's excellent study on this motif: "The Man

164

from Heaven in Johannine Sectarianism", *JBL* 91 (1972), 285-
313. This article will be discussed at the end of Chapter
Five.

21. I owe this to R. Brown, *op. cit.*, 350 (Vol. 29):

We note that "sin" is in the singular in vs. 21,
for in Johannine thought there is only one radical sin of which man's many sins (plural in vs.
24) are but reflections. This radical sin is to
refuse to believe in Jesus and thus to refuse
life itself.

22. Barrett, *op. cit.*, 281: "The singular (in v. 21) focuses
attention upon the cardinal sin of rejecting Jesus."

23. Bruce M. Metzger, *A Textual Commentary on the Greek New
Testament*, 224 (*ad loc*. John 8:34): τῆς ἁμαρτίας (C)

A majority of the Committee explained the absence
of the τῆς ἁμαρτίας from several witnesses of the
Western text (D it[b,d] syr[s] cop[bomss] Clement *al*)
as a stylistic improvement introduced by copyists
either (a) because τὴν ἁμαρτίαν occurs just a few
words earlier or (b) in order to make a closer
connection with the following general expression
ὁ δὲ δοῦλος.

24. Bultmann, *The Gospel of John*, 438, note 1.

25. The fact that this group did not *remain* (μείνητε in v. 31,
μένει twice in v. 35) in the Johannine community indicates
their defection. As for the scorn heaped upon them, *cf*.
Käsemann, *The Testament of Jesus According to John 17*, 63:
"Not even Paul, with his outbursts of anger and his irony,
exhibited the cutting iciness of the so-called apostle of
love, shown already in his style."

26. Bultmann, *op. cit.*, 439, has an excellent statement about
freedom as the eschatological gift one can accept only by
admitting his sin. Although this section, like much of
Bultmann's writing, is highly interpretative of the text,
it still provides us with some important insights. It puts
the words John ascribes to Jesus in 8:31*ff*. in this same
theological context as the conversation with Nicodemus. Sin
then, for John, belongs to the old world, τὸ κατώ, to those
who have not, or will not, be born ἄνωθεν. Hence sin is
seen in the light of the "dualism of decision."

27. J. Louis Martyn, *History and Theology in the Fourth Gospel*,

especially Part I, chapters 1 and 2.

28. Meeks, *op. cit.*, 303*ff*.

29. *Cf.* Barrett, *op. cit.*, 294, for a rabbinic parallel to the common belief in Judaism that sickness was caused by sin: Shabbath 55a. *Cf.* also Brown, *op. cit.*, 371 (Vol 29), and Strack-Billerbeck II, 528-29.

30. Martyn, *op. cit.*, 119.

31. In the Gospel of John, only in 5:14 do we find a connection between sickness and sin. This verse, however, is pre-Johannine, and is never developed in the rest of the Gospel. *Cf.* Fortna, *op. cit.*, 53-54, where he has assigned this verse to the pre-Johannine signs source.

32. *Cf.* George Johnston, *The Spirit-Paraclete in the Gospel of John*, 81:

> Only in the difficult passage 16:8-11 is any suggestion of a lawsuit found. But there the Paraclete is not the advocate for the disciples. He is a prosecuting counsel, listing the charges against the *cosmos* at the seat of God and securing a conviction.

Similarly, Bultmann, *op. cit.*, 561, note 4, cites the Testament of Judah 20 and Wisdom 1:7-9 as examples of the role of the Spirit as plaintiff, but denies them any parallel in John 16:8-9 because they lack John's cosmic dimension.

33. *Cf.* Bauer, *op. cit.*, 248; John's usage of this term recalls the earliest usage of it. Note also Barrett, *op. cit.*, 405, where he gives a parallel in Philo, Det. 146.

34. Judas Iscariot is referred to in John 6:71; 12:4; 13:2,26, 29; 18:2,35. In all these places he is irredeemably evil.

35. For references in the New Testament to light (φῶς) as an ethical symbol, *cf.* Matt 5:14; 6:23; Luke 11:35; 16:8 (sons of light); John 3:19,20,21; 8:12; 11:9-10; 12:35-36; Rom 2:19; 13:12; 2 Cor 6:14; Eph 5:8,9,13; 1 Thess 5:5; 1 John 1:5,7; 2:9-10.

36. See note 9 of Chapter Two.

37. *Cf.* Bultmann, *Theology of the New Testament* (ET), Vol. II, 21:

> each man is, or once was, confronted with deciding

for or against God; and he is confronted anew
with this decision by the revelation of God in
Jesus. The cosmological dualism of Gnosticism
has become in John a *dualism of decision*.

38. See below, pp. 63-64 of this study.

39. In the Gospel of John only *believers* have eternal life. *Cf.*
especially John 3:15-16,36; 5:24a; 6:40,47; (10:28 by implication); 11:25; (17:2 by implication); 20:31. In 1 John
5:12 we find the categorical expression of this important
Johannine principle: "He who has the Son has life; he who
has not the Son has not life." John 10:1 and 14:6b ("no
one comes to the Father but by me") also express the exclusive claim of salvation only through Jesus, the sole
bringer of the Father's life into an alienated world, where
believers *alone* have received him (*cf.* 1:11-13).

40. The various characters in the Gospel of John are types of
believers: *e.g.*, John the Baptist, Andrew, Peter, Nathan-
iel, the Samaritan woman, the Official, the Lame Man, the
Man born blind, Mary, Martha, Thomas, etc. Also there are
the antitypes who represent unfaith: The "Jews", Pharisees,
Judas Iscariot; and also some who are "in-between": Nicodemus and Joseph of Arimathea. All these characters in the
drama are more types than real, flesh and blood individuals
and perhaps represent actual historical groups within and
about the Johannine community during the time its Gospel
was being written.

41. *Cf.* Käsemann, *The Testament of Jesus According to John 17*,
11:

> The formula 'the Father who sent me' is, lastly,
> neither the only nor the most typical christolog-
> ical formula in the Gospel... In the Gospel, the
> formula 'the Father who sent me' therefore alter-
> nates continuously with the concept of the oneness
> with the Father, and the former receives its pe-
> culiar christological meaning through the latter.

Cf. also p. 24: "...the unity of the Son with the Father
is the central theme of the Johannine proclamation..."

42. *Cf.* John 17:3, the *locus classicus* of the Johannine concept
of the life-giving gnosis; more examples will be furnished
below.

43. *Cf.* Bultmann, *op. cit.*, p. 608, commenting on John 14:9,

> Jesus' answer shows him [Philip] the folly of this,
> by re-directing his attention to the indirect vi-
> sion of God in the Revealer (v.9). The implica-
> tion behind the reproachful question: τοσοῦτον χρό-
> νον κτλ. is that all fellowship with Jesus loses
> its significance unless he is recognized as the one
> whose sole intention is to reveal God, and not to
> be anything for himself; but it also implies that
> the possibility of seeing God is inherent in the
> fellowship with Jesus: ὁ ἑωρακὼς ἐμὲ ἑώρακεν τὸν
> πατέρα.

44. In designating the person or persons who believe in Jesus
as the Revealer sent from the Father, sometimes the singular is used, *e.g.*, ὁ πιστεύων (3:15,16,18,36; 5:24; 6:35,
40,47; 7:38; 11:25,26; 12:44,46; 14:12) and at other times
the plural, *e.g.*, φίλοι in 15:14; τοῖς πιστεύουσιν in 1:12b.
The difference is only stylistic, determined by the context
and not theological.

45. By the believer for whom the Gospel was written, we mean
not only those who have already confessed Jesus as the
Christ, and who consequently need the Gospel to strengthen
their faith, but those whose faith is still incipient, for
whom the Gospel was written in order to bring to full faith.
On the whole question of the purpose of John's Gospel, see
two important articles which present rather different views:
J.A.T. Robinson, "The Destination and Purpose of St. John's
Gospel", *NTS* 7 (1960), 117-31 (reprinted in *Twelve New Testament Studies*, 107-25) and Wayne Meeks, "The Man From Heav-
en in Johannine Sectarianism", *JBL* 91 (1972), 44-72. The
latter article is discussed below, at the end of Chapter
Five.

46. Bultmann, *op. cit.*, 58-60.

47. For the use of the term ἐξουσία in the Gospel of John, *cf.*
1:12 (quoted here); 5:27; 10:18; 17:2; 19:10-11. In all
these places the term refers to the authority and power
from the Father himself, *i.e.*, divine authorization and em-
powerment, to exercise a given act. In all these places,
except 1:12, this ἐξουσία has been given to Jesus. Only
here in 1:12 is it given to those who believe in him--to
enable them to share his sonship with the Father.

48. The pun contained in the term ἄνωθεν shows the depth of
Nicodemus' misunderstanding; his literal interpretation of
ἄνωθεν as "again" is contrasted with the Evangelist's obvious denoting of the term as "anew", or better, "from above."
3:31 makes it explicit that Jesus is ὁ ἄνωθεν ἐρχόμενος,
and hence he alone can bring new life to the believer.

49. Bultmann, *op. cit.*, 137-38. See above, note 38, and Chapter Two, note 43.

50. *Cf.* 2 Pet 1:4 γένησθε θείας κοινωνοὶ φύσεως, for a late New
Testament explicit statement of the possibility of man shar-
ing in the Divine Nature. The same notion seems to be implicit here in the Gospel of John.

51. *Cf.* Bultmann, *Die drei Johannesbriefe, ad loc.* on 1 John
3:9, p. 57:

> Gewiss ist wie in V. 6 das "Nichtsündigen" grund-
> sätzlich zu verstehen als die Verwirklichung der
> dem Glaubenden geschenkten Möglichkeit.

52. This likeness is expressed by the term καθώς, *cf.* John 17:
14,16,18; 20:21.

53. For the reason the aorist participle is preferred here, instead of the present participle found in some readings, *cf.*
Metzger, *op. cit.* (note 23), p. 218.

54. R. Brown, *op. cit.*, Vol. 29A, 545-47 (the outline of the
Farewell Discourse) enumerates four Paraklete sayings: 14:
15-17; 25-26; 16:26-27; 8-15.

55. *Cf.* Brown, *op. cit.*, Vol. 29, 510-12 on the μένειν motif.

56. I owe this insight, that παρέδωκεν τὸ πνεῦμα may have the
double meaning of (1) Jesus' expiring, and (2) Jesus' passing on of the Spirit to the community, to my teacher, Edward Hobbs. Chapter 20, verse 22 bears this out, with its
reference to "breathing" upon the disciples (ἐνεφύσησεν).

57. *Cf.* Bultmann, *Theology of the New Testament*, Vol. II, 16,
on the world as "existence in bondage." For the use of
κόσμος in John as signifying the emnity of unfaith, *cf.* 1:
10; 7:7; 8:23; 12:31; 13:1b; 14:17,22,27,30; 15:18-19; 16:
8,11,20,33; 17:6,9,11b,14-16,25; 18:36.

58. This vivid language found liturgical expression in the

"Prayer of Humble Access" in the rite of Holy Communion in the Book of Common Prayer, p. 82:

> Grant us therefore, gracious Lord, so to eat the flesh of thy dear son Jesus Christ, and to drink his blood...

59. The "vividness" referred to here seems to carry anti-doce-tist connotations. Note especially the use of the term τρώγω, meaning to "gnaw, nibble, munch, eat (audibly)" (Bauer, *op. cit.*, 836-7) and the use of σάρξ instead of σῶμα.

60. According to Bultmann, *The Gospel of John* (ET), p.234, 6:51b *ff.* is the work of a later editor.

61. The sacramental aspect of the eucharist, prominent in the latter section of chapter 6, remains undeveloped in the rest of the Gospel, and hence cannot be considered of primary importance for a general view of Johannine theology.

62. Being "in the bosom" of someone, as Lazarus with Abraham (Luke 16:22) or "the only-begotten God" with God (John 1:18) indicates the closest relationship of honor, reserved for the perfect. It is this relationship which the beloved disciple alone enjoys. This could indicate that only the Founder-Evangelist of the Johannine community (*cf.* 21:24) held this distinction; however, it could have been emulated by the rest of the community, if the beloved disciple also symbolizes the perfect believer.

63. The notion of having a special "place" with God is found often in gnostic literature, *e.g.*, "The Gospel of Truth 24:25 (Grobel edition, 96, 98):

> For the place where there is envy and quarrel-ing is a lack, but the place which is the Re-union is completeness.

Cf. Grobel's comments, *ad. loc.* The ideal place for the gnostic is reunion with the Unknown Father; for John it is being close to Jesus, who is from above, and will return thence, yet has been manifested in the flesh.

64. Although only in 3:16 is the world spoken of as the object of God's love, the same general idea is implicit also in 1:29; 4:42; 6:33,51 and 12:47. These are exceptional passages, however, to the main thrust of Johannine thought on

the world as man organized in emnity toward God. *Cf.* Note
57 above for the listings of this usage. Other understand-
ings of the term κόσμος are: (1) the neutral place where
Jesus' revelation takes place: 1:10a; 6:14; 7:4; 8:26; 10:
36; 11:9,27; 12:19; 13:1a; 14:19,31; 16:21,28; 17:11a,13,
18,21,23; 18:20,37; 21:25. (2) Where judgment, as the
light, occurs: 1:9; 3:19; 8:12; 9:5,39; 12:46. (3) Created
through the agency of the λόγος: 1:10b; 17:5,24.

65. Peace as an eschatological gift can be found especially in
Isaiah 26:12; 27:5; 52:7; 55:12; 57:19; 60:17. In the New
Testament *cf.* Luke 1:79; 2:14,29; Acts 10:36; Rom 5:1; 8:6;
14:17; 15:13 (with joy),33; Gal 5:22 (gifts of the Spirit,
the guarantee of the eschaton); *cf.* also the customary
greeting of Paul, "grace and peace", *e.g.*, Rom 1:7; 1 Cor
1:3; 2 Cor 1:2; Gal 1:3; Phil 1:2.

    Joy as an eschatological gift can be found in Isaiah 29:
19; 35:10; 51:11; 55:12; 61:7; 66:5. In the New Testament
cf. Rom 14:17; Gal 5:22.

66. *Cf.* 1 John 5:14 for the important qualification, "according
to his will" added to this doctrine.

67. Barrett, *The Gospel According to St. John*, 398, *cf.* 326.

68. See below, the discussion at the end of Chapter Five, on
the Johannine community's perfectionist self-understanding,
as delineated by Käsemann and Meeks.

69. *Cf.* Bultmann, *Theology of the New Testament,* Vol. II, 75*ff.*,
"Faith as Eschatological Existence."

70. *Cf.* Matthew 25:10-12, 34, 41, the parables of the Wise and
Foolish Virgins and the Great Judgment. On the last day
the division between the good and the evil is final and
complete.

71. *Cf.* Bultmann, *op. cit.*, 37:
        ...Jesus is the eschatological salvation-
        bringer...*his coming is the eschatological*
        event.

72. *Cf.* Rom 5:12*ff.* for another place where the term "death"
is used in a metaphorical sense. *Cf.* also Wisdom 2:24 on
the origin of "death" in the same metaphorical sense.

73. *Cf*. Psalm 110:1 and its use in the New Testament, referring to Christ's heavenly session, *e.g.*, especially Hebrews 12:2 and Romans 8:34, where he intercedes for man.

74. *Cf.* Kittell, *TDNT* (ET, Bromiley), Vol. 1, 112.

75. Especially in Käsemann, *The Testament of Jesus According to John 17*. See the discussion of this at the end of Chapter Five, below.

76. *Cf*. Brown, *op. cit.*, 135 and Barrett, *op. cit.*, 182.

77. *Cf*. IQS 1:9, "and so that they may love all the sons of light, each according to his part in the counsel of God, and hate all the sons of darkness each according to his guilt in the vengeance of God." (Translation from A.R.C. Leaney, *The Rule of Qumran and Its Meaning*, 117.)

78. *Cf*. Brown, *op. cit.*, 515, for this list and an excellent discussion of the φῶς/σκοτία motif.

79. *Cf*. John 1:37-38,40,43; 8:12; 10:4-5,27; 12:26; 13:36-37; 21:19-20,22. In the synoptic gospels the familiar motif of following Jesus after his call is found in Mark 1:8 (par. Matt 4:20; Luke 5:11); Levi's call, Mark 2:14 (par. Matt 9:9; Luke 5:28). On taking up one's cross, *cf*. Mark 8:34 (par. Matt 16:24; Luke 9:23). *Cf*. also Rev 14:4, the 144,000 "who follow the Lamb wherever he goes."

80. The same tradition is found in the Testament of Issachar 5:2 (Charles, *Pseudepigrapha*, Vol. II, 327):
    But love the Lord and your neighbor.
    And also *ibid.*, 7:6 (*ibid.*, 328):
    I loved the Lord;
    Likewise also every man with all my heart.
    Also in the Testament of Dan 5:3 (*ibid.*, 334):
    Love the Lord through all your life,
    And one another with a true heart.

81. See above, note 77.

82. *Cf*. Brown, *op. cit.* 660 *ad loc*. *Cf*. also Bauer, *op. cit.* under καθαίρω 1. (p. 387), the reference to Philo Agr. 10, Somn. 2,64.

83. *Cf*. *Theology of the New Testament*, Vol. II, 75:
    The demand for faith, therefore, is the demand

> that the world surrender the understanding it
> has had of itself hitherto--that it let the
> whole structure of its security which it has
> erected in presumptuous independence of the
> Creator fall to ruins.

84. In his *The Interpretation of the Fourth Gospel*, 179-86,
there is an excellent discussion of the term πιστεύω and
its background in both Greek and Hebrew literature, as well
as its use in John.

85. Brown, *op. cit.*, 512-15, discusses πιστεύειν together with
the terms εἰδέναι and γινώσκειν.

86. The noun phrase ὁ πιστεύων occurs in 3:15-16,18,36; 5:24;
6:35,40,47; 7:38; 11:25-26; 12:44-46; and 14:12. The term
ἡ αἰώνιος ζωή (or simply ζωή in 11:25) occurs along with
it in all but 3:18; 7:38; 11:26; 12:44,46 and 14:12. Sym-
bols of eternal life occur in 6:35 (bread, no hunger, no
thirst); 7:38 (living water); 11:26 (resurrection, not dying eternally); and 12:46 (not remaining in darkness, implying having the light of life, *cf.* 8:12b). Of those
where the term ζωή αἰώνιος does not explicitly occur, we
find that 3:18 is embedded in a context dealing with eternal life, which states that the believer is not judged, but
has life. In 12:44 we have part of a christological apologia, that believing in Jesus means believing in him who
sent him; the same type of apologia occurs in 5:19*ff.*, and
in 14:9b and 24b. Finally, the motif of the disciples doing the Son's work implies their spreading of the gift of
life which the Son brought, in 14:12.

87. *Cf.* Brown, *op. cit.*, 499, on the meaning of ἀληθιν-ή, ός.

88. *Cf.* Blass and Debrunner, *op. cit.* 442 (9), 229, on epexegetical clauses joined by καί.

89. *Cf.* Barrett, *op. cit.*, 250, commenting on the use of ἀκού-
ειν in 6:60, says that it "is here close to the meaning of
'obey' (as שמע in the Old Testament)." The same could be
said of its use in 5:24.

90. C. K. Barrett observes this fact in his commentary, *op.
cit.*, 362, commenting on 12:48.

91. *Cf.* Brown, *op. cit.*, 490, speaking of the section 12:44-50,

says:

>...this little discourse, which now comes at the end of the Book of Signs, nicely summarizes Jesus' message.

92. Sometimes the corollary is rather explicit, that unfaith (which involves the refusal to believe the right doctrine about Jesus) leads to spiritual death, *e.g.*, John 3:16.

93. Note that in 14:24b the teaching ὁ λόγος, is ultimately from the Father, *cf.* 12:44.

94. For the characterizations of the heretics in 1 John, see above, Chapter Two and below, Chapter Five. As for the other places where we find derogatory characterization of heretics, *cf.* 1 Tim 1:3-7, 9-10, 19-20; 2 Tim 2:16-18; 3: 1-9; 4:14-16; Tit 1:10-16; 3:9-11; 2 Pet 2:1-22; 3:3-7; Jude 8:23.

NOTES ON CHAPTER FOUR

1. *Cf.* Koehler-Baumgartner, *Lexicon in Veteris Testamenti Libros*, 234, on the hithpaʿel of הלך. The את in Gen 5:22, 24 is taken as *with*, indicating fellowship with God, which in turn definitely implies moral uprightness.

2. The actual assumption of Moses is not narrated in The Assumption of Moses, but reference to it may be found in Clement of Alexandria, *Stromateis* 6, 15, and is alluded to in Josephus, *Antiquities* 4, 8, 48 and in Philo, *De Vita Mosis* II, 291. *Cf.* Charles, *Pseudepigrapha*, Vol. II, 407-9, for his discussion about the composite nature of this work, *i.e.*, it is a testament and an assumption narrative, the latter existing only in allusions in isolated Greek quotations.

3. *Cf.* Philo, *De Vita Mosis* I, 1-2:

>I purpose to write the life of Moses, whom some describe as the legislator of the Jews, others as the interpreter of the Holy Laws. I hope to bring the story of this greatest and most perfect of men (μεγίστου καὶ τελειοτάτου) to knowledge of such as deserve not to remain in ignorance of it; for while the fame of the laws which

he left behind him has travelled throughout the
civilized world and reached the ends of the
earth, the man himself as he really was is known
to few...

(Quoted from the Loeb Classical Library, Vol. VI, 276-7.)

4. Noah, as the prototype of a new human race, created in
righteousness and possessing a virtually sinless nature,
is referred to thus in Jubilees 5:12,

And he made for all his works a new and righteous nature, so that they should not sin in
their whole nature for ever, but should be all
righteous each in his kind alway.

(Quoted from Charles, *Pseudepigrapha*, Vol. II, 20.)

Cf. Also the Noachic sections of I Enoch, in *Ibid.*, 168.
Charles list the following as "Noachic fragments preserved
in this book": vi-xi, liv-lv.2, lx, lxv-lxix.25, cvi-cvii.
For the Apocalypse of Abraham, see D. S. Russell, *The Method and Message of Jewish Apocalyptic*, 60. Here, according
to the usual apocalyptic literary device, Abraham is given
an audience with God, where he is told of the imminent des-
truction of the heathen and the ingathering of the elect.

5. The term םימת is used in the sense of ritual purity in Lev
1:3,10; 3:1,6; 4:3,23,28,32; 5:15; 6:6; 9:2,3: 14:10; 22:
19; 23:12,18. The foregoing all deal with sacrificial animals to be offered "without blemish." Similar passages
concerning such animals may be found in Numbers 6:14 (twice);
19:2 (red heifer); 28:3,9,11,19; 29:2,8,13,17,20,23,26,29,
32,36. Also *cf.* Ezekiel 43:22-23; 45:18,23; 46:4,6,13.
Note the important allusion to this in Heb 9:14, where
Christ alone is seen as the perfect, spotless (ἄμωμος) offering.

6. *Cf.* Josephus, Ant. 3, 278-9, for the *ethical* purity demanded of a priest, in addition to the ritual purity demanded of him and his ceremonial actions.

7. *Cf.* Sellin-Fohrer, *Introduction to the Old Testament* (ET,
10th edition), 260-72, for the classification of the Psalms
following Gunkel.

8. Job's yearning to recapture his lost fellowship with God,
in 23:3--"Oh that I knew where I might find him!"--is not,
of course, strictly mysticism, in the usual sense of onto-

logical union with the Divine, or even in the Greek sense
of enthusiasm. Nevertheless, the motif of fellowship *with*
God is strong in Job, just as it is later in 1 John.

9.   *Cf.* James M. Reese, *Hellenistic Influence on the Book of
     Wisdom and its Consequences*, 76:

> In stating that divine Wisdom teaches man the four
> cardinal virtues (8.7), he expresses the ideal hu-
> man perfection in terms of current hellenistic an-
> thropology rather than in those of the biblical
> tradition.

10. *Ibid.* Fn. 193 on p. 76, "...Wis is the only canonical book
     of the Old Testament to use the word 'virtue' in this way."

11. "His Day", according to Russell, *op. cit.*, 51-52, would be
     sometime in the middle of the first century B.C., since
     the first five chapters are generally held to be an intro-
     duction by the final redactor. Charles (*op. cit.* 170) be-
     lieved that chapters 1-5 consisted of parts of I Enoch
     written in Hebrew after 161 B.C., *i.e.*, after the Maccabean
     revolution had begun, when a revival of the national lan-
     guage, over and against Aramaic, took place:

> ...for when once a nation recovers, or is trying
> to recover, its independence, we know from his-
> tory that it seeks to revive its national lan-
> guage.

12. Matthew Black, *The Scrolls and Christian Origins*, 122.

13. A.R.C. Leaney, *The Rule of Qumran and Its Meaning*, 125.

14. See Herbert Braun for parallels in his *Qumran und das neue
     Testament*, Vol. I, 290-306.

15. *Cf.* Bultmann, *Theology of the New Testament* (ET), Vol. I,
     332*f.*, on Paul's union of the indicative and the impera-
     tive.

16. Walter Schmithals, *Gnosticism in Corinth* (ET), 181.

17. See above, note 15.

18. "Mature and whole-hearted" are the terms which come to mind
     when reading Delling's article in the *TDNT* (ET), Vol. VIII,
     73-74, on τέλειος. He uses the terms "undivided" and "to-
     tal" in speaking of the meaning of this term in Matthew:

> As God is unrestricted in His goodness, so ac-

cording to V. 48 the disciples of Jesus should be
total in their love, bringing even their enemies
...within its compass.

19. W. F. Albright and C. S. Mann, *Matthew*, Anchor Bible, Vol.
26, 71-72, translate τέλειος as "true" and comment:

The Greek word *telios* in this context does not refer to moral perfection, but "truth, sincerity"
(cf. Deut xviii 13). In this sense, the Greek
word is used in the LXX about Noah (Gen vi 9), and
Job (i 1). The Greek word in the LXX is linked
with *tāmîm*, and the meaning of the Canaanite-He-
brew word *tām*, "true", is the same in both pagan
and biblical literature. There are links in Hebrew between *tāmîm* and *'emeth* (truth), and also
in the LXX with the Gr. *alēthinos*, the "true" man.
It does not have here the later Greek meaning of
being "totally free of imperfection", which is
the meaning found in both the KJ and the RSV.

20. *Cf.* K. Stendahl, *The School of St. Matthew*, 137:

The obvious dependence upon Leviticus in the fifth
chapter of Matthew makes it reasonable to take Mt.
5:48 as an adaptation of Lev. 19:2. It may be
noted that the order of the ethical statements in
this part of the Sermon on the Mount is that of
the commandments in Mt. 19:18*f.*, where their climax is a parallel to Mt. 5:48 when it is said εἰ
θέλεις τέλειος εἶναι, Mt. 19:21.

21. *Cf.* Albright and Mann, *op. cit.*, for the use of the term
"overscrupulous" to translate ὑποκριτής-αί in Matthew, *ad
loc*. *Cf.* also the appendix on "*Hupokrisis, Hupokrites,
Hupokrinesthai*" on p. cxv.

22. τέλειος 5:14; 9:11; τελειότης 6:1; τελειοῦν 2:10; 5:9; 7:
19,28; 9:9; 10:1,14; 11:40; 12:23; τελειωτής 12:2; τελεί-
ωσις 7:11. This list is found in Allen Wikgren's article,
"Patterns of Perfection in the Epistle to the Hebrews, *NTS*
6, 159, note 3.

23. Wilgren, *op. cit.*, 160.

24. There is now a firm consensus among most scholars that the
Apocalypse of Adam, for example, is pre-Christian. This
designation does not necessarily indicate chronologically
before the time of Christianity, but rather independent of
any contact with it.

25. Hans Jonas, *The Gnostic Religion*, 44. *Cf. idem, Gnosis und
spatantiker Geist*, Teil I, 2. Kapitel, 4.c. *Erlosung*, S.

199-210, and Exkurs II. *Anthropologische Zwei-und Dreistufigkeit*, S. 212-214.

26. W. C. van Unnik, *New Discovered Gnostic Writings*, 68.

27. Hugh Montefiore and H. E. W. Turner, *Thomas and the Evangelists*, 115.

28. G. Van Groningen, *First Century Gnosticism*, 80.

29. Odes of Solomon, edited by Rendel Harris and Alphonse Mingana, Vol. II, 276-7.

30. Robert Grant, "The Odes of Solomon and the Church of Antioch", *JBL* 63 (1944), 374.

31. Clement of Alexandria, *Excerpta ex Theodoto* 78 (London: Christopher's, 1934), 88. It is quoted in English translation in Jonas, *The Gnostic Religion*, 45; see above, Chapter Two, Note 18, in this study.

32. Johannes Quasten, *Patrology*, Vol. I, 265.

33. According to Quastin, *op. cit.*, Vol. I, 260, Valentinus is dated by Irenaeus, *Adv. Haer.* 3,4,3:

    Valentinus came to Rome in the time of Hyginus
    (ca. 136 to 140 A.D.), flourished under Pius (ca.
    150 to 155) and remained until Anicetus (ca. 155
    to 160).

34. Irenaeus *Adv. Haer.* 1,6,4, in *Ante-Nicene Library*, Vol. I, 324.

35. *Ibid.*, 4,38,3 (*ANL*, Vol. I, 521-22). Here Irenaeus speaks of man as "making progress day by day, and ascending toward the perfect..." Further, Irenaeus states that man, "having been created, should receive growth..."

36. *Cf.* The Gospel of Philip, in *Sourcebook of Texts for the Comparative Study of the Gospels*, especially Logia 100 (p. 150) and 110 (p. 152). *Cf.* also Chapter Two, Note 17.

37. Again, *cf.* Chapter Two, Note 17.

38. *Cf.* Bultmann, *Theology of the New Testament* (ET) Vol. II, 37, "...*his coming is the eschatological event*." (Italics the author's.)

NOTES ON CHAPTER FIVE

1. See Chapter Three, Note 64 for the other uses of the term κόσμος in the Gospel of John.

2. *Cf.* Bultmann, *Die drei Johannesbriefe*, 82, commenting on 1 John 5:6,

   > Denn das besagt ja: der Sohn Gottes ist der his-
   > torische Jesus, der getauft worden und gekreuzigt
   > worden ist. Der Gegensatz gegen die Irrlehre
   > tritt deutlich hervor, wenn V. 6b hinzugefügt
   > wird: οὐκ ἐν τῷ ὕδατι μόνον, ἀλλ' ἐν τῷ ὕδατι καὶ
   > ἐν τῷ αἵματι. Denn damit wird offenbar der gnos-
   > tizierenden Anschauung widersprochen, dass sich
   > der himmlische Christus zwar in der Taufe auf Je-
   > sus niedergelassen, ihn aber vor dem Tode wieder
   > verlassen hat. Für die Wahrheit des echten Glau-
   > bens, der die paradoxe Identität des Gottessohnes
   > und des historischen Jesus bekennt, beruft sich
   > der Verfasser V. 6c auf das Zeugnis des Geistes:
   > καὶ τὸ πνεῦμά ἐστιν τὸ μαρτυροῦν.

   This corresponds to Cerinthus' heresy, according to Irenaeus, *Adv. Haer.* 1,26,1. *Cf.* Dodd, *The Johannine Epistles*, *ad loc.* 1 John 5:6, 130.

3. *Cf.* Dodd, *op. cit.*, 141.

4. *Cf.* Bultmann, *op. cit.*, 40-41, especially note 1 on p. 41.

5. Wolfgang Nauck, *Die Tradition und der Charakter des ersten Johannesbriefes*, 125:

   > Wenn der Verfasser sagt: "Sie sind von uns ausge-
   > gangen, aber sie wären nicht von uns; denn wenn
   > sie von uns gewesen wären, so wären sie bei uns
   > geblieben", so besagt das nicht nur, dass die Ir-
   > rlehrer jetzt die Gemeinde verlassen haben, son-
   > dern auch dies: Sie sind *von uns* ausgegangen, ihre
   > Lehre ist eine Verzerrung unseres Glaubens.

6. In 2 John the Elder apparently cannot excommunicate his op-
   ponents--he would if he could!--but can only *request* (not
   order) his followers not to welcome them. In 3 John we see
   that he lacks authority over Diotrephes.

7. *Cf.* A. E. Brooke, *A Critical and Exegetical Commentary on
   the Johannine Epistles* (ICC), xxxviii-xxxix, on The False
   Teachers. Brooke quotes Irenaeus, *Adv. Haer.* 1,26,1 on
   Cerinthus. *Cf.* also Schmithals, *Gnosticism in Corinth*,
   127, on the similarity of the supposed Cerinthian gnostics

in 1 John and Paul's opponents in 1 Cor 12:3.

8. On the meaning of χρῖσμα *cf.* Bultmann, *op. cit.*, 46-47,
commenting on 2:27. He states explicitly that it denotes
instruction (*Belehrung*).

9. *Cf.* Dodd, *op. cit.*, 58-65, his discussion on the meaning
of χρῖσμα. *Cf.* also Bultmann, *op. cit.*, 42-43, commenting
on 2:20-21, and Nauck, *op. cit.*, 123 (see Chapter Two, note
47).

10. Irenaeus, *Adv. Haer.* 3,3,4 (quoting from *ANL*, Vol. I, 416):

> There are also those who heard from him [Polycarp]
> that John, the disciple of the Lord, going to
> bathe at Ephesus, and perceiving Cerinthus within,
> rushed out of the bath-house without bathing, ex-
> claiming, "Let us fly, lest even the bath-house
> fall down, because Cerinthus, the enemy of truth,
> is within."

11. *Cf.* Conzelmann, "Was von Anfang war", *Neutestamentliche
Studien für Rudolf Bultmann*, Beihefte zur *ZNW*, ed. by Wal-
ther Eltester, Beiheft 21 (1957), 194-201, especially Conzelmann's excellent insight into the fact that the author
of 1 John looked back to the Fourth Evangelist as an authority, p. 198:

> Man versteht die Ausdrucksweise des Briefes m.E.
> nur durch die Annahme, dass der Verfasser das Jo-
> hannesevangelium bereits als feste Autorität vor
> Augen hat. Er fingiert zwar die Rolle des Evan-
> gelisten als eines Augenzeugen; er will gewiss
> nichts, als dessen Lehre wiederholen, einschärfen,
> anwenden!

12. *Cf.* Irenaeus, *Adv. Haer.* 1,6,2-3 (*ANL*, Vol. I, 324), comments thus on the abandoned morals of the libertine gnostics:

> For even as gold, when submersed in filth, loses
> not on that account its beauty...so they affirm
> that they cannot in any measure suffer hurt, or
> lose their spiritual substance, whatever the ma-
> terial actions in which they may be involved.
> (3) Wherefore also it comes to pass, that the
> "most perfect" among them addict themselves...
> to forbidden deeds...

13. Our chief and oldest source for the teachings of Cerinthus
is Irenaeus, *cf. Adv. Haer.* 1,26 (quoted by Brooke, *op. cit.*,
xlv):

> ...et post baptismum descendisse in eum ab ea
> principalitate quae est super omnia Christum
> figura columbae, et tunc annunciasse incogni-
> tum patrem, et virtutes perfecisse in fine au-
> tem revolasse iterum Christum de Jesu, et Jesum
> passum esse et resurrexisse, Christum autem im-
> passibilem perseverasse, existentem spiritalem.

An English translation of this can be found in *ANF*, Vol. I,
97*f*. Other references to Cerinthus are found in Irenaeus,
Adv. Haer. 3,2-3, Hippolytus, *Ref.* 7,21 and 10,17 (based on
Irenaeus' account), Epiphanius, *Haer.* 28, and Eusebius 3,
28.

14. *Cf.* Schmithals, *op. cit.*, 135-6:

> So far as the Gnostics held to a theological sig-
> nificance of the cross, an anathema was never
> aimed at the man Jesus--no matter how thorough-
> going the dualism was. Conversely, a disdain for
> his passion always ran parallel to the rejection
> of the man Jesus. In this connection I refer
> again to I John, where the polemic has preserved
> for us reports which are among the earliest that
> we possess about Christian Gnosticism. This po-
> lemic is directed not only against the rejection
> of Χριστὸς κατὰ σάρκα but also against the depre-
> ciation of his cross and suffering...

(He goes on to quote 1 John 5:6 and Irenaeus on
Cerinthus.)

15. See above, note 13, the quotation from Irenaeus on "incog-
nitum patrem." *Cf.* Jonas, *The Gnostic Religion*, 42, on the
main tenets of the gnostic doctrine of God, *viz.*, "The
transcendent God Himself is hidden from all creatures and
is unknowable by natural concepts."

16. Käsemann, *The Testament of Jesus According to John 17* (ET),
73; *cf.* also pp. 32, 38-39, 65.

17. *Ibid.*, 26; *cf.* also pp. 45, 66, 70.

18. *Ibid.*, 12.

19. *Ibid.*, 65.

20. This interpretation of John 1:14 I got from listening to
Professor Käsemann himself at a colloquium of professors
and graduate students in Biblical studies, at the Graduate
Theological Union, hosted by the Jesuit School of Theology
at Berkeley, on September 11, 1972.

21. Wayne Meeks, "The Man from Heaven in Johannine Sectarianism", *JBL* 91 (1972), 69-70

22. Explicit references to Christian prophets in the New Testament may be found in 1 Thess 5:20; Rom 12:6; 1 Cor 11:4;
12:10,28-29; 13:2,8; all of ch. 14; Acts 11:27; 13:1*f*; 15:
32; 19:6; 21:9-10. Ephesians 2:20; 3:5 and 4:11 seem to
be looking back at prophecy which has disappeared from the
life of the church the author of this epistle knew. Revelation 1:3; 22:7,10,18-19 all contain the title of this
apocalypse: [οἱ λόγοι] τῆς προφητείας τοῦ βιβλίου τούτου.
Other references to prophets and prophecy are found in Rev
10:7; 11:3,10,18 (note the two witnesses); 16:6; 18:20,24;
19:10 (the spirit of prophecy = the testimony of Jesus).

In the Didache we find references to prophets, who
seemed to have constituted a ministry parallel to the established ministry of apostles: *cf*. 11:3-12; 13:1-7; 15:1-
2. *Cf*. also Eusebius, H.E. 3:5, on the flight of the Jerusalem Christians to Pella:

> Furthermore, the members of the Jerusalem church,
> by means of an oracle given by revelation to ac-
> ceptable persons there, were ordered to leave the
> City before the war began and settle in a town in
> Peraea called Pella.
>
> (Penguin Classics edition, translated by G. A.
> Williamson, p. 111.)

In secondary literature, *cf*. Norman Perrin, *Rediscovering
the Teaching of Jesus*, 15:

> The early Church made no attempt to distinguish
> between the words the earthly Jesus had spoken
> and those spoken by the risen Lord through a
> prophet in the community...

Cf. also Ernst Haenchen, *The Acts of the Apostles* (ET),
395, note 2 (on 13:1, prophets as charismatic teachers).
All this is quite relevant to understanding the Gospel of
John, especially the discourses, as the words of the liv-
ing Christ spoken through the prophet-evangelist. *Cf*. M.
Eugene Boring, "How May We Identify Oracles of Christian
Prophets in the Synoptic Tradition?" *JBL* 91 (1972), 501-21.

23. *Cf*. Matt 7:15-23, the warning against false prophets; 1 Cor
12:1-3, a test of true charismatic prophecy; and 1 John 4:
1-3 another such test. In the Didache (cited above in

182

note 22) we find the itinerant teachers and prophets co-existing (somewhat uneasily--note ch. 12!) with the established ministry of bishops and deacons, mentioned in ch.
15.

24. Except for 3:16, a famous anomaly in John, we find that
love is just for the brethren in 11:5; 13:1 (he loved his
own); 14:21,23,28; 17:23. The beloved disciple seems to
represent the ideal Johannine Christian, as the special
recipient of Jesus' love, *cf.* 13:23; 19:26; 20:2; 21:7,20.
Furthermore, the members of the Johannine community are
told to love *one another* in 13:34; 15:12,17, with no mention of spreading that love outside the community. The
same goes for all the references to love in 1 John, note
especially 4:7*ff.* (love *one another*).

25. On the position of Diotrephes in his church, *cf.* Dodd, *op.
cit.*, 162:

> It seems, however, most natural to understand that
> Diotrephes either possessed or arrogated to himself
> the authority to excommunicate, and exercised it
> effectively. This authority belonged, so soon as
> the monarchical episcopate was fully established,
> to the bishop. Whether the church to which Diotre-
> phes belonged already possessed a fully episcopal
> constitution, we cannot say...

Also *cf.* Bultmann, *op. cit.*, 99:

> Der Diotrephes, von dem sonst nichts bekannt ist,
> wird als ὁ φιλοπρωτεύων αὐτῶν bezeichnet, also als
> derjenige, der in der Gemeinde (αὐτῶν) den ersten
> Platz einzunehmen beanspruch. Das Wort φιλοπρ ist
> vielleicht eine Bildung des Verfassers, durch die
> er herabsetzend den wirklichen Titel des Diotrephes
> vermeidet bzw. ersetz, nämlich den Titel ἐπίσκοπος.

Finally, *cf.* Massey Shepherd's commentary in 3 John, p. 941
of *The Interpreter's One-Volume Commentary on the Bible:*

> It should be noted that the elder accuses Diotre-
> phes, not of false teaching and heresy, but of
> resistance to the elder's authority. It is pos-
> sible of course that their differences are doc-
> trinal. But some interpreters think not. They
> see in Diotrephes an emerging leader--perhaps a
> bishop--of a local church who is concerned to
> keep his church free from outside interference.

26. One of the indications that the Johannine community was out
of the main stream of contemporary Christianity was *its*
mission policy in contradistinction to the rest of the

church; *cf*. Käsemann, *op. cit.*, 65, "Thus the world is the object of mission only in so far as it is necessary to gather the elect." and also Meeks, *op. cit.*, 70, "...it could hardly be regarded as a missionary tract..."

27. The Acts of John, sections 87-105, seem to represent an older, received tradition, which existed before the romance sections, and were incorporated into them. Perhaps this older tradition stemmed from the heretics who went forth from the Johannine community. *Cf*. Hennecke-Schneemelcher, *New Testament Apocrypha*, Vol. II, 224-35.

BIBLIOGRAPHY

Reference Works

Bauer, Walter. *A Greek-English Lexicon of the New Testament and Other Early Christian Literature*. ET by William F. Arndt and F. Wilbur Gingrich. The University of Chicago Press. Fourth Revised, and Augmented Edition, 1952.

Blass, F. and Debrunner, A. *A Greek Grammar of the New Testament and Other Early Christian Literature*. ET by Robert W. Funk. The University of Chicago Press. A translation and revision of the ninth-tenth German edition incorporating supplementary notes of A. Debrunner, 1961.

Braun, Herbert. *Qumran und das Neue Testament*. Tübingen: Theologische Rundschau 28, 1962.

Buttrick, George A., ed. *The Interpreter's Dictionary of the Bible*. Nashville: Abingdon Press, 1963.

Kittel, Gerhard, ed. *Theological Dictionary of the New Testament*. ET by Geoffrey W. Bromiley. Grand Rapids, Michigan: Wm. B. Eerdmans, 1964 +

Koehler, Ludwig and Baumgartner, Walter. *Lexicon in Veteris Testamenti Libros*. Leiden: E. J. Brill, 1958.

Moulton, W. F. and Geden, A. S. *A Concordance of the Greek Testament*. Edinburgh: T. & T. Clark, Fourth Edition, 1963.

Quasten, Johannes. *Patrology*. Three Volumes. Utrecht-Antwerp: Spectrum Publishers, 1966.

Strack, H. L. and Billerbeck. *Kommentar zum Neuen Testament aus Talmud und Midrasch*. München, 1924.

Young, Robert. *Analytical Concordance to the Bible*. New York: Funk & Wagnalls Company, 1936.

Source Books

Cartlidge, David R. and Dungan, David L. *Sourcebook of Texts for the Comparative Study of the Gospels*. Second Edition, revised and augmented. Society of Biblical Literature, 1972.

186

Charles, R. H. *The Apocrypha and Pseudepigrapha of the Old Testament*. Vol. II. *Pseudepigrapha*. Oxford at the Clarendon Press, 1913.

Hennecke, Edgar and Schneemelcher, Wilhelm. *New Testament Apocrypha*, Vol. II, *Writings Relating to the Apostles; Apocalypses and Related Subjects*. ET by R. McL. Wilson Philadelphia: The Westminster Press, 1964.

Works of Antiquity

Clement of Alexandria. *Excerpta ex Theodoto*. Edited with translation and notes by Robert Pierce Casey. London: Christopher's, 1934.

Eusebius of Caesarea. *The History of the Church From Christ to Constantine*. Translated with an introduction by G. A. Williamson. Baltimore: Penguin Books, 1965.

The Gospel According to Thomas. Coptic text established and translated by A. Guillaumont, H.-Ch. Peuch, G. Quispel, W. Till and Yassah 'Abd al Masih. Leiden: E. J. Brill, 1959.

The Gospel of Truth, A Valentinian Meditation of the Gospel. Translation from the Coptic and Commentary by Kendrick Grobel. Nashville: Abingdon Press, 1960.

Hippolytus of Rome. *Refutation of All Heresies*. Ante-Nicene Library, Vol. V. Edited by A. Roberts and J. Donaldson. Buffalo: The Christian Literature Publishing Company, 1886.

Irenaeus of Lyons. *Against Heresies*. ANL, Vol. I.

Josephus. *The Jewish Antiquities*. Loeb Classical Library, Vols. IV-IX, with an English translation by H. St. J. Thackeray. Harvard University Press, 1967.

Odes and Psalms of Solomon. Edited and translated from the Syriac by Rendel Harris and Alphonse Mingana. Vol. II. Manchester: At the University Press, 1920.

Philo of Alexandria. *Collected Works in Ten Volumes*. Loeb Classical Library, with an English translation by F. H. Colson. Harvard University Press, 1966.

Texts

The Greek New Testament. Edited by Kurt Aland, Matthew Black, Carlo M. Martini, Bruce M. Metzger and Allen Wikgren, in cooperation with the Institute for New Testament Textual Research. Second Edition. United Bible Societies, 1966, 1968.

Metzger, Bruce M. *A Textual Commentary on the Greek New Testa-*

ment. (Companion Volume to the above). United Bible Societies, 1971.
   The English translation of the Greek and Hebrew texts are genarally taken from the *Revised Standard Version*. New York: Thomas Nelson and Sons, 1946, 1952.

Secondary Literature

Albright, W. F. and Mann, C. S. *Matthew*. The Anchor Bible, Vol. 26. Garden City, New York: Doubleday & Company, Inc., 1971.

Barrett, C. K. *The Gospel According to St. John*. London: SPCK, 1962.

_____. "The Lamb of God." *NTS* 1 (1954-55), 210-18.

Bauer, Walter. *Orthodoxy and Heresy in Earliest Christianity*. ET of *Rechtgläubigkeit und Ketzerei im ältesten Christentum* (1934). Edited by Robert A. Kraft and Gerhard Krodel. Philadelphia; Fortress Press, 1971.

Bianchi, Ugo. *Le Origini dello Gnosticismo, Colloquio de Messina, 13-18 aprile 1966*. Studies in the History of Religions, XII. Leiden: E. J. Brill, 1967.

Black, Matthew. *The Scrolls and Christian Origins*. New York: Charles Scribner's Sons, 1961.

Braun, Herbert. "Literar-Analyse und theologische Schichtung im I Joh." *ZThK* 48 (1951), 262-91.

Brooke, A. E. *A Critical and Exegetical Commentary on the Johannine Epistles*. ICC. Edinburgh: T. & T. Clark, 1912.

Brown, Raymond E., S.S. *The Gospel According to John*. The Anchor Bible, Vols. 29 and 29a. Garden City, New York: Doubleday & Company, 1966 and 1970.

_____. *The Gospel of St. John and the Johannine Epistles*. Revised Second Edition. Collegeville, Minnesota: The Liturgical Press, 1965. (New Testament Reading Guide)

Bultmann, Rudolf. "Die Bedeutung der neuerschlossenen mandäischen und manichäischen Quellen für das Verständnis des Johannesevangeliums." *ZNW* 24 (1925), 100-46.

_____. *Die drei Johannesbriefe*. Meyers Kommentar. Göttingen: Vanderhoeck & Ruprecht, 1967.

_____. *The Gospel of John*. ET of *Das Evangelium des Johannes*. (With the Supplement, 1966). Translated by G. R. Beasley-Murray, R. W. N. Hoare and J. K. Riches, Philadelphia: The Westminster Press, 1971.

_____. *Theology of the New Testament*. ET by Kendrick

Grobel, Vols. I and II. New York: Charles Scribner's Sons, 1955.

Conzelmann, Hans. "Was von Anfang War", *Neutestamentliche Studien für Rudolf Bultmann*. Beihefte z. ZNW 21. Berlin, 1954, 194-200.

Deissmann, Adolf. *Licht vom Osten*. Tübingen: Verlag von J.C.B. Mohr (Paul Siebeck), 1923.

Dobschütz, E. von. *Johanneische Studien I, ZNW* (1907), 1*ff*.

Dodd, C. H. "The First Epistle of John and the Fourth Gospel." *BJRL*, Vol. 21, No. 1 (April 1937).

_____. *The Interpretation of the Fourth Gospel*. Cambridge University Press, 1953.

_____. *The Johannine Epistles*. Moffatt Commentary Series. London: Hodder and Stoughton Limited, 1946.

Eltester, Walter, ed. *Neutestamentliche Studien für Rudolf Bultmann*. (See above under Conzelmann.)

Feuillet, A. "Étude structurale de la première épître de saint Jean", in *Neues Testament und Geschichte: Oscar Cullmann zum 70. Geburtstag*. Zürich: Theologisches Verlag; Tübingen: Mohr, 1972, 307-27.

Flew, R. Newton. *The Idea of Perfection in Christian Theology*. Oxford University Press, 1934.

Fortna, Robert T. *The Gospel of Signs*. Society for New Testament Studies, Monograph Series 11. Cambridge University Press, 1970.

Georgi, Dieter. *Die Gegner des Paulus im zweiter Korintherbrief*. WMANT 11 (1964).

Grant, Robert. "The Odes of Solomon and the Church of Antioch." *JBL* 63 (1944).

_____. "The Origin of the Fourth Gospel." *JBL* 69 (1950), 305-22.

Haering, Theodore. *Gedankengang und Grundgedanke des ersten Johannesbriefs*. Theol. Abhandlungen, Carl von Weizäcker gewidmet. Freiburg i.B., 1892, Mohr.

Hoskyns, E. C. *The Fourth Gospel*. Edited by F. N. Davey. London: Faber and Faber Limited, 1947.

Johnston, George. *The Spirit-Paraclete in the Gospel of John*. Society for New Testament Studies, Monograph Series 12. Cambridge University Press, 1970.

Jonas, Hans. *Gnosis und spätantiker Geist*, I, II, 2. durchgesehene Auflage. Göttingen: Vandenhoecke & Ruprecht, 1954.

Jonas, Hans. *The Gnostic Religion*. Second edition, revised. Boston: Beacon Press, 1963.

Käsemann, Ernst. "Ketzer und Zeuge." *ZThK* 48 (1951), 292-311.

_____. *The Testament of Jesus*. ET of *Jesu letzter Wille nach Johannes 17* (1966), by Gerhard Krodel. Philadelphia: Fortress Press, 1968.

Kümmel, Werner Georg. *Introduction to the New Testament*. (Founded by Paul Feine and Johannes Behm). ET of *Einleitung in das neue Testament* (1965). 14th Revised Edition. Translated by A. J. Mattill, Jr. Nashville: Abingdon Press, 1966.

Leaney, A. R. C. *The Rule of Qumran and Its Meaning*. Philadelphia: The Westminster Press, 1966.

Martyn, J. Louis. *History and Theology in the Fourth Gospel*. New York: Harper and Row, 1968.

Marxsen, Willi. *Introduction to the New Testament*. ET of *Einleitung in das neue Testament* (3rd edition, 1964) by Basil Blackwell. Philadelphia: Fortress Press, 1968.

Meeks, Wayne. "The Man From Heaven in Johannine Sectarianism." *JBL* 91 (1972), 44-72.

Morris, Leon. "The Meaning of HILASTERION in Romans III.25." *NTS* 11, 33-43.

Montefiore, H. and Turner, H. E. W. *Thomas and the Evangelists*. Studies in Biblical Theology, Series 1, No. 35. SCM Press, 1962.

Nauck, Wolfgang. *Die Tradition und der Charakter des ersten Johannesbriefes*. Tübingen: J.C.B. Mohr (Paul Siebeck), 1957.

Noack, B. "On I John ii.12-14." *NTS* 6 (1959-60), 236-41.

O'Neill, J. C. *The Puzzle of I John*. London: SPCK, 1966.

Parker, Pierson. "Two Editions of John." *JBL* 75 (1956) 303-14.

Perrin, Norman. *Rediscovering the Teaching of Jesus*. New York: Harper and Row, 1967.

Reese, James M. *Hellenistic Influence on The Book of Wisdom and Its Consequences*. Analecta Biblica 41. Rome: Biblical Institute Press, 1970.

Robinson, J. A. T. *Twelve New Testament Studies*. Studies in Biblical Theology, Series 1, No. 34. SCM Press, 1962.

Russell, D. S. *The Method and Message of Jewish Apocalyptic*. Philadelphia: The Westminster Press, 1964.

190

Schmithals, Walter. *Gnosticism in Corinth*. ET of *Gnosis in Korinth* (FRLANT NF 48, 1956, 1st ed.) by John E. Steely. Nashville: Abingdon Press, 1971.

_____. *Paul and the Gnostics*. ET of *Paulus und die Gnostiker* (1965) by John E. Steely. Nashville: Abingdon Press, 1972.

Schnackenburg, Rudolf. *Die Johannesbriefe*. Herders theologischer Kommentar zum neuen Testament. Verlag Herder, Freiburg, 1953.

Schweizer, Eduard. "The Concept of the Church in the Gospel and Epistles of St. John", in *New Testament Essays in Memory of T. W. Manson*. Edited by A. J. B. Higgins. Manchester University, 1959, 230-45.
(ET of *Der Kirchenbegriff im Evangelium und den Briefen des Johannes* in *TU* 73, 1959, 363-81.)

Sellin, Ernst and Fohrer, Georg. *Introduction to the Old Testament*. ET of *Einleitung in das alte Testament* (1965), by David E. Green. Nashville: Abingdon Press, 1968.

Shepherd, Massey H. "The First Letter of John", in *The Interpreter's One-Volume Commentary on the Bible*. Nashville: Abingdon Press, 1971, 935-39.

Stendahl, Krister. *The School of St. Matthew*. Philadelphia: Fortress Press, 1968.
(First published in 1954 as Volume XX of *Acta Seminarii Neotestamentici Upsaliensis*.)

Turner, Nigel. *Grammatical Insights Into The New Testament*. Edinburgh: T. & T. Clark, 1965.

van Groningen, G. *First Century Gnosticism, Its Origin and Motifs*. Leiden: E. J. Brill, 1967.

van Unnik, W. C. *Newly Discovered Gnostic Writings*. Studies in Biblical Theology, No. 30. Allenson, 1960. ET of *Openbaringen uit Egyptisch Zand* (1958).

Westcott, B. F. *The Epistles of St. John*. F. F. Bruce and Marcharn, Manor Press. 1966 Edition. (Originally published in 1883, Cambridge and London: Macmillan and Co.)

Wikgren, Allen. "Patterns of Perfection in the Epistle to the Hebrews." *NTS* 6, 159-67.

Wilder, Amos. "Introduction and Exegesis of the Epistles of John", in *The Interpreter's Bible*, Vol 12. Nashville: Abingdon Press, 1957, 209-302.

Windisch, Hans. *Die katholischen Briefe*. Handbuch zum Neuen Testament 15. Tübingen: J. C. B. Mohr (Paul Seibeck), 1930.

NOTTINGHAM UNIVERSITY LIBRARY